JAPAN

Keiko Hirata
Mark Warschauer

JAPAN
The Paradox of
Harmony

YALE UNIVERSITY PRESS
NEW HAVEN AND LONDON

For information about this and other Yale University Press publications, please contact:
U.S. Office: sales.press@yale.edu   www.yalebooks.com
Europe Office: sales@yaleup.co.uk   www.yalebooks.co.uk

Set in Adobe Minion Pro by IDSUK (DataConnection) Ltd
Printed in Great Britain by Gomer Press Ltd, Llandysul, Ceredigion, Wales

Library of Congress Cataloging-in-Publication Data

Hirata, Keiko.
    Japan: the paradox of harmony/Keiko Hirata and Mark Warschauer.
        pages   cm
    Includes bibliographical references and index.
    ISBN 978-0-300-18607-9 (cloth: alkaline paper)
    1. Japan—Civilization—1945–   2. National characteristics, Japanese. 3. Harmony (Philosophy)—Social aspects—Japan.   4. Japan—Social conditions—1945–
5. Japan—Economic Warschauer, Mark. II. Title.
    DS822.5.H548 2014
    952.04—dc23
                                                                  2014007284

A catalogue record for this book is available from the British Library.

10 9 8 7 6 5 4 3 2 1

For Danny, Mika, and Noah

Contents

Note to the Reader   *viii*

Introduction   1

1 The Whistleblower   22

2 Grass-Eating Girly Men   59

3 Graying and Shrinking   88

4 Getting Along with the Neighbors   126

5 Meltdown   164

6 What We Learned at Lunch   202

Conclusion: Shaking Up Japan   240

Notes   *252*

Select Bibliography   *279*

Acknowledgements   *280*

Index   *283*

Note to the Reader

Japanese names can be written in English in various ways. In this book, we have followed the convention of first name first, family name last (e.g. Shinzo Abe). If only one name is listed, it is typically the last name for authors or public figures (e.g. Abe) and the first name for ordinary citizens used in descriptions of everyday life (e.g. Kenji, the student in chapter 6). In addition, though macrons are often used for long vowels in Japanese words or names, none are used in this book.

When converting yen to dollars, either we use the rate of 100:1, which was the approximate exchange rate in January 2014, or we simply state the amount of yen or dollars listed in the original source without converting. As for weights, Japan uses the metric tonne, equaling 1,000 kilograms (about 2,240 pounds), and that is the term we use throughout the book.

Introduction

After the March 2011 tsunami and earthquake, the world looked on in awe as the Japanese people displayed the resilience and respect they are famed for. With the subway system shut down, millions of commuters walked miles from their offices in Tokyo to homes in the suburbs. There was no reported looting. People stood in lengthy queues to buy food and drinks at convenience stores. Some bought bicycles to get home. Tokyo was packed with scared and exhausted pedestrians walking at a snail's pace without shoving, fighting, or arguing.

In the days that followed, the people of Tokyo lined up uncomplainingly for hours in stores to get bottled water or food for their families. Even after they had waited for hours, when items ran out they walked to other stores and waited at the back of the line. There was virtually none of the conflict or chaos that disasters like this often bring to other countries in the world, rich or poor.

Japan's collective resolve was even clearer in the coastal areas most affected by the earthquake. The coastal town of Hadenya was devastated, which led to many deaths and casualties.[1] Bridges, phone lines, and cell services were washed out, and the town was completely cut off from the outside world. Residents could not get supplies or information. The shivering survivors sheltered from the freezing cold in a hilltop community center, amid an 'apocalyptic landscape' of ruined houses and crushed vehicles. With little fuel or food, they immediately organized themselves roughly along the lines of their original community. Those men who had prominent jobs in the community assumed leadership and quickly started assigning tasks. Women boiled water and prepared food, while other men scavenged for firewood and gasoline.

Although they were cut off from the rest of Japan, the Hadenya survivors made contact with five other nearby centers sheltering another 700 refugees. Representatives from the centers met daily to swap supplies and assign tasks.

It took nearly two weeks for the authorities to construct bridges to reach Hadenya. According to the first reporters on the scene, 'tidy perfectionism' ruled the day, with immaculate toilets, cups, and soap neatly lined up, and boxes of supplies stacked in orderly rows. By all accounts, the rapid resumption of order, hierarchy, and a strict division of labor helped Hadenya survive.

Hadenya was not unique. Throughout the Tohoku region, people gathered in schools, community centers, and any other salvageable building. In Rikuzen Takada City, about a thousand evacuees gathered at Daiichi Junior High School. This was one of the largest evacuation centers, and it even appointed its own public relations person to deal with international reporters from CNN, Al Jazeera, and elsewhere. The daily log of the center's activities illustrates the attention to organization. They found an abandoned computer and began logging evacuees – 600 on the first day. They built dozens of makeshift toilets out of wood over the course of a week. They formed teams to find and distribute food from local convenience stores, and others to make and serve three meals a day of rice balls and bread. They recruited teams of elementary and junior high-school students to help with babysitting, formed groups that regularly cleaned the makeshift toilets, and held callisthenics sessions set to national radio broadcasts.[2]

The coastal areas also featured extraordinary tales of self-sacrifice. Takeshi Kanno, a 31-year-old doctor who risked his life to save dozens of his patients by moving them to the highest floor, refused to evacuate until everyone was saved. Three days after the earthquake, he made it back to his wife – just hours before the birth of their second child, whom they named 'Rei,' meaning 'the wisdom to overcome hardship.'[3]

'Not Losing to the Rain'

Such social solidarity is nothing new in Japan. With harsh terrain and little farmland, few natural resources, and more earthquakes and tsunamis than any other place on earth, the people of Japan have always had to come together or perish. Concern for the collective is part of the Japanese cultural DNA. It is encapsulated in one of Japan's most famous poems, 'Not Losing to the Rain,' discovered after his death in the suitcase of the famous Japanese poet Kenji Miyazawa, who died at the age of 37 in 1933 in the same Tohoku region that was ravaged by the 2011 earthquake:

not losing to the rain
not losing to the wind
not losing to the snow nor to summer's heat
with a strong body
unfettered by desire
never losing temper
cultivating a quiet joy
every day four bowls of brown rice
miso and some vegetables to eat
in everything
count yourself last and put others before you
watching and listening, and understanding
and never forgetting

in the shade of the woods of the pines of the fields
being in a little thatched hut
if there is a sick child to the east
going and nursing over them
if there is a tired mother to the west
going and shouldering her sheaf of rice
if there is someone near death to the south
going and saying there's no need to be afraid
if there is a quarrel or a suit to the north
telling them to leave off with such waste
when there's drought, shedding tears of sympathy
when the summer's cold, wandering upset
called a nobody by everyone
without being praised
without being blamed
such a person
I want to become[4]

That remarkable sense of collective resolve has allowed Japan not only to survive, but to thrive. After the Second World War, the nation was devastated. Some 3 million people died in the war – seven times as many as in the US, which had twice the population. Millions more were injured, missing, or ill from nuclear radiation. Much of Tokyo and other cities had been leveled by firebombing. The country's postwar GDP fell to less than $1,500 per capita, well below that of most Latin American countries.[5]

The Japanese people came together to rebuild their country. With an almost superhuman commitment to collective action and work, Japan became the second wealthiest nation on earth in only a few decades. And more than just riches, Japan has achieved remarkable success on almost every other metric of national well-being: a low crime rate, a high level of social equality, and the highest rate of adult literacy and numeracy in the world.

The downside of harmony

This book is about the remarkable success that Japan has achieved, thanks to the mass mobilization of capital and labor that norms of social solidarity helped make possible. But there is another side to the story – how aspects of those same norms now hold the country back. Indeed, as we argue throughout, Japan faces a crisis of harmony. Unless it makes changes to its traditional ways, the future of the nation is in danger.

How can harmony cause harm? To answer that question, we should return to Hadenya and the other small coastal towns of the Tohoku region. Just like Hadenya, those towns are disproportionately populated by 'old' people, and deference to the elderly is disrupting rational efforts to rebuild the region that was destroyed by the tsunami. Seniors want to spend their twilight years in their ancestral villages, so huge sums are being spent on reconstructing small and dangerous coastal communities populated largely by older people, rather than on supporting consolidated towns that could offer opportunities for the young.[6]

Hadenya's social organization rested on rigid gender roles, with women preparing food while men gathered firewood. Similarly, rigid gender roles have been evident throughout the country, and are certainly part and parcel of Japan's remarkable rise over the past five decades. Tireless efforts by women at home made possible the socialization and education of Japanese youth, while simultaneously allowing their husbands to put in exhausting hours in factories and on farms. Today, with Japan's population in decline, women are needed in the workforce; but Japan is having difficulty adjusting. Corporate glass ceilings limit women's contributions to the labor market, and heavy burdens at home discourage them from having children, thus contributing to Japan's demographic crisis.

Finally, Japan's social harmony is based on rigid 'insider/outsider' distinctions. One way to maintain harmony is by keeping outsiders out. For centuries, Japan's insularity protected it from conflict. Today, though, in an era of globalization, that same insularity shuts Japan off from the immigrants, ideas, and markets it needs to thrive. While other countries in Asia, such as Korea, China, and Singapore, are embracing globalization, Japan has stagnated.

Cooperation in a hostile land

Most people attribute Japan's social harmony to the nation's geography and agricultural history. Though the country consists of nearly 7,000 islands, most people live on four – Hokkaido, Honshu, Shikoku, and Kyushu. Japan is smaller than California, and three-quarters of the land is forested, mountainous, and unsuitable for settling. This pushes the entire population of 127 million people into largely coastal territory with an area smaller than that of Kentucky.

Japan is located in a volcanic zone in the Pacific Ring of Fire. The country has some 108 active volcanoes, or 10 percent of the world's total, and is hit by several bad typhoons every year. It also sits over an extremely unstable region of the earth's crust, where four tectonic plates interact. This makes it the site of nearly 10 percent of the world's large earthquakes, despite covering an area less than 0.1 percent of the world's total.[7] Tokyo is surprisingly prone to earthquakes: of the 1,500 per year that are big enough for humans to notice, 40–50 occur in Tokyo.[8] Earthquakes of magnitude 8 and above on the Richter scale have struck Japan in the years 684, 869, 1361, 1489, 1611, 1703, 1707, 1854, 1891, 1896, 1923, 1933, 1944, 1946, 1952, 1968, 2003, and 2011, typically killing thousands of people; in between those years, there have been hundreds of 'smaller' earthquakes (of magnitude 6–7), often quite deadly to populated areas.[9] In a nation of islands, earthquakes inevitably bring tsunamis – an especially cruel fate when such a high proportion of the population lives near the coast.

The small proportion of arable land, combined with the many natural disasters, kept Japan a poor country for much of its pre-industrial history. So for thousands of years, Japanese people have had to pull together to tend crops, protect themselves, and survive. They have developed a sense of fatalism, and seek to endure nature rather than conquer it. These attitudes are reflected in everyday language, with people stressing the importance of *gaman* (endurance, perseverance). Mothers tell their children, '*gaman shinasai*' (be patient, put up with what you are dealing with), and people will often say '*shikata ga nai*' (it can't be helped) or '*ganbatte*' (tough it out, be strong, do your best).

Japan has also been influenced by Confucianism, an ethical and political philosophy that emerged 2,500 years ago in China, from where it spread throughout Asia. The philosophy emphasizes the cultivation of ethics, rather than faith in God, and places special focus on both loyalty and social harmony – characteristics that were already important to Japan. Though Japan no longer sees itself as being as strongly Confucian as China or Korea, the lasting influence of Confucianism on the Japanese mindset is evident.

The history of *wa*

In Japan, the ideal of social harmony came to be known as *wa* – the creation and maintenance of peaceful unity and conformity within a social group, with a commitment to cohesive community taking precedence over personal interests. *Wa* is so central to Japanese history that the *kanji* character for it, 和, is an ancient symbol for Japan itself. When Prince Shotoku issued Japan's first constitution in the seventh century, he decreed in Article 1 that *wa* was to occupy a premier place in the value system, and he stressed the word several times in the document.

For a thousand years or so, *wa* was tempered by Buddhism and Confucianism, as well as by a feudal social system. From the twelfth century to the nineteenth, it found fertile ground in Japan's elaborate class structure, with merchants, artisans, farmers, and *burakumin* (outcasts) all dominated by a samurai warrior class. This military nobility considered itself followers of Bushido, or 'The Way of the Warrior,' which, like *wa*, emphasized such traits as benevolence, respect, honor, loyalty, obedience, duty, and self-sacrifice. The samurai class was licensed to enforce this by executing anyone they saw violating these principles – a regulation that led the other classes to cultivate a vague, indirect manner of speaking that can still be found today.

Though the caste system (and thus the formal leadership of the samurai) ended in the nineteenth century, the samurai assumed leadership in many areas of society, including in the administrative functions of the government, eventually occupying posts in the bureaucracy as 'servants' of the emperor. Japan's permanent bureaucracy, with little accountability to elected officials, has maintained a disproportionate influence in society ever since. At the same time, the values of the former samurai, such as loyalty, honor, obedience, and self-sacrifice, have continued to resonate throughout society. An example of this is provided by the isolated Japanese soldiers in Pacific island jungles who, for decades after the Second World War, refused to surrender. When they finally did come home, rather than being viewed as crackpots they were celebrated as national heroes, thanks to their extreme loyalty and perseverance on behalf of Japan and the emperor.[10]

Japan's history as an island nation also influenced the development of its culture. Surrounded by harsh seas, it was more ethnically homogeneous than many other countries. And with much coastline to defend and little area to retreat to, it had to be on guard against foreign intrusion. Two massive invasion attempts in the thirteenth century by Mongol forces with superior weaponry left their mark. Though the invasions failed, their centuries-long legacy was a deep suspicion of foreigners, including of the growing number of Christian missionaries, who, it was feared, were paving the way for a European invasion. Concerns about Christians from abroad were amplified by worries about the loyalty of Japanese Christians, especially after a large-scale Christian rebellion in Nagasaki against the regional government in the early seventeenth century.

These fears led to the drastic policy of *sakoku* (self-imposed isolation) in the 1630s. For two centuries, no foreigners (apart from Chinese and Dutch merchants) were allowed to enter Japan beyond a small artificial island in Nagasaki, and nor could any Japanese leave the country, on pain of death. Japan finally opened up in the 1850s, but only in response to treaties forced on the country by gunboat after US Navy Commodore Matthew Perry arrived in the Uraga Channel with warships and threatened Japan with cannon. The United States, Russia, the Netherlands, Britain, and France all forced unequal trade agreements on Japan in short order.

Commodore Perry's arrival was a wake-up call to the Japanese leaders, who saw how far they had fallen behind during the period of isolation. This realization, combined with the social and economic instability brought about by the imposition of the trade treaties, galvanized a revolutionary movement led by samurai in southwestern Japan. The samurai overthrew the Tokugawa Shogunate and established a modern imperial system, together with a professional army. The revolution came to be known as the Meiji Restoration, since the emperor (Emperor Meiji, emperor of 'enlightened rule') was restored to power, even though the revolutionary leaders, who then became oligarchs, actually dominated politics in the Meiji period.

Reversing the isolation of the *sakoku* period, the Meiji oligarchy reached out to the world aggressively. They invited foreign advisors to teach Japanese leaders Western science, culture, and languages, and sent large numbers of Japanese officials and students abroad.[11] However, continued fears of 'the other' dominated their policies. Their national slogans were 'Enrich the Nation, Strengthen the Military,' and 'Japanese Spirit with Western Technology.' In other words, they sought outside science and technology for the purposes of maintaining a strong nation and the 'Japaneseness' of the people.

Within a few decades, the Meiji oligarchy successfully transformed Japan from a feudal into an industrial society. Like other capitalist countries in the late nineteenth century, Japan sought markets, labor, and resources abroad. The country's growing economic and military strength, and its consequent expansionism, led to a series of conflicts with both Asian and European countries from the 1890s all the way through the Second World War.

Japan's colonization in East Asia also brought more foreigners to Japan, especially Koreans and Chinese. This, too, resulted in conflict. For example, following the Great Kanto Earthquake of 1923 – a quake of 8.3 on the Richter scale, accompanied by a 40-foot-high tsunami and a fire, which together claimed 140,000 lives – the Japanese people pulled together in social solidarity (as they so often have done in the face of tragedy).[12] However, this social solidarity did not extend to residents of other nationalities. In the aftermath of the tragedy, rumors spread that Korean immigrants were poisoning wells and plotting to overthrow the weakened Japanese government. Vigilante groups set up roadblocks and killed thousands of ethnic Koreans and hundreds of Chinese and Okinawans, and even Japanese speakers of regional dialects who were mistaken for Koreans. Once more, harmony among Japanese was accompanied by fear of and hostility toward 'the other.'

The components of *wa*

Some 1,400 years after *wa* was written into Japan's constitution, the concept remains widely accepted. *Wa* is not a collection of specific behaviors, and nor is it an ideology. Rather, it is what social scientists would describe as a set of culturally specific social norms: that is, standards of behavior that people in the culture are expected to adhere to and which are enforced through strong social pressure. As with other norms, *wa* suggests to people what is appropriate or inappropriate behavior in a given situation, thus helping to shape interpersonal interaction and relations.

Schools in Japan inculcate *wa* through a strong focus on character building, by having children share in cleaning and other duties from a young age. Japanese businesses encourage *wa* in the workplace, often providing new employees with several months of intensive training to indoctrinate them into the company's values, such as the value of solidarity, commitment, or community. Training focuses not only on technical matters, but also on molding 'Toyota man' or 'Ueda Bank man.'[13]

Wa permeates other aspects of life, too, such as sports. The American author and journalist Robert Whiting wrote a fascinating and humorous book called *You Gotta Have Wa*, which analyzed the differences between American and Japanese baseball.[14] Whiting describes such features of the game – known as *besuboru* – as obsessive ritualism, rigorous pre-game practices, and tolerance of tied games. Injured pitchers are encouraged to 'pitch through the pain,' all of which American players in Japan find completely baffling.

Individuals who break the idea of *wa* for personal gain are brought in line either overtly or covertly, by reprimands from superiors or by the tacit disapproval of family and colleagues. Hierarchical structures and a checks-and-balances system for ego in the workplace ensure the continuation of *wa*, and public disagreement with leadership is generally suppressed in the interests of preserving communal harmony.

Though *wa* is a complex behavioral and belief system, it can be understood largely in terms of a number of overlapping features, the first of which is *honor*. Drop a small scrap of paper in a restaurant and the waiter will likely chase you down for blocks to return it to you. Leave a dirty handkerchief behind and the same waiter may hand it to you washed, ironed, and folded when you next come in a month later. Leave a bicycle unlocked on the street and it just may remain there for weeks.

A behavior that is puzzling to many visitors to Japan is the wearing of *masuku*, or surgical masks. Foreigners often assume that people wear masks because they are afraid of catching colds. But in fact, the mask is only worn when someone wants to avoid infecting others, typically because they already have a cold or cough. Wearing a *masuku* is an honorable act of kindness and responsibility.

New York Times columnist Nicholas Kristof tells a wonderful story of honor in Japan:

> I would have mentioned my favorite example of how Japan is a society of high trust. It's the fact that the easiest people to steal from are the police. You see, you just walk up to any police box (*koban*) at a train station and say you need money to get home, and you'll get $20 or whatever in train fair [*sic*]. You have to give your name and promise to pay it back, but you don't have to show any ID. When I once asked a policeman why they didn't require ID, he looked at me as if I was very slow and said something to the effect: *People need train money because they've lost their wallets. But if they've lost their wallets, they don't have ID.* He added, though, that a day or two later, the borrower invariably comes by to repay the money.[15]

It is, of course, difficult to imagine a system like that working in the US.

Another aspect of *wa* is *self-reliance and service to others*. Children learn from a very early age how to become independent, in order to minimize their burden on others. In pre-schools and kindergarten, they learn how to get dressed and fold clothes by themselves. Many schools intentionally make children change their clothes before naptime, so that they learn how to fold their clothes on their own.

Even young children are assigned various tasks at school. At pre-school, for example, toddlers must take attendance, wipe the tables before lunch, and clean the cages of school rabbits. They develop pride in being the *otoban-san* (person in charge, on duty).

From elementary to high school, pupils clean their classrooms and bathrooms every day. Twenty minutes of cleaning time is typical, and students must bring a *zokin* (rag) to school for the purpose. They water flowers in the school yard and serve school lunches to their classmates, wearing an apron, hat, and *masuku*.

Finally, children must not be dropped off at school by car. From first grade on, they must walk to and home from school, no matter the distance, or else take public transportation. You might see first-grade children taking the subway by themselves, including transferring trains, to attend school.

It is important to note that self-reliance *within the Japanese system* is what matters most. The kind of autonomy typically valued in the United States – such as controlling one's own learning, pursuing technological or artistic creativity, or learning to make independent decisions in a new and unstructured environment – is less emphasized in Japan. Independence is valued insofar as it reduces your burden on others – so in fact, Japanese independence is forged from a communal interest. Independence for the sake of self-interest is aggressively weeded out.

This is because *wa* is also characterized by *rigid orderliness*. This is manifested in virtually every aspect of life. Japanese cities are stunningly clean and relatively quiet. People do not throw trash on the ground or talk loudly on cell phones. Minutely detailed rules, some explicit and others implicit, shape every aspect of life.

For example, children at a US pre-school may or may not need to bring a knapsack to school. In contrast, the material requirements of a Japanese pre-school are both numerous and detailed, involving a bedding set (consisting of several pieces and measuring exactly the correct dimensions), a precise uniform, two towels of specific sizes, a gargling cup, eating utensils, a wide array of footwear (shoes for walking to pre-school, outdoor shoes for use in the playground, indoor shoes for use at pre-school), and containers for all of the above ('a schoolbag, a blanket bag, a bag for eating utensils, a box for eating utensils, a bag for clothes, a bag for changing clothes, a bag for clothes after they have been changed out of, and a bag for shoes').[16] Each bag must be of a specific size, color, and material, and many of them are not available for sale in stores, so that preparing a child for pre-school involves procuring the materials and sewing the articles – a full-time job that can take weeks.

Another example is shoes. Some families in the United States ask people to take off their shoes when visiting, in order to help maintain a clean home. This is typically an informal arrangement. In Japan, though, the wearing, and the removal, of shoes is a highly structured affair. Shoes are completely banned inside the home and in many public buildings as well, such as schools and health clinics, most of which provide slippers for visitors to step into. Furthermore, there is a specific line of demarcation between 'shoe territory' and 'slipper territory.' Placing a shoe a centimeter into slipper territory will earn a reprimand or a startled stare. The same goes for placing a sock or a slipper in shoe territory, as it is then spoiled for its expected return to slipper land. Of course, these are mistakes that even a young Japanese child would never make, having implicitly learned the rules over the years. It is all frequently befuddling to foreigners, particularly since the demarcation lines are often in quite unlikely places, such as changing rooms in clothing stores. The bottom line is that in the US, whatever is not prohibited is probably allowed, whereas in Japan it tends to be the opposite: if it isn't specifically permitted, it's probably prohibited.

Rigid orderliness in Japan goes hand in hand with bureaucracy. There are more than a million Japanese civil servants, whose role includes making and implementing rules that everyone has to follow. Among these is a national registration system, under which all Japanese must regularly report to the government on numerous household issues, for example any change to the family's address. Within this administrative sector, there is an elite group of a few thousand, including several hundred at each key ministry, who hold huge sway over the country, operating with a great deal of independence from the country's elected officials. This elite set of permanent bureaucrats has much more power of policy-making than unelected officials in countries such as the US, Canada, or Great Britain, though it may be comparable to the powerful civil service of France.

Rigid orderliness overlaps with *enforced equality*. An example of this is found in Japanese public swimming pools, where even a completely bald man must wear a swimming cap. A rule is a rule; and just because there is no need for the rule, that is no reason for it not to be enforced. Similarly, Japanese children do not skip grades, no matter how talented; nor are they held back, no matter how poorly they perform.

Equality is emphasized not only in enforcement of rules, but in broader social norms. A popular Japanese saying is 'The nail that sticks up gets hammered down' (*Deru kui wa utareru*), and Japanese children learn not to be that nail.

Another feature of *wa* is *extreme loyalty*, as evidenced by the long hours of Japanese salarymen and their refusal to take allotted vacations. Interestingly, unlike in some other Asian contexts, such as China, loyalty is principally to the employer, rather than to the family.

The aftermath of the March 2011 earthquake revealed fascinating examples of workplace loyalty. Many people in Tokyo belong to food co-ops and thus have several crates of meat, fruit, vegetables, bread, and other products hand-delivered to their apartments every week. A couple of hours after the earthquake, a deliveryman was seen making his normal Tokyo deliveries. Though almost every elevator in the city was shut down, he had stayed on the job and was hauling crates – heavy not only with food, but also with ice – up many flights of stairs. The deliveryman apparently had a great deal of loyalty to his employer and felt he had to finish the job, whatever the challenges, even though that delayed his return to his family for several hours after the huge earthquake.

Company loyalty also has a negative side, as it discourages whistle-blowing, which is seen in Japan as a rare and shocking affront to corporate bonds. Bad corporate behavior ensues when no one is willing to speak out about it.

Wa is also characterized by *sharp hierarchies*. Everyone in Japan knows his or her place. A college student, for example, will not casually fire off an email to a professor, asking about an assignment. Indeed, the student may have no way of finding out the professor's email address, as that is privileged information and certainly beyond what a student has the right to know. Similarly a student, or even a visiting scholar, may not drop off a paper in a mailbox or leave it with a secretary for a Japanese professor to read later or to sign (unless, of course, he or she has first received explicit permission to do so).

Honor, orderliness, and hierarchy all come into play in Japan's ritualized bowing system, which involves different degrees of subservience in response to particular contexts among people of varying levels of importance. There is one type of bow for beginning a conversation with a co-worker, another type of bow from a retail worker to a departing customer, and a very different type of bow for expressing remorse.[17]

Though Japan is hierarchical, it is not as economically stratified as the US or many other countries. It has an unusually large middle class and comparatively little poverty. In the US, the average income of the wealthiest 10 percent of the population is 15.9 times that of the poorest 10 percent. By contrast, in Japan the difference is only 4.5 times – one of the lowest ratios in the world.[18] There is much less conspicuous consumption among corporate tycoons in Japan than in the US, and business leaders are often embarrassed to be paid too much. This may be one of the reasons why Japanese are comfortable with hierarchical corporate relations and demonstrate loyalty within them.

So does this mean that Japan is free of conflict? Far from it. Differences by class, gender, nationality, age, and political perspective divide Japan just as any other country, and examining the diversity and conflict within the nation is critical to understanding it.[19] In fact, rather than mitigating it, *wa* actually serves to intensify conflict in Japan, as the very rigidity of the Japanese system can amplify feelings of dissatisfaction, resentment, and humiliation until they explode. As noted in one famous sociological study of Japan:

> The harmony of the village has its cost. Underneath the placid landscape there are geological faults – a personal incompatibility, a clash of economic interest, a belief that one has been cheated – along with tensions built up which require occasional release.[20]

This brings us to the final and seemingly most contradictory aspect of *wa*: the drawing and maintenance of *sharp boundaries between the in-group and out-groups*, including redefining those groups through ostracism, expulsion, upheaval, and factionalism to enforce societal norms and expectations.[21] After all, how can harmony be maintained if the bad apples are not excluded from the barrel? So while, on the one hand, Japanese schools emphasize character, they are also noted for a particularly intense form of bullying of children who do not fit in.

Not surprisingly, this maintenance of in-group and out-group also contributes to Japan's suspicion of foreigners, as social stability among the Japanese is presumed to require diligence in walling out others. It is rare for foreigners to be perceived as Japanese – even those whose families have lived in Japan for several generations, such as many Korean immigrants. Skepticism of foreigners influences Japan's attitudes toward immigration, English teaching, study abroad, and many other issues pertinent to international competitiveness in the twenty-first century.

This issue could come into play during the 2020 Olympics, when athletes and tourists from around the world descend on Tokyo. For example, most Japanese have a very negative attitude toward tattoos, which are typically associated with gangsters. Recently, a Maori-language lecturer, in Japan for an academic conference, was denied entry to a bathhouse for having a tattoo on her face, in line with bathhouse policies forbidding anyone with tattoos from using the facilities.[22] This led a newscaster to ask how Japan could successfully host the Olympics when so many of the world's athletes sport tattoos.

A further example of Japan's insularity, as well as of the influence of the bureaucracy, is its stubborn whaling policy. Japan kills around a thousand whales a year, through a highly controversial 'scientific research' program, in a barely concealed attempt to contravene an international ban on commercial whaling. Despite condemnation and hostility from the outside world for this policy, the country has stubbornly resisted change. But whale is not even a commonly purchased food item in Japan. Much of the meat – about 100 metric tonnes a year – is channeled, at government expense, into school lunch programs, supposedly 'to teach children about the kind of school lunches Japan had in the past.'[23]

There seems to be little reason for Japan to continue whaling. The enterprise costs the country millions of dollars a year, while harming its attempts to enhance its international reputation. As it turns out, the whaling policy stems more from a desire by Japanese bureaucrats to defend the country's 'fish-eating' culture against outside 'meat-eating' cultures than from any Japanese interest in actually eating (or otherwise using) whale meat.[24] Attempts to change Japanese whaling policy are bitterly resisted by bureaucrats in the Ministry of Agriculture, Forestry, and Fisheries, who draw much of their power and influence from the management of whaling programs. The ministry's Fisheries Agency consists of people who have made a career out of defending Japan's supposed whale-eating culture (*geishoku bunka*). The ministry caused a public outcry in 2011, when it snuck a 2.3 billion yen (about $23 million) subsidy for whaling into a supplementary budget designed to revitalize the tsunami-devastated Tohoku region. Of that, 1.8 billion yen went to research whaling, and the rest was devoted to chartering a boat to monitor and block the activities of anti-whaling groups. According to local press reports in the area, 'no one understands why that money was spent on whaling when it should have been spent rebuilding our city or helping other people in Tohoku.'[25]

Whaling is far from the most pressing issue facing Japan, but it provides an example of the power of the bureaucracy and the challenges it creates for reform on issues such as immigration, gender, and education. With whaling, there is little economic rationale for continuing the current policy, and yet the policy remains unchanged. How will Japan tackle larger issues, in which the systemic obstacles to reform are much more overwhelming?

Honor, self-reliance, orderliness, and loyalty are very positive traits that the Japanese quite properly take pride in. These characteristics have helped make Japan one of the most successful countries in the world, whether measured by income level, social and economic equity, education rates, or health and longevity of the population.

But with Japan teetering on the edge of its former glory, have these qualities become overvalued to the point of crisis? How does the emphasis on *wa* discourage such traits as flexibility, diversity, and openness, which are so crucial in today's knowledge economy and information society? Unlike the industrial era, where vertical hierarchies prevailed, the post-industrial era of contemporary times favors far less formal horizontal networks. This is the paradox of harmony in Japan: by holding on so tightly to its traditional notions of harmony, Japan risks unraveling them. This book will explore how that process is taking place, and why.

*   *   *

We start in chapter 1 by looking at the system used for decades by postwar corporations to fuel the country's astronomical growth. Firms promised lifetime employment to Japan's salarymen, in exchange for slavish devotion to work above all else. The status quo was carefully maintained and was responsible for what was, without exaggeration, one of the fastest-growing economies in the history of humankind. But when that system fell apart, little changed. And now the very system that for decades worked in Japan's favor is leading it into decline. What happened? And why are so many Japanese companies having difficulty in retooling for a contemporary, interconnected, global economy?

From there, we will look at the intersection of economic change and gender relations in Japan. New forms of male–female relations are shaking up long-held assumptions for dating, marriage, and childrearing. Changes in the economy and family structure are also disturbing a long relied-upon safety net for Japanese women, who have been brought up to seek out husbands and raise children. Chapter 2 is about 'herbivorous girly men' – and the women they shy away from.

With childrearing in decline, in 2013 the elderly population hit a record 25 percent of the total. Market analysts told CNBC that adult diapers are expected to outsell baby nappies for the first time in 2014.[26] Naturally, policy-makers and citizens are worried about the decline in a working population, especially when the elderly need care. But an insular Japan is concerned that bringing in new workers will disrupt the *wa* – so what options are left? In chapter 3, we look at issues of immigration and other clumsy attempts to address the labor shortage in Japan.

Of course, Japan's economic troubles are starting to show in its international policy. The country has not had a traditional military for decades, and potential divisions between the political left and right were minimized by unity over the issue of 'yen diplomacy,' by which Japan's lack of military might was seen as secondary to its spending power. With Tokyo a humanitarian aid leader and relief provider, 'soft power' occupied a central role in diplomacy. But as Japan's economic power has declined, so has the country's diplomatic outreach. A return to a more active military role is being promoted not only by ultra-nationalists – who have long complicated Japan's pacifist posture by questioning whether the nation was actually responsible for its wartime atrocities – but also by the nation's center-right politicians. Chapter 4 examines the tensions that Japan faces as it is torn between its pacifist constitution and the rising pressure – including from its staunchest ally, the United States – to remilitarize.

It would be impossible to discuss the future of Japan without looking at its biggest postwar crisis: 3/11 – the earthquake, tsunami, and nuclear disaster of March 2011. Chapter 5 looks at how the nuclear crisis unfolded and how it came to be that many of the issues discussed in this book, including inflexible ideas of hierarchy and deferential treatment of superiors, only escalated the crisis. Was the disaster at Fukushima Daiichi a consequence of Japanese culture, or was it rather a result of the inherent danger and instability of nuclear power?

Finally, we examine one of Japan's greatest achievements, and one that is central to its harmony paradox: its educational system. The envy of most of the world, Japan's schools turn out graduates who are highly literate and accomplished in both math and science. The system has also been molding children into ideal citizens for generations, stressing civic responsibility and cultural identity as part of its curriculum. But along the way, the system has also cultivated the weaknesses of Japanese culture: intolerance of diversity, blinkered critical thinking, and a markedly poor grasp of the English language. Chapter 6 examines the Japanese education system and questions whether it is successfully preparing students for a globalized world.

We close by looking back at how Japan has managed its paradoxes over the last 75 years – through times of war and peace, boom and bust, glory and defeat – and ponder what may lie ahead.

CHAPTER ONE

The Whistleblower

Masaharu Hamada is a long-term employee of Olympus, a company famous for its cameras and medical equipment. After years at the company, and with an outstanding sales record in Japan and the United States, Hamada was stunned when he was suddenly demoted from his position as team leader of his sales division. Despite his talent for selling, he was assigned meaningless and solitary work, such as reading elementary training manuals and taking rudimentary tests designed for new employees. The intention was, in the condescending language of his supervisors, 'to educate Hamada.' He was denied a raise and promotion and was banned from contacting his former colleagues and clients. At one point, he was almost driven to a nervous breakdown, and he contemplated suicide.

Why would Olympus waste one of its top employees? To answer that, we need to go back to 2007, when Hamada discovered that his supervisor was trying to recruit an employee from a client firm who had classified information. Headhunting from a client firm is illegal in Japan, but his supervisor had already approached another employee from the same client. As a salesman, Hamada had been on the receiving end of complaints from his client. He brought the case before Olympus's compliance unit; despite the firm's privacy-protection rules, Hamada's name was leaked to the very boss he was complaining about.

A panicked Hamada wrote a letter to Olympus's president, Tsuyoshi Kikukawa, who would later be implicated in an accounting scandal. Kikukawa forwarded Hamada's letter to the personnel office, which suggested that Hamada's troubles may have been affecting his health. Personnel provided a doctor and insisted that he see only that doctor. The office had a plan: the doctor would diagnose Hamada as mentally ill, make him take extended sick leave, and then force him to quit. A justifiably anxious Hamada saw through the plot and refused to visit the doctor, which further angered the personnel director.

In desperation, he turned to the firm's labor union. The union director seemed supportive and sympathetic, but Japan's labor unions are company-based and are often tied to a firm's management. Such was the case with Olympus: even the union director pressured Hamada to see the company doctor. There was nobody left to turn to.

Reluctantly, in 2008 Hamada sued Olympus for its unfair reprisals. In 2010, despite pressure from the judge, he refused to settle with Olympus. He then lost his case in the lower court. But in 2011, the Tokyo High Court reversed the decision and ordered Olympus to pay Hamada 2.2 million yen ($22,000) in damages. In 2012, the Supreme Court rejected the appeal by Olympus and Hamada's former supervisor. Victory was assured. It was the first time that the Supreme Court had heard a whistleblower case.

Whistleblowers are a rarity in Japan, but Hamada was supported by some of the few that there are, including Hiroaki Kushioka, who had retired from a trucking firm in northern Japan after three decades of corporate harassment for talking to a journalist about a secret cartel among trucking firms that illegally inflated prices. For 30 years he was given menial work, such as gardening or shoveling snow, and his supervisors continually pressured him to quit. In 2002 he sued his firm in a district court for job discrimination and human rights abuses, and in 2005 he won. It was Kushioka's former lawyers – Japan's top attorneys on whistleblowing and labor law – who helped Hamada win in the Supreme Court.[1]

Hamada's plight is not over yet. In a testament to Japanese corporate loyalty, he still loves Olympus and is not ready to quit his job. His former supervisor now serves as an executive director at the company. Even after the Tokyo Bar Association warned Olympus about its abuse of Hamada's human rights in 2012, he continued to be assigned demeaning work, so that he was obliged to turn to the Tokyo Bar Association a second time. The following year, another Olympus employee filed a lawsuit after he, too, was given a menial job (in this case, working under Hamada). He claimed that it was a form of psychological pressure and harassment to get him to quit.[2]

Japanese companies tend to work like clans, and whistleblowers quickly become outcasts. As the firms globalize, they must seriously address corporate governance and transparency issues. And to do that, they need to understand that whistleblowing is an invaluable aspect of good governance. It should be encouraged as a way of eradicating unethical practices and elevating companies to higher standards. The silver lining in Hamada's case is that the public is now more aware of whistleblowing problems, and the publicity has ensured that it is on Hamada's side. Hopefully, the Supreme Court's ruling will set a precedent for Japanese firms in dealing with whistleblowers. Hamada's next challenge is to push the Diet (Parliament) to enact laws penalizing firms that abuse whistleblowers. 'We need a society where honest hardworking people don't lose out,' says Hamada.[3] His struggles continue.

Japan's miracle economy

Hamada and Olympus can only be understood within the broader context of Japan's economic development and business culture, as it has developed over the past seven decades. After the Second World War, nearly half of Japan's industry and national infrastructure lay in ruins. The United States, frightened that the Soviet Union would find ample ideological territory in the communal society of postwar Japan, contributed food, production supplies, and transportation materials to Japan's reconstruction efforts, in order to bolster its resistance to Soviet influence.

Japan's priorities shifted from fighting the US to fighting poverty. Early on, Prime Minister Shigeru Yoshida (1946–47, 1948–54) guided this trend through the 'Yoshida Doctrine,' which prioritized recovery and growth, limited funding for national defense, and relied on America for protection. By the mid-1950s, Japan had already returned to its pre-war levels of industrial production. After that, its GDP increased more than fifty-fold between 1955 and 1990. The Yoshida Doctrine steered Japan out of poverty and ruin, into a land of skyscrapers and bullet trains and toward the world's second-largest economy at the time.

This burgeoning economy required corporate workers who would devote themselves tirelessly to the expansion and recovery effort. Soldiers (and a generation of children raised to become soldiers) found a new niche as corporate warriors. They worked long hours and demonstrated the same kind of loyalty to their firms and their bosses as was once reserved for the emperor and the nation. Having experienced the desperation of poverty during and immediately after the war, they worked (and overworked) to improve their lives and rescue Japan from the shame of its defeat.

Workers were given lifetime employment, and promotion was based on a combination of seniority and personal talent. The salary-men trusted that their lives would improve year by year. Giving less than all of their energy in return would have displayed ingratitude.

By the 1980s, Japan seemed to be an unstoppable force in global economics. Having recovered from the 1970s' oil crises, it had accumulated huge international trade surpluses, most notably with the US. Tense American lawmakers insisted that it stop free-riding on America's open market and security protection. American economists argued that the Japanese should spend more time on leisure and less time at work, in order to stimulate domestic consumption and reduce the lopsided trade balance with the US. Scholars warned about Japan's close government–business alignments and urged the US to deal with it more aggressively.[4] Japanese management became a hot subject for research, and Japanese language courses became popular among college students in the US and other countries.

America had to react. And in September 1985 it did. An agreement between the US, Japan, and three European powers – the Plaza Accord – effectively raised the value of the yen to reduce Japan's mounting trade surplus with the United States. The Japanese government relaxed interest rates to stimulate Tokyo's export-led growth. Easy money flowed into Japanese real estate and stock investments. Prices skyrocketed. By 1990, the aggregate value of land in Japan was said to be 50 percent higher than the total land value of the rest of the planet.[5] The emperor's palace in central Tokyo alone was worth more than all of California. Japanese firms went on real-estate shopping sprees, grabbing foreign landmarks such as the Rockefeller Center and Columbia Pictures. Fear of Japan was palpable in the United States. An over-the-top scene from the post-apocalyptic 1990 film *Prayer of the Rollerboys* showed the Harvard University campus being airlifted to Tokyo by Japanese helicopters.

Young women (dubbed 'office ladies' or 'OLs') went shopping, too. Though they usually had entry-level jobs and no career ambitions, they were armed with a strong yen and a penchant for upmarket fashion. With savings and bonuses from their meager jobs, these women traveled to major cities in the US, Europe, and Asia to shop for expensive brand-name bags and clothes. Tourism in cities like Honolulu came to depend on such women.

The 1980s was a euphoric era in Japan, and for many people the question was when, not if, Japan would overtake the US as the world's economic giant. But as we all know, Harvard University never ended up in Tokyo. The ever-expanding Japanese economy had to pop.

Bursting the bubble

The inevitable burst came in 1990–91, with the collapse of the stock and real-estate markets. People soon realized that their affluence had been an illusion, built on easy credit and speculation. When it went up in smoke, most people returned to their traditional habits of frugality. Banks went out of business and property values went into freefall. The frenzied rush of domestic spending came to a halt as the free money dried up.

Japan entered its 'lost decade' (actually two decades) of economic recession. Japanese real estate lost 90 percent of its value; jobs became harder to find; and a new generation of Japanese shoppers increasingly eschewed Luis Vuitton for cheap goods in 100-yen ($1) stores.

Japan saw slow growth and deflation through the 1990s and 2000s. Between 1994 and 2006, its share of the global economy almost halved – from 18 percent to 10 percent. By 2012, China had more Fortune 500 companies than Japan.[6] When it comes to per capita income, Japan has fallen behind many other advanced industrial countries: from second in 1993, it fell to eighteenth place in the 2008 international rankings. In terms of GDP per capita adjusted by purchasing-power parity, Japan was passed by the Asian Tigers: by Singapore in 1993; Hong Kong in 1997; and Taiwan in 2010.[7] Rising national debt forced the government to cut back on safety nets for the increased number of those in need.

Before the bubble burst, fresh graduates in Japan had plenty of options. There was a market for regular full-time employees with high-school or college degrees, and firms would provide specialized job training for new recruits. Male graduates typically faced no problem in finding guaranteed lifetime employment. Meanwhile, female workers were expected to become 'office ladies', or to take menial or clerical work for a few years until they got married.

Since the 1990s, however, many young men have joined the fastest-growing segment of the Japanese labor market – the so-called 'irregular' (part-time or temporary) workers at the bottom of the labor hierarchy. Irregular jobs used to be dominated by *shufu* (housewives), who would re-enter the labor market part time once their children started school. Today, many young men compete with these housewives for low-paid, part-time, dead-end jobs largely in the service sector.[8] Japan's labor market is thus largely bifurcated: permanent salaried employees on the one hand; irregular workers on the other.[9] Both groups face serious challenges.

The salaryman's slog

It's 10 p.m. and a haggard middle-aged man is dozing on Tokyo's subway. His gray suit has wrinkled over the course of his workday. His mouth hangs open and his legs are outstretched, despite the etiquette reminders hanging throughout the train. His napping head slides slowly downward until it rests on the left shoulder of a young woman. She moves an inch to the right, but his head slides again and again settles on her shoulder. This is a common scene on Tokyo's subway.

He is just one of hundreds of salarymen, Japan's white-collar businessmen – corporate warriors fighting for the companies on which their lifestyle depends. The salaryman makes up the majority of the male workforce in Japan.

The man on the subway is Toru Kato, 49 years old, a white-collar manager at an office maintenance and cleaning company in Shinjuku, the buzzing business district of Tokyo. He wakes at 6 a.m. to get to the office by 8:30. He'll often stay in the office, finishing extra work or joining an obligatory drinking party with business partners, before catching the last train home. Tonight was his lucky night: he may be home by 10:45 p.m.

Toru works about 60 hours from Monday through Friday; but like his colleagues, he only declares some of his overtime work. The unpaid work (called 'service overtime') is considered necessary and obligatory at times of high demand. Like most salarymen, he rarely takes the two weeks of vacation he is offered, as he feels guilty about burdening his colleagues with extra work while he is away.

Toru and his family live in Saitama City, a suburb of Tokyo. He commutes into work for an hour, a typical commute for the Tokyo area. He is committed to his family, but admits that he is not often available as a father. Even on weekends, he often plays obligatory games of golf with his business clients, or else studies for an exam required for promotion. Currently, he is preparing for the TOEIC (Test of English for International Communication), a popular international test for business people, to improve his previous score.

Toru's firm promises the security of lifetime employment. In addition, it provides twice-a-year bonuses, monthly subsidies for transportation and housing, and generous retirement benefits. Toru can expect to climb the corporate ladder, with steady pay rises based on a seniority system that rewards loyal workers.

Toru's wife, Satomi, is a stay-at-home mom who takes care of their children, aged 15 and 17. She is responsible for the household budget, and she gives Toru a monthly allowance of $400 (out of his monthly take-home pay of $4,000) that he can spend on after-work drinking and golf. To save money, Satomi prepares a lunch box, or *bento*, for Toru every morning, alongside her children's. When the household is sent off, Satomi leaves for her part-time receptionist job at a neighborhood dentist.

Toru's family enjoys middle-class life, with his children going to Kumon to study math, and then on to piano and swimming lessons. He is plagued by overwork, long commutes, and a lack of sleep, but he is proud of his achievements at work and of his role as the breadwinner in his family.

To most Japanese men, the ideal life means having a full-time white-collar job. Though at first glance, the idea of loyalty-based promotion and lifetime employment may seem a wonderful way to live, the salaryman's life is far from easy. He typically works 60–80 hours per week, and rarely sees his children.

The salaryman is a conundrum of hard work and wasted effort. With a workforce so willing to dedicate themselves to extreme endurance efforts on behalf of their firms, one might imagine that Japanese companies would be just as unstoppable now as they were during the boom years. But these same salarymen struggle to survive the enormous workloads and the emotional toll of their work obligations. And lifetime employment within the system (for those lucky enough to have it) has created an environment where merit is shunned in favor of perseverance. The social cost is an underutilized, exhausted workforce and a wasted generation of human capital – all of which deprive the country of the innovation and imagination it needs to thrive.

Within Japanese corporate culture, it is difficult for employees to take vacation or leave the office early, even on a 'No Overtime Day' (see below). Some say it has become harder to take time off: workloads have increased since companies have cut back on staff to save on costs. One of the world's largest market research firms, IPSOS Global, ranked Japan as the most workaholic of 24 major countries in its 2010 report.[10] Only 33 percent of Japanese workers use up all their vacation, in contrast to 89 percent in France. The United States ranked the fifth most workaholic nation, with 57 percent vacation utilization.

Working long hours, having an obligatory golf outing on Saturdays, and never taking a vacation, overworked salarymen are prone to extreme exhaustion. Many, especially those in the Tokyo metropolitan area, commute for two hours on crowded trains, catching some sleep if they are lucky enough to be able to sit down. Many spend Sundays at home asleep, in an effort to recover and regain their strength for the coming week. Workloads and work hours have increased since the bubble burst in the early 1990s, and excessive overwork is common among young people struggling to keep full-time positions. If they don't keep up, they fear they'll face *risutora* (restructuring of an organization, i.e. firing) in the tight economy. Traditionally, the younger employees are also expected to help keep down the workloads of older employees; a fresh employee who is not the first to arrive and not the last to leave is off to a bad start.

If these workdays seem superhuman, they are. Even a lifetime of cultural acclimatization cannot train a body to operate on the brink of exhaustion for decades. Fatigue can create mental and physical problems, and some salarymen suffer from (usually untreated and stigmatized) depression. Others develop high blood pressure and hardened arteries. Fatigue can also trigger suicide. This is known as *karo-jisatsu*, 'suicide from overwork.' Of the more than 30,000 suicides recorded in 2011, a third were believed to be work related, according to the National Police Agency (though this number may include people who committed suicide after losing their jobs). Overall the suicide rate in Japan is nearly twice that in the United States (despite the Japanese having much less access to guns), and is among the highest in the Organisation for Economic Co-operation and Development (OECD). Suicide is the leading cause of death in Japan for males aged 20–44.[11]

Overwork can also lead to sudden heart failure or cerebral hemorrhage, even among workers still in their prime. *Karoshi*, or 'death from overwork,' is the 'salaryman's sudden death syndrome,' as victims often die without any record of serious illness. Perhaps the best publicized *karoshi* cases involve hamburger chain McDonald's Japan and Toyota Motors. In 2007, the manager of a McDonald's restaurant died of a brain hemorrhage at the age of 41. The Kanagawa Labor Bureau ruled that she (a rare 'salarywoman') was a victim of *karoshi*, as she had worked more than 80 hours of overtime per month for six months before she died: 20 extra hours every week, four hours per day, for six months.[12] Another McDonald's case involves a manager in Kawasaki City, near Tokyo, who in 2009 died from overwork at the age of 25. He was working 17 hours straight – from noon to 5 a.m. – before he died. After taking a seven-hour break, he returned to work and collapsed. The *karoshi* stories of Toyota men are similarly tragic. An employee died from overwork in 2002 at the age of 30, having put in more than 80 hours of overtime per month for six months before his death. In his final month, he had logged 106 extra hours at work.[13] Another Toyota case involved a 45-year-old elite engineer, who died in 2006 having worked more than 80 hours of overtime per month to develop a hybrid version of Toyota's blockbuster Camry line.[14]

No doubt *karoshi* is the gravest and the most horrific problem within Japanese corporate culture, but overwork also has broader effects. Exhausted employees are in no position to brainstorm, create, or think freely. The constant stream of work and physical fatigue leaves them drained. It is no surprise that employees are hesitant to suggest new projects or ideas that might help the company, since taking on board those suggestions would only increase an already crushing pile of work. Exhaustion is killing staff, but it is also killing ideas. Studies show that Japan has among the lowest per hour labor productivity rates of any major developed country, and some attribute this in part to its reliance on overtime work.[15] Reducing overtime may actually increase labor productivity.[16]

'No Overtime Days'

Japanese firms seem reluctant to address these underlying factors. Some companies have ignored the problems, while others have paid them lip service. For example, an American worker at Canon explained that the company introduced a 'No Overtime Day' on Wednesdays. Normally a chime would sound each day at 5:15 p.m. to announce that the workday was over, but on Wednesdays the chime was followed with the announcement: 'Today is a No Overtime [*zangyo*] Day.' However, as the American explained,

There was no admonishment to leave the office and no managers came around telling people they should go home. More importantly, the managers kept on working, and as long as they were there, none of their subordinates were going home... No Overtime Day was purely for show. Not once did I see any Canon employee leave at 5:15 p.m. on No Overtime Day.[17]

The example of 'No Overtime Days' makes it clear how difficult it is to change social norms in Japan's world. No matter what the official policy, peer pressure to stay in the office late is strong. Junior workers (*kohai*) are obligated to impress their superiors (*sempai*) by remaining in the office, the *sempai–kohai* tradition being drilled into men and women throughout their years of education. In any case, given the heavy workloads of salarymen, leaving early would only shift the burden to the following day. The only people who leave the office on time are the OLs (who have no time-sensitive work), non-regular workers (discussed below) and regular salarymen who take their work home, doing *furoshiki zangyo* or 'briefcase overtime.'

Can workers refuse to do overtime? Those who try may lose their jobs. A Hitachi employee, Hideyuki Tanaka, was fired in the late 1960s after refusing to work overtime. He took his case to court in 1978 and won, but in 1986 the Tokyo High Court overturned the lower court's decision, supporting Hitachi's claim that collective agreements with its employees gave it the right to impose overtime work and that individual consent by an employee was not necessary. In 1991, the Supreme Court upheld the Tokyo High Court's decision.[18]

During the boom years, Japanese companies had working hours from Monday through Saturday (with Saturday a half-day). When the government introduced the five-day working week in 1989, it was supposed to reduce working hours. But that never happened: workers just stayed in the office for longer during the five days of the week, in order to make up for the lost half-day; the total hours per year remained the same.

Overwork is just one of the myriad challenges the salaryman faces because of stringent corporate rules and norms in a culture of hierarchy. Blind obedience is expected. The following is from the personal blog of a young salaryman:

> Got up at 6 a.m. Commuted to work at 7:30 a.m. Started working at 9 a.m. Made a series of careless mistakes in the morning and got scolded by my supervisor. My colleagues were amazed at my stupidity ... My supervisor shouted, 'You are so useless!' and kicked my desk. Female workers sneered at me as I, red-faced with shame, profusely apologized to him. At noon, I wanted to be away from my colleagues for lunch ... I went to a restaurant at the Matsuya Department store, but left more than half of my order. Sitting at a one-person table and seeing my fatigued self in the window, I thought, 'How long am I going to have this life, until 30, 40, 50, or 60? Am I going to continue to be mocked by my colleagues?' At 9:40 p.m., after finishing the mandatory overtime, I left the office for home.[19]

As difficult as the salaryman's lot is, at least it provides economic and social security for the employee and his family. The alternative lifestyle – that of the part-time or temporary workers known as '*freeters*' – has its own set of problems.

Life of a '*freeter*'

It is 10 p.m. in Tokyo, and Kenta Yamamoto, a 25-year-old college graduate, is in his tiny apartment, tired but getting ready for work. Tonight is one of his night shifts at FamilyMart, a convenience store chain where he works part time. He pulls jeans over his skinny legs and dons a white T-shirt. Having no money to spare, he spends less than $13 per day on food, a tough task for a young man in Tokyo. Earlier today, he ate two leftover *bento*, given to him by his supervisor.

Kenta grew up 200 miles away, in Nagano, and he often wonders how he came to have such an insecure lifestyle. He was an average student at his college in Tokyo, where he majored in economics. Like his friends, he expected a few decent job offers during his third year in college. He did the rounds of companies, but no offers were forthcoming. Whereas most students land something in their junior years, Kenta continued his job hunt into his senior year, visiting dozens of job-seeking seminars for college students. He was short-listed by a small construction company during his senior year, but the final offer never came, and he graduated without any prospect of regular, full-time employment.

Kenta felt humiliated. Such cases are on the rise. He believes he is a victim of Japan's recession, but he also suspects that his family's lack of *kone* (connection) worked against him: that is, he didn't know anyone who could introduce him to a business contact.

While still at college Kenta started part-time work at FamilyMart. Since graduation, he has stayed at the same job, while increasing his hours: he now works 39 hours a week, including three night shifts. With no girlfriend, he fights loneliness and fears for his future alone.

Kenta is a *freeter* – a portmanteau term coined by Hiroshi Michishita in the late 1980s from the English word 'free' and the German word '*Arbeiter*' (worker). The term *freeter* typically applies to people below 35 who are engaged in part-time work, and usually excludes housewives and students, even if they work part time.

Kenta and the salaryman Toru (whom we met above) are two poles of the Japanese male workforce. They are both college graduates, but they have different lifestyles. And their lives tell the story of Japan's economic transition. On the one hand, the traditional expectations of corporations and employees have for years maintained a status quo of growth and satisfaction. But in a new economy, the old ways are keeping many Japanese men and women out, struggling to break into a system that mostly refuses to change. Meanwhile, companies are trapped in the amber of stale ideas.

Freeters have always existed in Japanese society, and have often been considered dreamers or 'moratorium individuals.' Dreamers would pursue unconventional career paths as musicians, singers, artists, actors or athletes, while working part time – think of the familiar stereotype of an aspiring jazz musician working in a coffee shop. The 'moratorium individual' would opt for part-time jobs because he did not want to join the corporate rat-race straight from school, and would put off full-time work for a year or so after graduating from high school or college. To both the dreamers and the moratorium individuals, being a *freeter* was a matter of choice. It appealed to people who often preferred a flexible schedule.[20]

But now the dreamers and moratorium individuals are outnumbered. Most *freeters* today *want* a full-time, permanent job, but they cannot find one. They have no alternative but to accept part-time employment without benefits.[21]

Impoverished temps

The non-regular workforce in Japan also includes *haken* ('dispatch workers' or 'temps'), hired by human resource agencies and then sent to companies on fixed contracts for short stints. Though they may work full-time hours, they are temporary employees, and are not eligible for many benefits. According to one study, the *haken* population increased from 27 percent to 40 percent in the manufacturing industry between 2002 and 2007.[22] Another report suggests that temporary work nearly doubled from 20 percent in 1990 to 34 percent in 2008.[23]

Japan's Cabinet Office estimates that there are about 4.2 million people in non-regular work – mainly *freeters, haken*, and part-time housewives. Young people have been hit hardest. In 2010, 45 percent of workers aged 15–24 held part-time or temporary jobs, a leap from 17.2 percent in 1988. There are almost twice as many irregular workers among young people as in older age groups.

Japanese companies are hiring more temporary and part-time workers to cut costs – and are reducing the number of fresh graduates they take on permanently. This places another unexpected financial burden on college students: since Japanese firms seek the newest graduates, some college seniors perceive a frozen jobs market and prefer to stay on at college to await a thaw.

Some of the problems stem from boom-year policies. Back in the mid-1980s, when Japan's economy was still flourishing and jobs were plentiful, the Japanese government peeled away some regulations to accommodate cost-cutting businesses. In 1985, the Worker Dispatching Act allowed temporary *haken* staffing on project-based work in 13 sectors that faced worker shortages; the law was extended to 26 sectors in 1996, and by 1999 it covered all occupations, except the manufacturing, construction, medical, and legal sectors. In 2004, the government lifted the remaining ban on temps working in the manufacturing sector.

Life is difficult for such workers, especially if they do not have a well-paid spouse. According to Japan's Ministry of Health, Labor, and Welfare, non-regular workers earn approximately 62 percent of the wage of regular workers.[24] The emergence of the working poor and the income gap between regular and irregular workers have made the terms *waakingu-puaa* (working poor) and *kakusa* (income gap) household words.

Living just above the poverty line in a country with very high rents, many young irregular workers cannot afford an apartment. Renting in Japan incurs steep up-front costs, including an agent's fee, a nonrefundable 'gift' to the landlord (called 'key money'), and a security deposit, all of which taken together can be the equivalent of three to six months' rent. The luckiest live with their parents, but some are what the Japanese call 'net café refugees' or 'the cyber-homeless': they sleep in internet cafes, in rooms designed for hard-core gamers. The small private compartments offer access to showers, the internet, games, DVDs, comics, and even unlimited soft drinks.

A night at a net café costs around \$15 to \$35 and is affordable for poor young workers.

Non-regular jobs are insecure. Workers usually retire without benefits and they are rarely protected by labor unions against rule-breaking and sudden dismissal. Japanese labor unions are enterprise unions: rather than representing workers across an industry, they represent the members of a single firm or corporate group (e.g. the Toyota Group). The union's top priority is typically to protect the interests of the regular workers, who generally see the cheaper non-regular workers as a threat.

Young people in the non-regular workforce, like all non-regular workers, are too poor to tax, which reduces the take of national tax revenues. In addition, male non-regular workers are considered undesirable as future husbands and have a difficult time finding a wife. This then contributes to the country's low birth rate. (Female non-regulars avoid this problem, as women are not considered breadwinners in any case.)

The longer someone stays in non-regular work, the harder it is to get out. Firms are notoriously rigid on hiring. They normally reserve permanent regular positions for fresh graduates at specific ages: 18 years for high-school leavers, 22 for college graduates, and 24 for postgraduates. As *freeters* and *haken* workers reach their late twenties, their chances of getting a regular job dwindle. A small number of companies have added opportunities for long-term, full-time employment for people in mid-career, but non-regular workers do not have the requisite skills or work experience to fill these positions. They have not been given job training and they lack a stable employment record. And even if they have that kind of experience, non-regular workers may find it a challenge to get a regular position. Martin Fackler of the *New York Times* tells the story of a promising auto engineer who won praise for his design work on advanced biofuel systems. Nevertheless, like many young Japanese, he was a 'so-called irregular worker, kept on a temporary staff contract with little of the job security and half the salary of the "regular" employees,' most of whom were much older than he was. After more than a decade of trying to gain regular status, the engineer finally quit – not only his job, but also Japan: he moved to Taiwan to study Chinese and to look for a job there.[25]

The Japanese government's response to the labor market problem has not done much to encourage an open-door culture. In 2010, the Welfare Ministry advised firms to expand the definition of a 'new graduate' to cover three years after graduation; thus a 25-year-old candidate with a bachelor's degree would qualify as a 'new' graduate. The ministry even offered subsidies of up to $22,000 per person to large firms that gave regular jobs to new graduates.[26] But these measures do nothing to help non-regular workers who are over 25.

Rigid hierarchies

Japanese firms have their own cultural reasons for ensuring that new salarymen are hired young. Offices typically run on a strict hierarchy, revolving around age and time with the company. Foreign workers in Japanese offices are often surprised at how well their co-workers have learned their colleagues' birthdays, which are often published on an in-house list. The subtle suggestion of the birthday list is that those with earlier birthdays have more authority and need to be respected by younger workers. Adding middle-aged hires to the office disrupts that unspoken hierarchy. If a 35-year-old worker comes into an office on the bottom rung of the ladder, a Western company would not bat an eyelid at asking him to do tasks that are expected of new employees. But in Japan, younger workers who had been there longer would be in the awkward position of having to defer to an older worker who knew far less about the company. This would make employee training difficult and would cause problems for the harmonious balance of the office.

There is also the stigma of corporate disloyalty. A worker who makes a mid-career shift may be suspected of having been disloyal to his previous employer, which in itself makes that worker undesirable. If work conditions in the old job were poor, it would hint at a lack of endurance; if work conditions were good, it would suggest lack of loyalty. There is little incentive for workers to make mid-career shifts, and so few companies offer the opportunity to do so.

Japan's rigid labor market has serious implications for the economy and society. By privileging older workers in the lifetime employment system, Japanese firms fail to incentivize youthful, creative minds at the very time when Japan needs fresh ideas. This is a problem for companies, but it ripples outward into the economy as a whole.

Living the salaryman lifestyle is hard, but it is also tough to be shut out of the system. For most men in Japan, it is a choice between extremes: the extreme hours of the salaryman or the extreme insecurity of the non-regular worker. This dilemma leads some youth to opt out of the economy completely and to become so-called NEETs ('not in education, employment or training') as they lead a reclusive *otaku* (a homebound anime/game/computer geek) lifestyle. However, not surprisingly, this is not sustainable, as is illustrated by this online chat discussion, translated from the Japanese:

> Person A: These days I only feel like becoming a NEET or *freeter*, even though my parents allowed me to go to college. What's it like to live a NEET or *freeter* life?
>
> Person B: I'm in between the *freeter* and the NEET worlds and I feel like ending my life every day. Get a job! Please! You shouldn't become like me. Once you miss the full-time employment opportunity upon college graduation, that will be the end of life in Japan.
>
> Person C: Usually, at first it's fun [to be a NEET or *freeter*] because you have the time to watch as much anime as you want or to play as many computer games as you want, but it becomes a life in hell when you run out of money.[27]

For those who land a permanent full-time position, the pressure of clinging to job security helps shape their personality and behavior. The ideal salaryman is not aggressive or argumentative, but is quietly determined. He needs to be smart without showing off his talents, and should work diligently. He should be reliable and punctual and respectful to his bosses, supporting their decisions and garnering support for them in his department. He understands the importance of the corporate hierarchy and never voices his opposition to managers, even if he secretly disagrees. Individuals with this type of personality usually get promoted smoothly, and may end up becoming a section head by their thirties and then a department head in their forties.

Not all regular employees are ideal super-salarymen. Some drop out when they can't keep up physically or psychologically with their overtime work. Others quit when they can't meet their sales quotas, or can't get along with their colleagues or superiors. Some workers are forced to quit because they do not fit into the corporate culture. But once they quit, they are in freefall. They will probably never again have the comforting promise of lifetime employment, and instead end up as *freeters* or temps.

For this reason, some employees won't quit even under extraordinary duress. This gives corporations enormous power, which in turn helps make them intolerant of independent opinions or challenges to authority. A general sense of inflexibility permeates the Japanese corporate world. Firms may offer severe reprisals, but employees have little choice but to stay. This discourages the kind of flexible, bottom-up creativity that is required for innovation in a knowledge economy. And it strongly discourages the kind of whistleblowing discussed earlier in the chapter that is necessary to keep corporations honest and to limit unethical behavior.

Of course, not everybody falls into the salaryman vs. *freeter/haken* dichotomy. As in other countries, there are many small business owners who may work long hours but who are not subject to corporate control. At the same time, public employees – especially those working for local government – tend to have a shorter workday than the typical salaryman (albeit longer than their US counterparts). There is also variation among companies, with some demanding more extreme hours than others. However, the general pattern holds true, with most employees either working grueling hours as salary-men or else subject to the vagaries of part-time or temp work.

Women in the workforce

The Japanese corporate world is not friendly to women who want to pursue a lifetime career *and* have a family. Despite some recent legal changes, Japanese women still lag far behind salaried workers in other industrialized countries, in terms of employment and promo-tion opportunities.

Most working women in Japan are non-regular workers, that is *haken, freeters*, or *pato* (housewife part-timers), with low pay, no job security, and few benefits. Non-regular employment among women increased from 32 percent in 1985 to 54 percent in 2008.[28] Now women account for about 70 percent of the non-regular workforce.[29] They often deliberately earn just enough to maintain their special status as dependent spouses in the national pension program: under a 1986 amendment to the National Pension Law, a dependent spouse does not pay pension premiums if she does not earn enough to support herself (annual income of under 1.3 million yen).

About 8 percent of non-regular female employees are *haken* contract workers.[30] A female *haken* worker earns much less than her male counterpart, as women are usually sent on short-term contracts for low-paid clerical and sales work.

Most regular female workers occupy non-career-track – *ippanshoku* – positions, with no opportunities for promotion or training. Unlike *haken* positions, these *ippanshoku* jobs are guaranteed until retire-ment, but most women quit them after getting married or having a child. Only very few members of the female workforce are in career-track positions, *sogoshoku*.

A durable glass ceiling

The 1986 Equal Employment Opportunity Law (EEOL) was designed to increase the number of career-track women. It was intended to encourage Japanese companies to hire female college students under the same working conditions as new salarymen. Specifically, the EEOL prohibited discrimination against women in five areas: 1) recruitment and hiring; 2) assignment and promotion; 3) training; 4) fringe benefits; and 5) retirement age, resignation, and dismissal.[31]

But critics view the law as a great disappointment, arguing that it has not kept women in the labor force or helped them reach positions of authority. Despite some revisions in the 1990s and 2000s, the law is pretty toothless, lacking any enforcement mechanism. There is no system to help women who claim that their employers have violated the law. The only recourse is the public shaming of violators, but that has done little to change their behavior.

Two fundamental problems create barriers for women. One is the infamous length of the workday: most mothers required to work ten hours a day (let alone twelve or more) quit. Some can do it, with the help of parents, relatives, or hired babysitters (who charge $30–40 per hour per child in the Tokyo area). If these women live near their company, they might have dinner with their children and then return to work. Or some women with small children may utilize public institutions such as *hoikuen* (combination pre-school and daycare for working parents), which are open until 7 p.m. or 8 p.m., Monday through Friday, and until 2 p.m. or later on Saturdays. Mothers with anything less than a full support network, however, often struggle to keep up. The burden of those long hours forces most career-track women to quit before they reach management-level positions. If women avoid overtime for the sake of their children (for example, leaving work at 6:30 p.m. to pick up their children from daycare), they may be passed over for promotion and/or pushed into dead-end clerical jobs.

The second barrier to women's career advancement is one of the standard practices for career-track workers at large firms: domestic and international geographical transfers (*tenkin*). Japanese salary-men are often transferred to another branch of their firm at short notice. This typically happens every three to five years. Many salary-men with older children (particularly if they are of junior-high or high-school age) go alone to their new posting, so that their children's education is not interrupted (a practice called *tanshin-funin*). Working women who move with their children may end up far from childrearing support networks of parents or relatives, and they may have to change their children's schools. Most companies do not consider workers' personal circumstances, and so if women want to remain in their career-track positions, they have no choice but to follow the firm's order and move to the new location.

Some Japanese websites discuss what it means to be a career woman. They advise career-minded female students to avoid positions in the finance sector and trading companies, since (in their view) these are notoriously anti-woman. Other sites warn women that they should expect to live apart from their future husband, since career-track positions often require transfers to different offices. Still others argue that the biggest problem facing career-track women is not the shortage of childcare facilities (which the government tends to focus on, in order to encourage female employment), but the corporate transfer system imposed on workers. It is a commonly expressed opinion on the websites that women need to comply with their company's transfer orders if they want to be treated equally; some chide women for complaining about transfers, saying 'that's why women cannot work like men do.'

Not infrequently, career-track women are unsympathetic toward other career-track women who are thinking of quitting their jobs.

The argument usually goes something like this: companies make investments in career-track women, so if a woman quits simply because she can't relocate, executives will hesitate to hire another woman. Career-track women earn a lot more than non-career women; but if women quit the career track only a few years in, then companies might think they are in it to make money fast. One long-time career-track woman sums it up: 'The enemy of women in the workplace is women themselves!'

While the Japanese work environment usually makes it difficult for women to have a family life and a career, a few jobs are considered female friendly. These include local public sector (*chiho komuin*) jobs (i.e. municipal government). These jobs require only light overtime work and few or limited geographical transfers. They provide generous maternity leave and other benefits, and they treat women and men almost equally in terms of promotion. The only drawback is that local fiscal deficits have recently sparked cuts in public sector jobs. Teaching posts – also local, public sector jobs – are particularly popular among women, especially at the elementary level. Most school teachers work hard, but their hours are not as long as those of salarymen.

Female job-seekers with skills in English or another foreign language also flock to foreign companies, which are popular because they do not discriminate on promotion or salary and accept older applicants. Some Japanese websites praise the corporate culture of foreign firms: no unpaid overtime work and no meddling in personal affairs (e.g. boyfriends and marriage) – something many Japanese firms engage in. Nor do foreign firms demand non-work-related things: whereas a Japanese boss might send a junior employee off to stand in a park and 'hold' a spot from where the cherry blossom can be viewed to best advantage, such errands would be unthinkable at foreign firms. The advantage of Japanese firms, according to these websites, is their guarantee of lifetime employment, which foreign firms do not provide.

Many career-oriented women try to get a job at a company with many female employees. Shiseido, a global cosmetics company, provides a woman-friendly working environment and is extremely popular among female career seekers.

Shiseido has four women for every male employee, and the company's leaders offer incentives for female career-track workers to stay at the firm. These include a daycare facility at its headquarters in Tokyo, a flexi-time system, and a system of parental leave of up to three years for a single child and five years for two or more children (the national law mandates that working mothers with newborn babies be given 14 weeks of paid and one year of unpaid maternity leave). Shiseido does not transfer employees who have either small children or elderly parents in need of care, and has made it easier for employees to take leave if their spouse gets transferred to another city. By 2010, 20 percent of Shiseido's managers were women, a significant increase from less than 12 percent in 2003.[32] While Shiseido has become a model for retaining female workers, such female-friendly workplaces are extremely rare, and most women employees find themselves in a difficult working environment.

The good news for women is that Japan does not have enough managers to fill the available posts. This shortage could help bring about change in corporate employment practices and encourage more substantial employment opportunities for women. Some media sources report that a small but increasing number of Japanese companies are starting to bring more career-track women into management. Some experts argue that women should account for 20–25 percent of career-track positions.

A number of legal issues intersect with women's participation in the workforce, especially in relation to long work hours and forced geographical transfers (tenkin). Unpaid overtime work is illegal and is in violation of the Labor Standard Law, but the ban goes largely unenforced. As for tenkin, the Japanese courts ruled in the mid-1980s that companies can compel workers to accept geographical transfers, unless the move is deemed unnecessary or illegal, or unless it would cause the worker extreme hardship. In 2006, Japan's Equal Employment Opportunity Law was amended to prohibit certain forms of indirect discrimination, including weight and height requirements, and the requirement for applicants for managerial positions to accept transfers to any geographical location in Japan. But the EEOL is limited, and (as mentioned before) it lacks any 'teeth.' Further amendments are needed to give it greater power.[33]

Two additional laws were passed in 1999 in an attempt to enhance women's participation in the workforce. The first was the Childcare and Family Care Leave Law, which allows women and men to take one year of childcare leave from work, as well as three months of family leave; the other was the Basic Act for a Gender-Equal Society, which outlaws discrimination against women. For all that, successful legal challenges to discriminatory practices on the part of corporations remain very limited.

The government has also promoted the concept of 'work–life balance' (WLB) in the private sector. It set up a task force to incorporate WLB into corporate life, and in 2007 it adopted a Work–Life Balance Charter and Action Guidelines for Promoting WLB (e.g. to halve the number of companies that impose a 60-hour (or longer) working week, and to increase to 10 percent the number of men taking parental leave), with the aim of helping Japan become a more family-friendly nation. The government has been promoting WLB under the aegis of the Gender Equality Bureau in the Cabinet Office, with the slogan 'Change Japan' (*Kaeru* Japan). But the charter and guidelines are simply intended to serve as an inspiration: they lack any legal teeth to enforce or incentivize them. The government hopes gradually to encourage people to embrace WLB, but it has failed to make any significant or meaningful change to revitalize the Japanese economy and workforce.

A rise in the proportion of two-income households would do much to halt the decline of the Japanese economy, and a surge in the number of female graduates means the potential for this exists. But Japanese companies – and society as a whole – have been slow to embrace the change. The long hours and sacrifices required in the typical Japanese office are incompatible with the responsibilities of childrearing. Women are thus forced to choose between a career and children. They are caught between their traditional roles as mothers and wives and the growing problem of raising a family on a single income.

The old Japan and the Olympus saga

Japan's future survival will be built on the back of Japanese companies, but only if they adjust to the twenty-first-century economy. Judging by corporate practices and working women's struggles, though, these companies face a monumental battle to invigorate themselves and regain a competitive edge in the world market. In many ways, Japanese companies seem ideologically attuned to the Bushido ethics of the nineteenth century, where loyalty, endurance, and silent acceptance of orders were valued over ideas, energy, and letting the best concept win.

Olympus, where whistleblower Hamada works, represents the old ideas of 'Japan, Inc.' Besides Hamada's case, Olympus has faced scrutiny over another high-profile whistleblowing case involving the firm's former chief executive and president, Michael C. Woodford. The Woodford case is not just about whistleblowing: it casts light on broader issues of corporate governance in Japan. The Woodford case highlights the insularity of Japanese organizations and their lack of transparency, the extremes of corporate loyalty, and the collusion between interests in the Japanese business world. The case is not merely about Olympus; it offers insights into the culture of the many corporations that work in the same way.

The scandal started with the abrupt dismissal of Woodford, a Briton, allegedly due to cultural clashes between him and the rest of the board of directors over his Western style of management. Tsuyoshi

Kikukawa, Woodford's predecessor and successor, complained that he was too 'Western,' and often bypassed the heads of divisions to give orders directly to the rank and file.[34] But that wasn't the whole story.

In fact, Woodford was dismissed because he raised questions about a suspicious acquisition deal in 2008 that involved a British medical equipment company and a couple of advisory firms. Two things caught his attention. The first was the staggering cost – $2.2 billion paid to acquire the British Gyrus Group. The second thing was the exorbitant fees paid to two mysterious, now-defunct Cayman Islands-registered advisory companies. A $2 billion deal might have attracted a 1 percent fee for advisors; but Olympus paid out $687 million – about 31 percent of the purchase price – the highest percentage ever paid as a mergers and acquisitions fee![35] Woodford found other suspicious transactions from 2006, when Olympus had spent hundreds of millions of dollars on buying three unprofitable Japanese companies that dealt with face creams, microwave cookware, and waste disposal – areas that Woodford struggled to associate with Olympus's camera and microscope businesses. Olympus quickly wrote off three-quarters of the value of the companies after the acquisitions.[36]

Woodford discovered these irregular transactions in articles published in a small Japanese business magazine called *FACTA*, which had obtained information from an unidentified informant within Olympus.[37] This whistleblower had not gone through Olympus's internal compliance unit to address the irregularities – understandable in the light of whistleblower Hamada's bitter experience with the same company – but had instead turned to a journalist.

Woodford pressed his fellow board members to explain the irregularities, but he was stonewalled. After the independent auditor PriceWaterhouseCoopers confirmed his suspicions, Woodford demanded the resignation of the entire board. It responded by firing him. The board members summoned him the day after his call for their resignation and 'let him go' in a ten-minute meeting at which he was not allowed to speak.

That is when Woodford went public, in an interview with *Bloomberg Businessweek*:

'Do you know how extraordinary it is to sack a [company] president in Japan?' Woodford says. 'Do you know? Unless you commit some terrible crime, it just doesn't happen. What were they doing in there? What were they scared of?'[38]

Olympus's independent inquiry – headed by a former Japanese Supreme Court judge and established after shareholders demanded an open investigation into the allegations – found that the company had cooked the books for two decades and had inflated its performance. It had attempted to use all of these transactions to dispose of secret investment losses it had made during the bubble years – approximately $1.7 billion worth. Rather than reveal heavy losses in open balance sheets, Olympus had crafted a *tobashi* ('flying away') scheme to hide them. This is also known as a 'hot potato' scheme: if you have a hot potato, you don't want to hold on to it – you want to pass it on to someone else. During the 1990s and early 2000s, like many other Japanese firms (most notably Yamaichi Securities, which hid more than $2 billion in losses and collapsed in 1997), Olympus sold its loss-bearing investments to 'special purpose vehicles' (i.e. dummies) that did not have to be included on its books. However, *tobashi* was banned in the early 2000s. Anticipating changes in the Japanese accounting regulations, Olympus's Kikukawa realized that he had to end the scheme. He cleared the balance sheet by purchasing non-performing companies in order to mask Olympus's bubble-era investment losses.[39] The company's independent investigation committee concluded that the firm's management was 'rotten at the core.'

Seven people were arrested, including Kikukawa, the executive vice-president, and the corporate auditor. Olympus decided to pursue around 70 individuals involved in the fraud, including a dozen board members, for tens of millions of dollars in damages. Shareholders filed a lawsuit against the company over the scandal, and the Tokyo Stock Exchange fined it 10 million yen ($100,000). Meanwhile, its stock price plummeted by almost 50 percent.

The investigation of the Olympus fraud continues, with the Tokyo Metropolitan Police and the Tokyo prosecutor's office investigating where the massive advisory fees went. Major newspapers such as the *New York Times* and Japan's *Sankei Shimbun* have reported that some money may have ended up in the hands of organized crime syndicates, including the Yamaguchi Gumi, Japan's largest *yakuza* (mafia) group.

The Olympus scandal is not an isolated incident. There have been many corporate frauds in Japan, such as the case of Kanebo, a now-defunct cosmetics conglomerate. In 2005, Kanebo admitted that it had had negative net worth for nine years, but had disguised its troubles by declaring as much as $2 billion in non-existent profits.[40] Another recent example is Daio Paper, which in 2011 sued its former chairman for confiscating $140 million from subsidiaries for his gambling debts. In addition, a Madoff-style Ponzi scheme was found in 2012 with a pension-fund investment advisory company, AIJ Investment Advisors. AIJ had been hiding trading losses for about a decade and had falsified performance records to lure new clients. There are more and more stories like these, going back to the early 2000s and 1990s.

Do Japanese corporations care about ethics? The Olympus case shows how corporate loyalty counts for more than ethics and law. As Woodford found to his cost, Kikukawa was the emperor of the Olympus dynasty: all Olympus employees were obedient to him, and the management was a Kikukawa regime.

'Without a Westerner who could articulate and express the problems and was willing to risk his career, to risk anything, the Olympus scandal would never have gotten out. How many more Olympus' there are is a matter of speculation,' said Woodford.[41]

Olympus's case demonstrates the Japanese government's lack of appropriate oversight. Japanese corporations favor the interests of insiders rather than those of shareholders. The insiders at Olympus – including even the auditors who approved the balance sheets – attempted to hide massive investment losses. Japanese firms have too few independent directors on boards (Olympus had three, but none of them questioned Woodford's dismissal).

GMI, a New York-based research group, ranked Japan 33rd of 38 countries in corporate governance in 2011 – behind even Russia and China. Almost half of the Japanese firms studied by GMI did not have a single independent director on their boards. This contrasts sharply with industrialized European countries, where 70 percent of the companies studied have majority independent boards.[42]

The Japanese government has doubled the penalties for accounting fraud, which can now attract ten years in jail. The top fine for individuals has risen to 10 million yen ($100,000), and 700 million yen ($7 million) for firms. However, penalties are still considered lenient. In the Kanebo case, for example, the individuals charged with the fraud received suspended sentences of up to two years.[43]

As *The Economist* wrote:

Can Japan Inc. be trusted? Of course crime happens everywhere; there might even be a bit less of it in Japan than elsewhere. That is not the issue. The question is what happens when crimes are discovered. Do the institutions of authority act with the necessary degree of integrity? . . . Olympus, and the response of Japanese officialdom, is less about a single sad incident as it is a view about the malleability of rules, and the subjectivity of their enforcement. Until Japan's institutions of governance – those internal to the corporations, as well external regulators and prosecutors – change, Japan cannot change.[44]

So what happened to Michael Woodford, Olympus's former chief executive? Although foreign shareholders called for him to return to the Olympus board, he abandoned his bid to do so after key

Japanese institutional shareholders (such as Sumitomo Mitsui Banking Corporation, Nippon Life, and Bank of Tokyo–Mitsubishi UFJ) refused to give their support. These Japanese institutional shareholders were among the largest stakeholders in Olympus, and they did not speak 'one single word of criticism [of Olympus], in complete and utter contrast to overseas shareholders who were demanding accountability,' said Woodford. The Japanese institutional shareholders even kept on those former directors of the board not directly implicated in the scandal. After giving up his plans to return to Olympus, Woodford sued the firm in a British court for wrongful dismissal and was awarded $15.4 million in settlement.[45]

Woodford summed up the scandal:

> Prime Minister Noda spoke out about the Olympus scandal, but he said, 'please don't think that Japan works differently from other capitalist markets.' With the greatest respect, Mr. Noda, it *does*.[46] (italics added)

Reluctant globalization

How can Japanese firms break out of the shell of insularity and promote corporate transparency and accountability? Perhaps the best people to do this are those with overseas experiences – perhaps those who have studied or grown up in other countries and who have acquired different modes of thinking. Open-minded individuals with overseas experience may be able to introduce fresh air into Japan's stifling corporate culture.

But sadly, various reports indicate that the number of Japanese studying abroad has steadily declined since around 2004. *The Economist* writes that in 1997, roughly equal numbers of Japanese, Korean, and Chinese students (including postgraduates) were studying at Harvard University.[47] But by 2011, there were about five times as many Chinese as Japanese at Harvard, and three times as many

Koreans. Overall, the number of Japanese studying abroad fell from 83,000 in 2004 to less than 60,000 in 2009.[48]

Why do Japanese young people not want to study abroad? Quite simply, they are worried about getting a regular, full-time career. The Japanese job market is brutal after two 'lost decades.' Japanese college students have only one shot at job hunting, and the recruitment season is getting earlier and earlier. Today, college students start the hunt in the summer of their junior year. If they study abroad, they miss the recruitment season. Not getting a job before graduation can have a serious long-term impact on their career, and most students do not want to take the risk. Some who study abroad deliberately delay their graduation for a year so as not to harm their recruitment chances.

Because of the tight job market, young people may be more concerned about negative corporate attitudes toward job candidates who have studied overseas. Insular Japanese companies often prefer to hire graduates from domestic institutions, as Western-educated youth may be considered too aggressive and individualistic to value conformity and harmony. A recruiter for the Bank of Tokyo–Mitsubishi UFJ, which in 2011 took on fewer than 20 applicants with international experience (out of 1,200 fresh graduates), told the *New York Times*: 'We're cautious, because we emphasize continuity and long-term commitment to the company.' He went on: 'Especially in finance, we don't want people who are focused on short-term gains.'

Some students and adults fear that an education in Western ways might scare employers off, because foreign experience carries a stigma. The phrase '*nihonjin rashiku nai*' ('doesn't act Japanese') may be whispered about some job-seekers who have spent what seems like too much time overseas. This attitude is the bane of those who are already a bit too old to find solid work, but who might have hoped that their experience abroad would have made up for missing the entry window. According to one software engineer who returned to Japan after working in Los Angeles: 'In the eyes and minds of most

Japanese, if you go abroad for anything more than a short vacation you are treated like tainted meat when you come home.'[49]

Japanese firms are losing their competitive edge through their reluctance to hire qualified candidates with overseas experience. For as long as conformity and harmony are valued above skill and creativity, Japanese firms are unlikely to change.

Abenomics

A number of recent Japanese prime ministers have tried to find ways of shaking up the economy – none more so than Shinzo Abe, who has led the government first in 2006–07 and again from December 2012. Abe, who studied public policy at the University of Southern California in the 1970s, has pushed hard to jolt Japan's stagnant economy, using what are widely described as 'three arrows': easing monetary restrictions, massive fiscal stimulus, and sweeping structural reforms.[50] These approaches fall squarely within the demand-side liberal interventionist framework of British economist John Maynard Keynes and have thus been applauded by today's prominent liberal economists, such as Paul Krugman.[51]

The easing of monetary restrictions in Japan is designed to overcome deflation, which has plagued the country for some 15 years. The Consumer Price Index remained flat or fell from 1996 to 2009, with consumer prices actually lower at the end of that period than at the beginning.[52] Though deflation would seem to be a positive thing for consumers, in fact it is widely accepted among economists that it has a negative effect on growth, because it amplifies the expense of debt and thus discourages investment. In Japan, this deflationary period corresponded to the so-called 'lost decade' of negative economic growth. To overcome deflation, Abe successfully lobbied the Bank of Japan to set a 2 percent target rate for inflation and to dramatically expand its purchases of Japanese government bonds, treasury bills, and other assets.[53]

Parallel to this, the Japanese government has engaged in fiscal stimulus by greatly increasing public spending on infrastructure and renewable energy. The goal of this is to lay the groundwork for future growth and to create temporary jobs. A 10.3 trillion yen stimulus package was announced in January 2013. It included a combination of construction projects (such as repairing school buildings and aging roads), subsidies to companies to develop new technologies, and loan guarantees for small businesses. Much of the early spending focused on reconstruction to recover from the earthquake, tsunami, and nuclear catastrophe, and to strengthen the country's defenses against natural disasters.[54]

Structural reform represents the third 'arrow' of Abenomics, and includes both regulatory reform and the creation of economic partnerships with other countries. To this end, Abe convened committees of economists, business leaders, and politicians to draft a reform package. In June 2013, his government announced its policy agenda, which included lifting a ban on the online sale of drugs, and the creation of deregulated and lightly taxed economic development zones around the country. Some economists voiced disappointment that the reforms did not include broader business and labor market deregulation measures, such as simplifying dismissal rules or mandating the inclusion of outside directors on corporate boards.

One of the main pillars of structural reform centers around free trade. Japan's protectionist policies have long been harmful to the country's economy, but have proved resistant to change. This is especially so in the area of agriculture. There are only 2.5 million farmers in the country, and of those only a fraction – about 400,000 – work full time.[55] Yet rural bias in Japan's electoral system means that those 2.5 million farmers are highly influential in deciding the outcome of elections. For that reason, no politician wants to cross them.

Due to postwar land reform, the average Japanese farm is tiny – only 1.9 hectares (4.7 acres) – and is thus very inefficient. In contrast, US farms are, on average, more than a hundred times as large.[56] Rice farms in Japan are even tinier. Yet it is virtually impossible to sell imported rice, due to a ludicrously high tariff of 777.7 percent. The retail price of white rice is thus about $2 per pound in Japan, compared to about $0.70 in the US. Since rice is a main staple of the Japanese diet, this represents a huge tax on consumers and benefits just a tiny group of farmers. A number of politicians did hope to change this, but the agricultural lobby, supported by the Ministry of Agriculture, Forestry, and Fisheries, has proved too powerful.

In spite of the obstacles, Abe has put free trade on the agenda, at least to some extent. In particular, he insisted on Japan's joining the Trans-Pacific Partnership (TPP), a comprehensive free-trade agreement in the Asia-Pacific region, led by the US. Participation in the TPP was bitterly opposed by farmers' groups in Japan,[57] but was supported by the country's broader *Keidanren* (Federation of Business Organizations), which seeks a larger export market around the world. Finally, after sitting on the sidelines as an observer through three long years and eighteen rounds of negotiation, Japan officially joined the TPP as a negotiating member during the nineteenth round, in August 2013. However, within the TPP negotiations, Japan has been insisting that tariffs on rice, wheat, beef and poultry, dairy products, and sugar be exempt from the treaty. Even within these limitations, Japan's joining the TPP negotiations provided a huge boost to what could turn out to be one of the broadest trade agreements in history.[58] The 12 countries currently in the TPP make up about 40 percent of global gross domestic product and about a third of world trade, and more nations are poised to join. One expert has noted that Japan's participation could 'triple the economic gains' that the United States gets from the treaty.[59] Abe's chief cabinet secretary, Yoshihide Suga, calls TPP 'the biggest pillar of reform' in Japan.[60]

Abenomics got off to a strong start. Japan finally started to break out of its deflationary spiral, with consumer prices growing by 1.2 percent in November 2013 compared to a year earlier – the most they had increased in nearly five years. The dangerously overpriced yen also fell about 25 percent in value – from its autumn 2012 price of 77 to the dollar, back to a more reasonable 100 to the dollar in autumn 2013 – thus giving Japanese exports a big boost. Tokyo's main stock exchange, the Nikkei 225, approximately doubled in value from mid-2012 to mid-2013. The country's GDP rose at an annualized rate of 3.8 percent in the second quarter of 2013, and the rate of unemployment fell to its lowest level for four years, also 3.8 percent. It remains to be seen whether these figures represent lasting improvements to the economy or were simply a short-term fix, resulting from a large infusion of public funds.

Conclusion

Though its deficit spending causes many economists to fear for its sustainability, Abenomics is undoubtedly breathing fresh air into Japan's economy. Yet as the stories of Toru and Kenta, the sorry state of opportunities for women, and the depressing Olympus scandal all reveal, Japan's business environment still has a long way to go, both to meet the needs of the Japanese people and to be globally competitive. Today's economy requires flexible interactions within and across teams and countries. It requires rapid decisions in response to changing contexts and circumstances. The informality of a company such as Google – where what you know is more important than your credentials, and where serendipitous interactions between staff of all levels is positively encouraged – would shock Japanese salarymen. The type of community that gives rise to companies in the mold of Google, Apple, Facebook, and Amazon is to be found not in Japan, but rather in the US, UK, Canada, France, Australia, Brazil, India, Russia, Singapore, Germany, and Israel – not a single Japanese city is among the world's top 20 'start-up' incubators.[61]

Of course, there is more to life than being rich, and perhaps Japan's emphasis on social accord and harmony can serve the nation in other ways. Let us move, then, from the economy to take a look at how the most intimate bonds for the future of a nation are faring – those between young men and women.

CHAPTER TWO

Grass-eating Girly Men

Haru is sitting in the back of a tiny café, looking like a ghost in a blouse and tight pants. His demeanor is meek, and he barely talks to his companion, a more traditionally dressed friend of about the same age. Haru's long hair – with streaks of dark red highlights, applied by a professional – is kept up by a hair clip. A touch of dark makeup circles his eyes. Haru flicks ash from his cigarette into an ashtray, his pursed lips silent when the waiter asks if he'd like anything else. His friend orders him another cup of coffee.

A visitor to Japan might see the morning rush of salarymen, all in black suits and white shirts, as proof of the country's homogeneity. There's a sense of conformity in Japan that makes it easy to assume that everything is done the same way; that the entire nation is middle class; and that the women are at home while the men work. But beneath the surface, there is more diversity than one might expect at first – including a rejection by many of Japan's young people of the country's traditional gender roles.

Some believe a shakeup and rejection of traditional Japanese gender roles is liberating after years of rigid and restricted expectations. But it carries consequences for Japan that have already crept into a wide spectrum of Japanese society, from popular music to employment statistics. Perhaps the most troubling manifestation lies in empty wedding chapels.

Diversifying men

While the Japanese economy is changing, the idealized expectations of Japanese men are not. Old ideas persist: a man should find a company and spend his life there, supporting his family with his income and deriving personal satisfaction from his office work, while his wife takes responsibility for the household and children, whether or not she works. Despite the outliers discussed in chapter 1, the salaryman is still the template for men.

But these men have an image problem and they are losing respect. In the boom days, salarymen were viewed as earnest, selfless, hard-working cogs making up the engines of economic growth. Today, they're just schlubs. In countless movies and graphic novels, the salaryman is a trapped, spineless slave of his company. He endures insults like *shachiku* ('corporate livestock') or *kaisha no inu* ('corporate dog'). In TV shows, such as 2004's *Salaryman Neo* (aired on conservative broadcaster NHK), he comically kowtows to bosses and clients. The salaryman is shown relieving the stress by drinking with colleagues, droning on about work as his face turns ever deeper shades of red, oblivious to the annoyance he is causing his female colleagues.

Salarymen are considered offensively uncool when it comes to fashion. Older, middle-aged (*oyaji*) salarymen 'release bad odor' and wear boring dark suits and ties. Some have adopted the *choiwaru* ('little bit wild') look, including smart suits in their wardrobe and making bold fashion experiments, such as a light-yellow shirt; but they are the exception that proves the rule.

Beyond unfashionable, salarymen are often viewed as borderline absentee fathers. They are pigeonholed with the well-known proverb 'a good husband is healthy and absent.' Many wives want the salary, but not so many want the man.

Nowadays, though, many men reject the corporate credo of self-sacrifice, in favor of a lifestyle that suits their interests and passions. Some cross traditional gender lines into the beauty and fashion worlds; others immerse themselves in manga, anime, or video games. Fashionable men and anime men (*otaku*, see below) are usually employed, but only in order to support their true passions. They work to live, rather than live to work.

Herbivores

Scattered between the black suits of salarymen waiting for an afternoon train, one might find a handful of younger men like Haru, in tight jeans and with earbud wires trailing from a well-groomed head of hair. Their clothes could be seen in any American hipster enclave: thrift-store flannels, white T-shirts, floppy sneakers. They are young, effeminate, and fashionable – the antithesis of a salaryman.

In 2006, Maki Fukasawa coined the term 'herbivore men' (*soshoku-kei danshi*) to describe these 20–30-year-olds of the post-bubble generation.[1] Megumi Ushikubo popularized the phenomenon in her bestseller, *Herbivorous Girly Men Are Changing Japan*. The title refers to their passivity: grass-eaters are content to graze on whatever grows naturally around them, rather than aggressively pursuing their ambitions and desires.

Herbivores have been described as 'metrosexuals without the testosterone.'[2] While Western stereotypes of them as asexual are exaggerated, they are generally passive in pursuit of sex and relationships.[3] That passivity may be a factor – though far from the only one – in Japan's perilously low birth rate (see next chapter).

Salarymen are content with drab personal hygiene, but grooming is the mark of herbivores. They go to beauty salons to have their hair done, whereas salarymen go for ten-minute-guaranteed haircuts. Herbivores may watch their weight and skip meals to maintain slender figures. They invest in beauty products and bodycare lotions, nail buffers, and tweezers for plucking their eyebrows. Cosmetic companies such as Shiseido, Otsuka, DHC, and Mandom all have products catering to men; but herbivores have adopted girls' products as well. One billboard for a popular hairspray advertises the claim that, while women will want to use it, it's only for men. The message that the herbivore niche market is being targeted is re-inforced by a picture of a spiky-haired, androgynous young man and the slogan 'NO WOMEN.' While you might well find one wearing a hair clip and texting on a pink cell phone, herbivores are specifically *androgynous*, not transgender. They adopt 'girly' things because they find them cute, not to change their gender identity.[4]

Having grown up in the post-bubble era, herbivores are skeptical of expensive purchases, seeing them as excessive and tacky. They might carry around 'points cards' to save money at stores.[5] They seek out bargains, even in beauty products, and keep purchases to the bare essentials. Well-groomed herbivores may be influenced by popular young male idols – singers and actors who are typically slender, pretty, and cute. In the Japanese entertainment industry, soft, delicate men are in vogue, while masculine and strong men are considered outdated.

After watching the bubble generation work hard to earn money that eventually turned into debt, herbivores are not interested in devoting their lives to a company at the expense of their inner life. It is said that they lack ambition. They work, but maintain a spiritual independence. They see their jobs as a way to get by, rather than as a source of emotional satisfaction. Their identity is more likely to be invested in hobbies than in performance goals. They reject most corporate norms (which can be a source of generational tension). Consider the obligatory after-work drinking: if a herbivore must accept a boss's invitation to a drinking party, he might order sweet drinks instead of beer. This is of symbolic significance: raising a glass of beer for a toast is supposed to unite colleagues in their battle within the merciless corporate world. Herbivores do not crave unity with their bosses. Choosing a melon soda over a beer, however, may be seen as a subtle insult, an unwillingness to 'loosen up' and open up with the rest of the staff. Many middle-aged salarymen deplore herbivore co-workers for their selfishness, and are shocked that they are not chained to Japanese principles of self-sacrifice.[6]

If the social world of salarymen is made up of their office colleagues, herbivores prefer a network of friends. They favor the close, personal, and familiar. They would rather cook and host a dinner party, decorating their homes to be welcoming to guests than drink after work. Ushikubo writes that herbivores love their home-towns and often stay close to their families, usually living with their parents until (and if) they get married. They are not attracted to the Western lifestyle that is typically admired in Japan, i.e. large houses and material affluence. Herbivores prefer domestic trips to traveling abroad, which they consider dangerous and exhausting.

Herbivores are described as gentle, unassuming, and sensitive. Ushikubo writes that they do not boast like typical salarymen and are not afraid to be vulnerable. They make friends with women easily, which is not a common thing within Japan's gender-segregated society. While salarymen might talk of nothing but work, herbivores can hold their own on subjects like fashion, art, or interior deco-rating. If herbivores have a girlfriend, they are likely to 'go Dutch' on the bill; if they get married, they will expect their wife to work. They treat women as equals, whereas salarymen tend to see women as fragile things in need of protection.

Finally, herbivores avoid risk in their careers and personal lives. While they do not have strong career ambitions, they are careful not to rock the boat. They do the bare minimum required to get by. While not indebted to their companies, herbivores would be happy to hold one job for their entire working life.

How many herbivores are there? Ushikubo estimates that about 60 percent of men aged 20–34 are herbivor*ish* – that is, not a perfect herbivore stereotype, but with some herbivore tendencies. A consulting company to Japan's largest advertising firm estimates that the proportion who consider themselves herbivores ranges from 60 percent of men in their early twenties to at least 42 percent of men aged 23–34.[7]

The herbivore phenomenon hinges on Japan's changing society and economy. In the post-bubble era, families have had fewer children and schools have fewer students. In a less competitive environment, young people have grown up more comfortable with themselves. They have received the attention they craved, and are more secure. They do not seek validation in competition with their school peers, and this attitude is carried through into their adult lives.[8]

This makes the herbivore a reverse image of the salaryman in another way: Ushikubo found that herbivores were fairly popular among women in their twenties and thirties. Herbivores are the 'healing type' (*iyashikei*) – in her words, 'pure, gentle, and shining.' This stands in sharp contrast to the typical salaryman, whose masculine ideals would forbid any expression of gentleness, and who are considered tired and dull, rather than shining.

Ushikubo argues that during the bubble years, women wanted men of three 'highs' (*ko*) for marriage: high education level (*kogaku-reki*), high income (*koshunyu*) and high height (*koshincho*). In contrast, a new generation of women seeks lows (*tei*): low posture (gentle and respectful to women), low risk (with preference for stability and security at work), and low dependency (particularly on women, in terms of household work). Others argue that modern women are pursuing average (*hei*) men: ordinary appearance, average income, and a mediocre lifestyle. Many herbivores fit in comfortably with these lows and averages. Thrifty, committed to family and community, and not interested in gambling, drinking, or womanizing, herbivores are naturally attractive to today's young women. Their willingness to perform household chores and to prioritize family life over corporate life is also appealing. Some consider herbivores to be the ideal type of man and recommend them as husbands for women who want a career.

But herbivore men are also notoriously shy and hypersensitive to rejection.[9] One herbivore blogger wrote about meeting his current wife. He was extremely shy when he started dating her, a 'carnivore girl' whom he had met at a singles' party (see *konkatsu* below). After almost two years of dating, he wanted to propose to her, but he couldn't pluck up the courage. One day, frustrated with his indecisiveness, she finally ordered him to marry her: 'Hey, you have to marry me!' He did.[10]

The passivity of the herbivore generation in romance is backed up by national surveys. According to a 2010 study by the Japan Family Planning Association, 36.1 percent of males say they are 'indifferent or averse' to having sex, compared to 17.5 percent in 2008.[11] A 2010 survey conducted by the National Institute of Population and Social Security Research found that 61.4 percent of never-married men aged 18–34 had no girlfriend, compared to 52.2 percent in 2005, and 27.6 percent of men in that age range said they are not even looking for a mate. As for those in their late thirties, more than 25 percent of unmarried men and women between 35 and 39 say they have never had sex.[12] Though the significance of these findings has been questioned,[13] comparisons to previous surveys by the same organizations point to a downward trend in male–female relationships among young people in Japan.

A number of reasons have been put forward to explain the rise of the herbivores. Most agree that the phenomenon points to Japanese men becoming more feminized. Herbivores mark a rejection of the salaryman culture and the adoption of a more humble (albeit fashion-sensitive) lifestyle that centers on home and community. They may also be a harbinger of a slow drift away from the corporate world that has dominated and defined masculinity in Japan for decades. Now, as the corporations struggle to keep up, so do the gender roles they maintained.

The Johnny's

The entertainment industry feeds and thrives on the proliferation of 'girly men' in Japanese society, with their canny but voracious consumption of music and entertainment. Male celebrities have opened the gender gateway, encouraging men to adopt traditionally feminine purchasing habits: herbivores, and even progressive salary-men, now dabble in hair salons and use skin care products, now that male celebrities have embraced an approach to beauty once reserved for women. You can see it across genres – from popular male idols to cross-dressing 'visual-*kei*' heavy-metal bands (such as X Japan and Color). With their androgynous styles and makeup, these would remind Western observers of KISS, David Bowie, or Boy George. In addition, the Japanese entertainment industry is filled with 'trans-women' superstars – popular transgender (or 'new half') models (e.g. Ayana Tsubaki), beauty consultants (e.g. Ikko), singers (e.g. Ai Haruna), and comedians (e.g. Matsuko Delux). Perhaps it is easier to 'perform' one's identity across gender lines in Japan. After all, Japan is a country of traditional *kabuki* theater, where respected male actors perform women's roles.

Though Japanese men do not normally adopt the style of these cross-dressing or transgender stars, they do follow the fashions of more mainstream male idols. Typically, teenagers or slightly older male idols are not masculine by Western standards, but tend to be cute, slender, and smooth-skinned, capturing a sense of gentleness. To many Westerners, they seem effeminate or androgynous, and some Japanese male idols could be mistaken for female pop stars. One commenter describes them as innocent-looking, 'flower-like' boys. While they would hardly be accepted as an ideal image of masculinity in Western societies, these idols are embraced in Japan and throughout Asia.

The 'pretty-boy' phenomenon started in the late 1960s with a boy band, Four Leaves, produced by the talent agency Johnny &

Associates.[14] Founded in 1963 by Johnny Kitagawa, the kingmaker of Japanese show business, Johnny & Associates has produced countless singing and dancing male idols. Kitagawa's marketing strategy was to use exclusively young, pretty, and gentle-looking men – and it has worked brilliantly. Since the mid-1980s, he has produced phenomenally successfully bands in this mold, including Shibugakitai, Shonentai, the roller-skating boy band Hikaru Genji, SMAP, Tokio, Arashi, Hey! Say! JUMP, and KAT-TUN. These singers – collectively known as 'The Johnny's' – all look pretty and androgynous. Teenage girls and young women adore and worship them, and young men in their teens and twenties, especially herbivores, fashion themselves after the idols' hairstyles and mannerisms. Now almost all male idols look androgynous.

Kitagawa has faced numerous serious allegations over the years, including of pedophilia, sexual abuse, and rape. Though he lost a libel suit against a magazine that accused him of sex with minors, he has never been prosecuted.[15] He has continued to lead Johnny & Associates and to produce many more boy bands. One of his latest creations is a band consisting of boys aged from 12–18 years, defiantly named Sexy Zone. Despite the serious accusations leveled at Kitagawa, the empire of Johnny & Associates thrives, and pretty boys continue to dominate Japan's show-business world, with many young Japanese men following their fashion.

Otaku *men*

If you look around a subway car in Tokyo, you might find another kind of man – one in between the herbivores and the salarymen. Rushing onto the train early to grab a seat, then instantly pulling out a portable gaming system and donning headphones, he seems oblivious to standard etiquette. Easily mistaken for a texting herbivore, save for the furious tapping of his thumbs, we have spotted a young man who is often dismissed by those around him with the word *otaku*.

The *otaku* is a geek. He (it usually is a man) is a nerd or a gamer who has a keen interest in pop culture such as anime, manga, or video games. The *otaku* (literally meaning 'your home' – the 'o' indicating politeness) was originally used for reclusive people who spent much of their free time at home. The word was coined in the 1980s and caught on internationally after a 1993 cover story in *Wired* magazine that described the *otaku* as 'socially inept but often brilliant technological shut-ins.'[16] Today, it has a broader meaning, generally referring to anyone who takes a hobby to passionate extremes – anime, games, trains, military equipment, idols in the entertainment industry, and much more. You may encounter middle-aged *otaku* men standing in line with school children at a train museum, or waiting with cameras on a railway platform to photograph the *shinkansen* (bullet trains).

To some, the term has negative connotations of reclusive people shut off from social lives, living in an anime or game-based fantasy world. By the end of the 1980s and early 1990s, it was associated with the brutal crimes of a serial killer, Tsutomu Miyazaki. This was an *otaku* who, in 1988–89, murdered four little girls aged between four and seven and molested their corpses. Miyazaki was said to have collected and watched about 6,000 anime and other videos at home before the murders. With the horrific deaths of these girls, he established a stereotype of *otaku* as mentally ill and possibly dangerous. Miyazaki was put on trial in 1990 and was hanged in 2008, but he shaped the perception of *otaku* for more than a decade. *Otaku* became synonymous in the public imagination with *lolicon*, being attracted to underage girls (the word is a contraction of 'Lolita Complex,' referring to Vladimir Nabokov's novel *Lolita*, in which a middle-aged man becomes sexually obsessed with the book's eponymous 12-year-old).

Despite the stigma, the *otaku* population has grown since the 1990s, and *otaku* have slowly come to be more accepted. Tokyo's Akihabara district has become a national hub for *otaku*. It is lined with stores selling *otaku* culture, welcoming *otaku* fans, and hosting *otaku* cultural festivals.

The media have come to portray *otaku* men more positively as well. The popular 2005 TV drama *Train Man* is a case in point. It is billed as a true story about an unfashionable *otaku* man trying to approach the stylish and beautiful office lady whom he had protected on the train from a drunk. In the story, which is based on a collection of discussions on the famous 2-Channel ('2chan') online forum, the *otaku* man was portrayed as kind but extremely shy. He had never had a girlfriend, and so he seeks advice on the 2-Channel forum, which helps him eventually to win her heart.

With the growth of the *otaku* population, more women are meeting *otaku* men and finding that they don't know how to date them. Advice websites abound: Can the *otaku* handle married life? Can he give up his hobby once he gets married? How compatible is the *otaku* if a woman has an active social life? What basic knowledge of anime should a girlfriend of an anime *otaku* have to maintain a good relationship? Which anime can be recommended for beginners? What would you do if your boyfriend turned out to be a 'coming-out *otaku*'? What would you do if you found your boyfriend has a hobby of collecting anime figurines of young female characters that may remind you of Barbie dolls or may lead you to suspect he is *lolicon*? Would you accept such a hobby or would you tell him to give it up?

Some women dislike *otaku* men and would never date them. Others have an *otaku* boyfriend but are too embarrassed to let others know it, and may become furious if their boyfriend drops anime or cosplay (costume play) jargon into a conversation in more 'respectable' company.

Relationship experts have advice for women who are dating *otaku*. A typical suggestion is for the woman to realize that the *otaku*'s hobby is a part of his identity, and to accept that she is not his top priority. Typical advice assumes that, if presented with an ultimatum, the *otaku* will choose his hobby over his girlfriend. If she hopes he'll give up his hobby when he gets married, she may be sorely disappointed, the experts suggest. They reckon it is pointless to urge him to abandon his interests, and say that belittling *otaku* culture can damage the relationship.

So what is an *otaku* girlfriend to do? Accept the man's hobby and realize that it offers one great advantage if she marries him: he'll be so preoccupied with his hobby that he won't have the time or interest in finding another girlfriend. Sugoren (a dating advice website) carried out a survey of Japanese women who had dated *otaku*. The results reinforced the view that the men are generally not the flirty type. As one respondent summed it up: 'If *otaku* boys cheat on me, it happens only in the second dimension (not with real girls).'[17]

Some view *otaku* men as suitable for marriage because of everything they *don't* do: apart from rarely cheating, according to surveys of women they are typically not gamblers or heavy drinkers.[18] Experts urge the non-*otaku* wife to develop her own hobby to make her happy without him. 'Do not depend on him,' says one specialist on the topic. 'If you really cannot tolerate his collecting anime figurines, tell him not to show them to you or not to carry them with him when you two go out.' The wife of an *otaku* man adds:

> Marriage and dating are not the same, so you need to be realistic when it comes to marriage. I wanted to be a housewife. And my husband supports me financially, and this is great because I don't have any special skills necessary for getting a job. Also, he doesn't enjoy gambling or sleeping around, so he is just fine for me.[19]

While this kind of gender separation is traditional in Japan, some suggest a more egalitarian strategy of sorts: that the non-*otaku* girlfriend or wife should become an *otaku*. Respect his hobby and embrace it to become a true partner who understands him. 'The river between the *otaku* man and the non-*otaku* woman is very, very deep,' writes Toko Shirakawa, a columnist for the bulletin board of *Yomiuri Online*, Japan's largest online newspaper. 'It's not easy to cross the river, so if you truly think his hobby is rubbish, you should not consider him as your marriage mate.'[20]

Idol otaku

Just as pop culture feeds and reflects the tastes of herbivores, so the same cycle exists for *otaku*. One subcategory is growing: idol *otaku*, who are obsessed with Japan's popular girl bands. Today, many idol *otaku* are passionate about AKB48, a girl group with 48 (or more) singers aged 14–25 that is by far the most popular idol group in Japan. AKB48 and its sister bands, also called '48s' and managed by the same company, are the female counterparts of The Johnny's, but they have an even larger following. And while The Johnny's have marked a significant shift in gender norms for their audience, the '48' bands reflect the very traditional gender expectations of their audience.

AKB48 is one of the world's highest-earning pop groups, with CD and DVD sales in 2011 alone exceeding $212 million – more than the Irish band U2. Initially, it was conceived as a girl group targeting the *otaku*, and the singers often wore schoolgirl uniforms, like anime characters. But AKB48's popularity extends to scores of non-*otaku* men and young girls who want to look like their favorite members. By all accounts, AKB48 has become a mainstream J-pop group.

AKB48 is named after Akihabara, the geeky *otaku* district of Tokyo mentioned above, where the group was formed. It consists of three 'teams,' A, K, and B, each of which initially had 16 female members. The three teams take turns performing almost daily at the AKB48 Theater in the Don Quixote discount store in Akihabara. As well as the 'regular' members, there are 'non-regular' trainees ('research students'), who bring total AKB membership to almost a hundred girls. Thus AKB48 has been certified by Guinness World

Records as the world's largest pop group. It also has sister groups in three other Japanese cities, as well as in Shanghai and Jakarta.

AKB48 members are selected by their fans, and membership changes annually. Unlike in female pop groups in Korea, a typical AKB singer looks like the girl-next-door, not a superstar. Even though the group's singing and dancing are not perfect (again in sharp contrast to the sophisticated South Korean girl bands), fans forgive this and cheer the girls on to do their best.[21] The AKB48 girls are 'idols you can meet', and many *otaku* visit the AKB Theater to do just that. After each show, the performers line up to say goodbye to their fans.

Some fans have gone to extremes – a typical trait of the *otaku*. Websites show them flaunting bulk purchases of the latest AKB48 CD, having spent millions of yen on thousands of CDs. The reason? Each CD has a voting slip for the annual contest to determine the most popular AKB48 members (who then go on to larger roles in the group). Fans also buy merchandise (from T-shirts to autographed towels and pen cases); make pilgrimages to the AKB48 cafés; check their idols' blogs; and record the TV shows on which they appear.

'No AKB48, No life!' writes one fan on a bulletin board for the group. 'AKB is like Disney,' writes another, adding that the AKB world is 'like a dream land that brings you fairy tales, it's an unreal space.' Idol *otaku* men support their favorite AKB girls through frenzied participation in the group's annual poll to determine who will become the lead singers. By watching these girls working tirelessly and achieving success, *otaku* men are said to be inspired in their own lives, finding hope for their own future.

Idol *otaku* are challenging to date, since they usually prioritize their idol's diary, such as meet-and-greet events and concerts. *'Hatsugen Komachi'* ('Talk Town'), a sub-site on *Yomiuri Shimbun*, Japan's largest newspaper, features stories of perplexed girlfriends and wives of idol *otaku*. One woman confesses that she had been unable to understand why her boyfriend was frequently 'too busy to go on a date' with her. On discovering that he had concealed from her his frequent participation in idol events at weekends, she asks online what she should do. Another woman on 'Hatsugen Komachi' complains that her boyfriend didn't want to celebrate her birthday, because he wanted to go to his favorite idol's birthday event on the same day. She can't consider him for marriage, she writes: he might someday prioritize an idol's birthday party over his own child's birthday party!

Overall, the partners of idol *otaku* do not cope very well if the man is too obsessed with his idols. They feel saddened or pained to see their partners so completely absorbed in the idol worship of teenage girls. Many women say they find it incomprehensible that adult men should fantasize about teenagers, and some are disgusted to think that their partners could be *lolicon*. However, others argue that so-called 'light' *otaku* – those who are not overly obsessed – can actually make good mates, since they are likely to be sympathetic to working women and may help out with children and around the house more than a work-obsessed salaryman. As Megumi Ushikubo (author of the herbivore book) warns, 'don't go to the red ocean,' where women fight bloody wars among themselves to hunt men with high incomes, high expectations, and high education. Ushikubo urges women to 'turn to the unexplored blue ocean' (where the light *otaku* may swim).[22]

The expanding range of careers and lifestyles among Japanese men has certainly complicated the dating life of Japanese women. Expectations of courtship have changed. Women have new opportunities, but find that they come with new strategies. Many have learned to be more assertive, creative, and strategic in dealing with shy and reluctant herbivores or *otaku*.

Diversifying women

Of course, changes to the Japanese economy are not segregated by sex, and Japanese women are diversifying, too. The traditional idea that all women will be office ladies until they become housewives is no longer true. Adult women may be roughly categorized into three cultures, each reflecting unique world views and challenges that transcend economic status: single women, housewives, and working mothers.

Single women

As we have seen, Japanese society often has an unkind view of single women over 35 years of age. One woman tells of sarcastic remarks from married female colleagues, who bluntly ask why she doesn't marry or if her standards might be too high, a grave insult in a country that values humility. Others on 'Hatsugen Komachi' stereotype older single women: they are too choosy about men, even in 'old' age; they depend on parents for money; they are so-called 'parasite singles' (a term coined by sociologist Masahiro Yamada) who do not seriously think about their biological clocks. Some conservative men see single women as selfish and self-indulgent burdens on a society that ends up supporting them.

For single women worried about financial security, the poverty statistics present a frightening snapshot of their future – not least because so many are irregular workers. Among single women aged 20–63, nearly a third (31.6 percent) live below the poverty line (i.e. earn less than 1.25 million yen ($12,500) per year). For those over 64, the rate is even worse, at 52 percent.[23]

Destitution aside, living alone has been portrayed as a public health issue in the Japanese media, which inadvertently fan fears about lonely deaths (kodoku-shi) whenever they report on people whose bodies are only found weeks after they die. These people are the nightmare endgame of female singlehood: they live alone in urban apartments, with no friends, relatives, or close neighbors to rely on. Recent stories about the solitary deaths of female celebrities have built on these fears. Nobody knew about veteran actress Reiko

Ohara's death in 2009 until the police and her brother found her body – two weeks after she died. Other solitary death stories include the 2012 passing of former CNN headline newscaster Yoshie Yamaguchi at the age of 51, and the 2008 death of popular adult movie actress Ai Iijima at the age of 36. Conservatives in the media and social media seize on these stories, accusing women of bringing these sad ends upon themselves by forgoing marriage, and warning other women to avoid the same fate.[24] Though elderly men also die alone, of course, there is less media focus on them.

A Japanese cottage industry of books warns women of the dangers of valuing a career over marriage. One bestseller, *The Croissant Syndrome* (1988), recalls the popular women's lifestyle magazine *Croissant*, dedicated to the 'new female lifestyle' in the 1970s and 1980s and featuring stories of single, fashionable, career-centered women. The magazine idealized single life and had a large following. The term 'croissant syndrome' has come to refer to unmarried career women who, under the influence of the magazine, once rejected traditional family lifestyles and never married or had children, but who then came to regret their decision in their forties, when it was already too late to bear children.

In a similar retrospective, Shiho Tanimura wrote a book in 1990 celebrating single-minded career women in their twenties and thirties and entitled *The 'I May Not Marry' Syndrome*. Her follow-up book in 2003, *The 'I May Not Marry' Syndrome, 10 Years Later*, described how most of the women in the first book, herself included, had after all ended up marrying and having a typical family. All this advice stands in marked contrast to that normally given to single men, who are encouraged in popular bestsellers to shed the home loans, debt, and burdens of family life, and replace them with a carefree 'Latin life,' dedicated to personal fulfillment.[25]

Other books offer advice to single women, such as the bestselling *Distant Howling of the Loser Dogs*, which suggests that the unmarried over 30 should accept that they are 'loser dogs' and, rather than howl or bluff, simply admit that they have lost the battle against married women with children ('winner dogs') and take pride in who they are.[26] In a more positive vein, feminist sociologist Ueno Chizuko offers practical suggestions on positive aging to women who expect to live alone: how to manage their finances, choose a place of residence, and choose nursing care for themselves. Her bestselling book, *Ohitorisama no rogo* (*A Guide for Singles, Life after Retirement*) popularized the term *ohitorisama* ('a person alone') to describe women who live comfortably on their own, resisting the pressures of marriage. The popularity of the term spawned a 2009 TV drama, *Ohitorisama*, which explores the lifestyle of an unmarried high-school history teacher who is perfectly capable of doing things by herself and who happily and passionately pursues her career. In recent years, a slew of businesses have emerged that target *ohitorisama* women, providing comfortable environments for them to dine in restaurants, go to the movies, or attend karaoke bars alone.

Housewives: End of a tradition?

Despite glimmers of acceptance, single life is still stigmatized. In contrast, housewives have traditionally been praised as the selfless, hardworking, and devoted mothers who helped bring about the country's economic miracle. They made sure that their children were educated and that their husbands stayed focused on their careers. There was a clear division of labor between men and women, with the role of women being to nurture and strengthen children and men.

Many people still expect women to fulfill this role. Japanese companies are generally unsympathetic toward women who try to balance career and family, and 70 percent of working women leave the labor force when they have a child, with some then taking part-time jobs once their children are at school or grown up.[27] Female workforce participation in Japan is thus represented by an M-shaped curve, where women quit their jobs in their late twenties or their thirties, and then rejoin the labor force once their child is older, with a peak in participation from 45 to 49.[28]

Housework is the domain of the Japanese wife. Mothers spend most of their time on childcare, cooking, and cleaning. A housekeeper is too expensive for most families, and with salarymen husbands working late evenings, wives are the only ones left to clean up.

Japanese women generally take great pride in their housework. Though women usually learn cooking skills from their mothers, some housewives take cookery lessons to prepare fancy meals for their husbands and children.[29] They make super-decorative *bento* (lunch boxes) for their children. Kindergartners in Japan bring *bento* to school every day, and many housewives prepare elaborate lunch boxes with five or six little dishes, including rice balls that look like pandas or bears. These types of *kyara-ben* ('character *bento*') are labor-intensive, often taking 30–45 minutes or more to prepare.[30] Women may plan, shop, and organize dinner, keeping in mind leftovers for the next day's *kyara-ben*. This is not just a lunch box: it's a work of art, expressing the mother's creativity, devotion, and love for her child.

Some housewives care for senior family members who live with them. And, outside the family, they may be kept busy attending their children's school events and volunteering for Parent–Teacher Association activities.

While these roles are still the norm, the prolonged recession has changed expectations. Many families, especially young ones, can no longer survive on the husband's income alone. Housewives are pinching the pennies and giving their husbands less pocket money. Many take on part-time or temp positions.

The image of the housewife has also grown less reverential. One prevalent new stereotype – that 'every day is a holiday for the housewife' – depicts them as napping the day away, wasting their time on supposedly frivolous activities like language classes or tennis lessons, and blithely spending their husband's hard-earned money on leisure and fashion goods. Since these housewives are thought to live in a very narrow world of housework and daily errands, they are caricatured as not understanding how society works and as unable to talk about anything but the mundane.

Housewife bashing doesn't stop there. After the bubble burst, housewives were also blamed for Japan's fiscal problems. One book, *Give Me a Break, Full-Time Housewife*, argues that housewives are free-riders on the nation's pension and healthcare systems.[31] This book (and others) rails against legislation that provides income tax exemption and generous healthcare, social security, and pension benefits to families, but only if a woman's salary falls below 1.3 million yen ($13,000) a year. Critics argue that the law deters women from working, but attempts to change it have thus far failed.

Many housewives, especially those without children or the elderly to care for, are made to feel guilty or ashamed for not working. Some critics sarcastically compare them to the young people 'not in education, employment, or training,' with the jibe that NEETs depend on their parents, while housewives depend on their husbands. When asked 'What do you do all day?', many housewives become uncomfortable and lie, claiming that they are too weak to work, or that they are 'freelancing.'

But going back to work can be difficult for housewives. They can work only during the hours when their children are at school, and there are few jobs that can accommodate this schedule, nearly all of them poorly paid and irregular. One graduate from a well-regarded university who recently took a part-time position in an elementary school cafeteria lamented to the authors that she had to become an *obasan* (middle-aged woman), who cooks and cleans and barely earns the minimum wage.

Housewives may become an anachronism in Japan, as more families depend on two incomes. Many Japanese men today want their wives to work full time to help meet family expenses. Social media debates ponder the fate of Japan in a post-housewife era. Some believe a greater role for women in the workforce will revitalize the country's economy, increasing demand for corporate childcare, nursing care, restaurants, cleaning services and maid services, since a family of two wage-earners has more disposable income. Others worry that Japan will suffer from even lower birth rates as both husband and wife put in long hours. Still others argue that housewives entering the labor pool will take jobs away from university graduates looking for a permanent job.

Struggling working mothers

Having a career and a family might seem as though it would make a woman's life more financially secure and emotionally satisfying; but that is not necessarily the case. Working women in Japan remain saddled with a hugely disproportionate share of housework and childcare, making the life of the working mom daunting.

The question of work–life balance for women is not a new one in Japan. In the late 1980s, a popular singer, Agnes Chan, started bringing her infant son and her nanny to work. Bringing a baby to work was considered practically revolutionary at the time, and a nationwide debate ensued about the role of mothers in the work-place. Though the TV producers gave her permission to bring the baby and nanny to the set, Chan was widely castigated, especially by unmarried career women, who argued that children were a private matter that should not encroach on the public sphere, and that work-places could not afford to accommodate a surge in children.[32] Slippery slopes were also greased: 'if her behavior is hailed, very soon people will start dragging their disabled elderly to work.'[33] Feminists took Chan's side, offering their support for mothers who were torn between work and family. The 'Agnes controversy' thus led to discussion on the childcare challenges faced by women across the nation.[34] But more than a quarter of a century since the Agnes controversy broke, not much has changed. The number of working mothers has grown, but their options have not expanded.

Japanese women still have a hard time finding childcare. Though affordable, full-time childcare facilities (*hoikuen*) are, in theory, available for full-time working parents, demand outstrips supply, and children are sometimes turned away. In that case, most mothers have no option but to stay at home with their children. Some large companies, such as Shiseido, offer their employees private childcare (see chapter 1), but such support is rare.

Even if she does secure a childcare place, there are further challenges facing a working mother. Her schedule may keep her in the office when the *hoikuen* closes, and – with little immigrant labor and no tradition of young Japanese taking such jobs – hiring a nanny or housekeeper is difficult and extraordinarily expensive. Most women are expected to cook and do the other housework with the help of neither their husband nor a domestic worker. On average, working mothers in Japan spend more than four hours a day on housework and childcare, while working fathers spend 30 minutes.[35]

Despite the childcare challenges, Japan's economic difficulties are pushing mothers into the workplace. The current catch-phrase is thus 'work–life balance' (WLB, see chapter 1), which is based on the idea that people should balance love, marriage, family, and career. The leading advocate of WLB is Yoshie Komuro, CEO of Work Life Balance Co. Ltd. Her company acts as a consultant to companies and the general public about balancing work and life. This typically boils down to increasing employee motivation and productivity, so as to shorten work hours and offer more time at home. Komuro speaks of WLB as if it were a societal revolution: women could secure careers, men would participate in child-raising, and Japan's birth rate would rise as couples with more free time become more positive about having and raising children.[36] She also calls for men to be 'trained' to do more housework. Unfortunately, her own life belies her company's goals: previously an employee at Shiseido, she worked 60-hour weeks while pregnant, took less than three weeks off work around the time she gave birth, and wrote instructions to her employers from her hospital bed.

Inspirational business books for women fly off the shelves, but many of them are profiles of supermoms, such as Fumiko Hayashi, a high-school graduate who climbed the ladder from car sales to become president of BMW Tokyo and mayor of Japan's second-largest city, and Kuniko Inoguchi, a mother of twins and a professor who became a cabinet minister and upper-house representative. Publications about such women are popular, but they can create unrealistic expectations for working mothers who lack the financial means and social support of Japan's business and government elite.

Konkatsu: Marriage hunting craze

As time goes by, Japanese people marry later or (increasingly) never marry at all. The average age of first marriage rose from 1993 to 2012 by more than two years for men (28.4 to 30.8) and by more than three years for women (26.1 to 29.2). Women now typically have their first child at age 30.3 (2012 data), compared to 25.7 in 1975.[37]

Nearly half (47.3 percent) of men and more than a third (34.5 percent) of women between the ages of 30 and 34 were unmarried in 2010. That same year, 35.6 percent of men and 23.1 percent of women aged 35–39 were unmarried. All these figures were the highest ever recorded. The so-called 'lifetime singlehood rates' (*shogai mikon-ritsu*), which are based on the proportion of 50-year-old men and women who have never been married, are also on the rise, reaching 9.7 percent of women in 2010 and a startling 18.9 percent of men (compared to only 3.4 percent of women and 2.2 percent of men in 1975).[38]

During the postwar years, unmarried women over 25 were stigmatized as 'old maids' (*orudo-misu*) and compared to Christmas cakes: in Japan, families buy a Christmas cake on 23 or 24 December. After 25 December, nobody wants a cake anymore.

These days, few women wed before they are 25. It is not that Japanese women don't want to marry: in a 2010 government survey, about 90 percent of single women and 87 percent of single men aged 18–34 said they would want to marry some day.[39] But the economy has created serious obstacles to finding a mate. Male salaries steadily declined in the so-called 'lost decades', and more men are taking temporary or part-time jobs. As men have lost the confidence to date (and the wherewithal) because of their low income, women have fewer men to choose from. To make matters worse, the extremely long hours of professional careers and the irregular hours of part-timers can make meeting people something of a challenge. Among working couples, dates sometimes need to be arranged weeks or even months in advance, eliminating spontaneity and dampening enthusiasm. And many men lack the charm, confidence, and enthusiasm required to cultivate romance or attraction.

Unrealistic expectations play a role, too. As the income of Japanese men has dwindled, women have not always adjusted to the reality of the post-bubble era. Some of them want to become stay-at-home moms, like their mothers were in the 'Showa style' of the 1960s to the 1980s – Japan's golden age.[40] That requires a husband who can support a family, and these women want a man who can keep them in the comfort to which they have been accustomed while living with their parents. It is difficult to find a well-paid young man in modern Japan. That is why so many relationship books advise women to lower their standards – better an imperfect marriage than none at all.

To find a lifetime partner, people in their twenties through to their forties engage in *konkatsu*, short for *kekkon katsudo* ('marriage hunting'), itself a spinoff word from *shukatsu* or *shushoku katsudo* ('job hunting'). Coined in 2007, the term *konkatsu* has twice been nominated as Japan's most popular word of the year. *Konkatsu* is distinct from mere dating, the purpose of which is to meet people and have fun. Instead, *konkatsu* conjures up the grueling work of job hunting, requiring a similar level of planning and strategy to find a suitable romantic partner. The concept has spawned countless maga-zine and newspaper articles and bestselling books that discuss *konkatsu* tactics, while TV dramas on *konkatsu* are also popular.

Traditionally, family and friends would introduce potential partners in a formal *omiai* ('matchmaking') setting. If the couple liked each other, they would start dating and perhaps marry several months later. Today, young people think traditional matchmaking old-fashioned, and it accounts for only about 5 percent of current marriages. If they can afford it, singles instead turn to professional marriage brokers – a booming industry in post-3/11 Japan, as young people, aware of their mortality after the tragedy, seek *kizuna* ('bonding'). Men and women register and pay a fee to the marriage broker, and provide information about themselves and their preferred partners (such as income, height, and education).[41] The broker will introduce men and women with matching preferences, and will typi-cally organize social events, such as dinner parties, golf games, or hikes where clients can meet and socialize. These events are pitched at people who are openly seeking marriage partners, and so serious discussion of marriage and straight-to-the-point questions can arise within minutes of first acquaintance.

Efficiency is the name of the marriage game. After all, dating costs time and money that many people simply do not have. Men and women may hurry through the 'getting to know you' phase. This can lead to interactions that might seem shockingly direct to a Westerner. If a potential partner must care for ailing parents, for example, that could be a deal breaker, so the topic is addressed early on, in a bid for maximum efficiency. *Konkatsu* event participants' profiles are often available ahead of time to other participants, so they can more or less instantly home in on the most interesting individuals and plunge straight into conversation.

Those who are less well off may skip brokerage agencies (whose fees can be in the thousands of dollars) and instead attend the popular (and cheaper) *omiai* speed-dating parties, which allow them to meet a large number of people in a single session. Some large events can attract up to 1,000 participants on a single night, perhaps spread out across various designated venues in a city, where participants are given some visible marker of participation (such as a special wine glass or a pin). *Omiai* events include 'travel parties' to amusement parks or the mountains, 'large parties' involving dozens of people who mingle and talk, and formal 'petite parties,' at which suitors fill out a profile card and have a short chat with the other participants, with men moving around women in the manner of sushi on a conveyor belt. People who want to save even more money may turn to online matchmaking sites for 'net *konkatsu*.' These typically incur a monthly fee of 2,000–4,000 yen ($20–40) and provide a service similar to online dating sites in the West.

Konkatsu can be exhausting. Speed-dating with a few dozen suitors in an hour can be a dizzying and stressful process. Active *konkatsu* daters may feel drained from repeated failure. With such a small amount of time to make conversation at a *konkatsu* party, participants often find themselves judging suitors by shorthand evaluations of age or income, leaving them feeling dissatisfied. The inner life of the individual is lost in the barrage. In light of this, it is not surprising that many participants in these *konkatsu* get-togethers look down on the other people there, assuming that anyone present has been unable to find a partner anywhere else. The irony of seeking a mate at an event where participation itself makes potential partners less attractive is not lost on the participants.

Many websites offer forums for women in their thirties and forties to discuss the finer points of *konkatsu*. Discussion frequently turns to the precise opportunities that women of different ages and backgrounds have, and the strategies they should thus pursue. According to one commenter, in Tokyo a 32-year-old may stand a good chance, whereas in the countryside even a 28-year-old might have difficulty in finding a suitable husband. Another woman, assessing her own age and looks, writes: 'I learned that my marriage market value is similar to that of a man who earns just 3 million yen a year [$30,000 – an amount on which a family would struggle]. No wonder I haven't been successful in my *konkatsu* activities.' The economic and social realities of Japan have spawned a culture of disappointment and diminished expectations. The brutal but typical refrain across message boards targeting aging single women is that women over 35 have to settle for men who are less than ideal.

For certain singles, romantic life carries an air of desperation, largely because Japan's social organization relies so heavily on families. As women age, so romance is replaced by a sense of catastrophe about a life spent in isolation – not only rejected by men, but without the safety net of marriage. The common idea in Japan is that single life is fun for the young, but becomes increasingly dire with each passing decade. Some 20-year-old women are financially independent and can travel or have comfortable lives alone. They have many friends and few responsibilities. But in their thirties, those same friends get married, bear children, and have little time to socialize. As single women enter their fifties, they face a slew of professional anxieties. People over 50 often fear that they will be fired by companies trying to cut labor costs. For single women without a husband's resources, this could spell financial ruin, especially if their parents fall ill or die. As women age, so the independence of their youth becomes a burden. Many women, seeing this long-term life arc, begin to panic: without a husband or family, they fear they may be dependent on social welfare to survive. That looming threat of isolation can spawn anxiety in all but the most independently minded women. Single men also face the anxiety of growing old alone, but they typically have more financial resources to fall back on, as well as a larger dating pool of potential partners their age.

Japan is, of course, a large and diverse country, and each of its 127 million people has his or her own story. Not every single woman is looking for a man, and nor is every single woman over 35 desperate. Take, for example, Makiko, a 50-year-old professor at a university in

Tokyo. Makiko has a high income, a good pension pot, and an economically secure future. She works long hours, but has much vacation time throughout the year, which she spends traveling around Japan, Korea, and the United States, where she has many relatives and friends. She happily pursues her hobbies and dotes on her nephews and nieces without a thought of *konkatsu* or of pursuing a husband. Makiko – and many others like her – are the antithesis of the desperate single woman.

Wa, gender, and family

By some definitions, male–female relations and family life in Japan are the epitome of harmony. The teen birth rate in Japan is the lowest in the world (just one-eighth the rate in the United States).[42] The rate of single-parent households is also among the world's lowest (only one-third the rate in the US).[43] The divorce rate is half that in the US.[44] In Japan, crime against women (as indeed all crime) is rare: the rate of reported sexual violence is a quarter that of Hong Kong, one-seventh that of South Korea, and one-tenth that of Germany.[45]

Japan has a relatively relaxed attitude toward both premarital and extramarital sex, without the misogynist double standards that exist in many other parts of the world. Gays and lesbians are treated with greater tolerance than in many Western countries, and issues related to homosexuality are not politicized in the country.[46] Transsexuals and transgender people are increasingly accepted as well. Hate crimes against sexual minorities in the country are virtually unheard of.

In the postwar era, life in Japanese families was orderly. Men and women knew their roles. Clear expectations reduced conflict, and there was a high degree of consensus among husbands and wives as to family matters, just as there is consensus in other aspects of Japanese life. Men dominated the work domain, but women were the main decision-makers in most other aspects of family life, including childrearing.

Rigidly defined gender roles and harmonious family relations served Japan well in the postwar period and contributed to the nation's rapid economic growth. Men worked extreme hours to build Japan's economy, while women fed them and raised children to contribute to the country's human capital.

Today, though, this archetypal harmonious family is facing challenges. The new, usually *involuntary* roles for men in the workforce, as *freeters* or *haken*, are paralleled by new *voluntary* roles for men in society, as herbivores and *otaku*. These men are typically passive in romance, thus making it harder to form relationships. Meanwhile, many women must choose between raising children alone while a husband works long hours, joining the workforce while taking sole responsibility for household work and childrearing, or staying single with an unpredictable social and economic future. In other words, just as the economic order of the postwar era no longer functions, so the social order that has governed gender relations in the postwar period is also facing serious cracks.

The problems that men and women are having in developing stable relationships have undoubtedly been exacerbated by two decades of economic stagnation, and perhaps these problems will ease if the country returns to a period of economic growth. If not, they could contribute to the troublesome demographic trends that threaten Japan's future. To those demographic trends we now turn.

CHAPTER THREE

Graying and Shrinking

In 2010, Sogen Kato was believed to be the oldest man in Tokyo – a very respectable 111 years. However, when local officials went to his family home to celebrate 'Respect for the Aged Day', his daughter sent them away – and with good reason. The local police later received a tip-off from Kato's guilt-ridden grandson. When they went round, it was to find a mummified body lying in his bed. For 30 years, Kato's family had lived with his corpse so that they could continue fraudulently to collect his pension.

Kato's case sparked a national inquiry into centenarians and pension fraud. After a thorough evaluation and a series of follow-ups, officials found that 230,000 centenarians were missing from the records, presumably either dead or living abroad. Hundreds of them had allegedly reached the age of 150, and there was one man who had supposedly been born in 1810. And Kato's was by no means the only instance of families living with decomposing relatives in order to benefit from their pensions.

Kato's case, and the investigation it spawned, revealed just how neglected many seniors are. The revelations rocked Japan, the world's 'grayest' nation. With almost a quarter of its population over 65, Japan had already been shouldering the burdens of an aging population – a rickety social security system, a shortage of senior care facilities and personnel, poverty among the elderly, crimes by seniors, and social disconnection. Now people were adding pension fraud and poor official accounting for seniors to the list of problems.

Gray Japan

The city of Nagasaki is not yet a ghost town, but it is typical of aging Japan. A look at the boutiques in the shopping arcades reveals a heavy emphasis on the fashion of the 1980s, as favored by *obaachans* (grandmothers). The Nagasaki branch of the Tamaya department store has even closed its children's section, instead using the available space to expand its range of elderly care products, such as hearing aids. Scanning faces on a typical day downtown, one strains to find an unlined one. There is little evidence of youthful nightlife. The young people there wear high-school uniforms and most leave town as soon as they graduate: seven in ten of those who go on to college depart to study in some other town, and over half of the young people find jobs elsewhere, especially in Osaka and Tokyo.[1] By 2040, a total of 39 percent of Nagasaki's population is expected to be 65 or older, compared to 26 percent in 2010.[2]

Nagasaki is just one harbinger of changes in Japan's demographics, which are shifting upward as baby boomers reach retirement age. The National Institute of Population and Social Security Research, a governmental think-tank that provides a 50-year demographic trend every five years, has estimated that the proportion of seniors (people aged 65 and older) in Japan will jump from 23 percent in 2010 to 39.9 percent in 2060.[3] For comparison, sociologists consider any population where 21 percent or more are aged 65-plus to be 'a hyper-aged society'[4] – so Japan, already a hyper-aged society, is aging at warp speed. The National Institute of Population and Social Security Research reckons that the workforce population (15–64-year-olds) will shrink to nearly half of Japan's population by 2060 (from

63.8 percent in 2010 to 50.9 percent in 2060). This means that each senior will be supported by a mere 1.25 working-age individuals. The institute also predicts that Japan's peak-time population of 128 million (in 2010) will shrink to 94.6 million by 2060.

Japan is not alone. Other industrialized countries, particularly in Europe, are watching anxiously as their median age rises. Italy and Germany have low birth rates on a par with Japan (within the range of 1.25 to 1.40 per woman) and face similar social problems, such as a shrinking potential workforce and a rising number of pensioners. But in this race, Japan has them beat: its population has aged more rapidly than that of any other industrialized country, bar Monaco.[5] As of 2011, Japan has the world's highest proportion of old people (23.1 percent of the total population), surpassing Germany's 20.6 percent and Italy's 20.3 percent.

The country also has among the lowest proportion of young people in society: only 13.1 percent of Japan's population is below 15 (lower even than Germany's 13.3 percent or Italy's 13.8 percent). It thus has by far the biggest gap between the number of old (65+) and young (under 15), with a ratio of 1.74:1 (compared to Germany's 1.54:1 and Italy's 1.47:1).[6]

The graying population is due both to a rise in longevity and a decline in the birth rate. Japan's women have been ranked top in terms of longevity in every year since the mid-1980s: as of 2012, a Japanese woman can expect to live to the age of 86. The typical Japanese man will live to be 79 years old, a male life expectancy that is in the top ten in the world. Of course, extended life expectancies are a 'good thing' – the desired consequence of advanced medical technology, higher living standards, and universal healthcare. But an aging population and a declining birth rate are a problematic combination, making Japan's population older while shrinking the general population pool.

Senior power, senior poverty

The rapid aging of Japanese society is evident. Visit a typical elementary school in Tokyo, and its teachers will tell you there are fewer children than a decade ago. Go to a hospital, and you can see large crowds of senior citizens waiting for a handful of doctors, who run from room to room in their efforts to care for so many patients. Visit the countryside, and you will likely see lots of seniors, few children, and boarded-up schools.

There are actually two parallel and seemingly contradictory problems related to seniors in Japan: elderly people in the country are simultaneously too powerful and too poor.

Their immense power is seen in the voting booth, where seniors exercise greater influence than in any other country in the world. This stems from three factors. First, they represent a higher proportion of the population than in any other country: 23.1 percent, compared to only 12.9 percent in the United States. Think for a moment how much influence older votes have in US elections, and start by doubling that.

But it gets worse. As in the United States, there is a huge voter turnout gap by age. In 2000, approximately 35 percent of people aged 20–24 turned out to vote in Japan, compared to about 78 percent of those aged 65–69.

Finally, it is the rural areas of Japan that are the grayest, as young people move to the cities in order to further their studies and to seek careers and opportunities. Yet the rural districts of Japan are also greatly overrepresented in Japan's Diet. This is because districts were originally set up after the Second World War, when some two-thirds of the population lived in rural areas. Today only one-fifth does. Japan's voting system has undergone reform since then, but not sufficient to keep up with these population shifts. The number of representatives varies from prefecture to prefecture, but not nearly enough to represent the population variations. As a result, rural and thinly populated

Tottori Prefecture has roughly 240,000 voters per representative, whereas Tokyo has more than a million per representative.[7]

It is easy to see how this situation is self-perpetuating. Seniors are so powerful at the polls that they are able to resist change to make the electoral system fairer – for example, through a more representative carving out of legislative districts. As in other countries, seniors also vote in their own interests, which may not be consonant with policies directed at aiding young families. Disproportionately based in rural areas, seniors tend to favor protectionist policies that help elderly farmers, but hurt the pocketbooks of young urban families. They also typically press for greater expenditure on public pensions than on education.[8] These policy choices increase the cost of raising children and thus depress birth rates, thus helping to ensure that the country gets even grayer, and that the cycle continues.

Disproportionate influence by age also has a negative impact on the workforce. The hierarchical Japanese *wa* accords great respect and influence to those who are older. For that reason, pay and power in companies are largely determined by how old a person is, rather than by the quality of their work or ideas. Influence by age and seniority is not unique to Japan, but it is especially strong there. For example, one study examined the backgrounds of 150 CEOs of the top 50 enterprises in Korea, China, and Japan. The CEOs in Japan were the oldest, with an average age of 63.1, compared to only 51 in China. The Japanese CEOs also had the least education: only 18 percent had graduate degrees, compared to about 50 percent of the Korean CEOs and fully 70 percent of the Chinese. These discrepancies were attributed to Japan's 'unique corporate culture,' where 'experience is valued.'[9]

The hierarchical system in Japan leaves far fewer opportunities for the young. A total of 45 percent of those in the workforce aged 15–24 held irregular jobs in 2011, up from 17.2 percent in 1988 and roughly twice the rate of workers in older age groups. According to the Ministry of Economy, Trade, and Industry, just 9.1 percent of Japanese entrepreneurs in 2002 were in their twenties, compared with 25 percent in the US. Japan has 'the worst generational inequality in the world,' according to one expert, who added that it 'has lost its vitality because the older generations don't step aside, allowing the young generations a chance to take new challenges and grow.'[10] Not surprisingly, this situation has contributed to wide-scale disillusionment and even depression among Japanese youth.

Ironically, though, the power of seniors in Japan has not led to their prosperity. Simply put, the lower the ratio of working-age population to elderly, the fewer resources there are to support seniors' healthcare and welfare. And in Japan the ratio of working people to older people is the lowest in the world – and is decreasing year by year. Of course, in Japan the problem is exacerbated further by the fact that a smaller percentage of working-age women hold jobs than in most other developed countries.

To cope with the difficult situation, the government is cutting senior benefits, shifting the burden of care to the elderly themselves. The Diet has passed a series of healthcare laws that require upper-middle-income seniors, aged 70 and above, to pay 30 percent of their medical bills. Though many Japanese seniors enjoy relatively good corporate pensions, others receive more meager state pensions or no pension at all. About 540,000 seniors living alone were on state welfare in 2012. This figure, though, is estimated to represent only about 30 percent of the elderly who actually need state assistance. For many needy seniors refuse public help: they feel there is a stigma attached to welfare and are too ashamed to seek it out.[11]

In addition, though older workers usually have a lot of power in the workforce, more and more firms are seeking ways to lay them off or fire them, since their seniority-based salaries weigh heavily on companies. Workers in their fifties or sixties who are laid off in Japan have an extremely difficult time finding a new job. As a result of firings and government cutbacks, elderly homeless people are to be seen throughout Japan at subway stations, under bridges, and in underground shopping malls. These homeless seniors are common in large cities and are increasingly showing up in small ones, too.

Those slightly better off come together in places like Sanya,[12] a Tokyo district that used to attract laborers because of its cheap hostels, and now has housing projects that accommodate approximately 5,000 poor seniors who cannot rent regular apartments. Seiji Omata, 80 years old, is typical of Sanya residents. He worked as a plumber for 50 years until his retirement at the age of 70. After retirement, his income plummeted to $300 per month, all in pension. He had to sell his house to survive, and when he ran out of that money a few years later, he finally went to the local government for welfare assistance. That is when he was introduced to this housing, which is run by a non-governmental organization. Omata now receives $1,400 per month in total (i.e. pension and welfare stipends) and spends it all on the housing and meals provided by the housing staff.[13]

Poverty and desperation sometimes drive seniors to crime. Though still low compared to the United States, criminality among older people is rising rapidly in Japan, where it used to be virtually unknown. The number of seniors in the country who were the subject of criminal investigation went up six-fold from 2001 to 2011, reaching 16 percent of all those investigated, and the number of assaults committed by that age group jumped nearly fifty-fold in the same decade. Meanwhile, the general crime rate has been falling by about 5 percent a year. Elderly crime has been growing much faster than the national crime rate, but it has also been rising even faster than the population of seniors.[14]

This has resulted in a 'seniorization'[15] of Japanese prisons, as the share of the incarcerated elderly rises. Most imprisoned seniors commit their first crime after the age of 65. Three-quarters of senior prisoners are repeat offenders: they mostly commit serial petty crimes, such as shoplifting for food or picking pockets, to cope with cuts in government welfare spending and rising healthcare costs. A quarter of senior offenders have been arrested ten times or more and have returned to prison within a year of each release. By international standards, Japan has an unusually high rate of offenders aged 60 and above – about 12 percent, compared to a typical rate of 5 percent in other advanced industrialized countries.[16] Low incomes and weakening social ties are usually cited as the main causes of elderly crime. Many seniors live on their own, impoverished and socially isolated. Indeed, about 70 percent of seniors on government welfare live alone.

One survey found that many older people fear social isolation and despondently expect to die alone.[17] This sounds strange in a country that traditionally respects its elderly. But it is the case that many young people move away to seek economic opportunity elsewhere, and falling incomes over the past two decades have left younger families less able to support their parents. Postwar Japan's traditional extended three-generation family living under one roof has gradually been replaced by the two-generation, nuclear household.

This situation is not likely to get better soon. While 30 percent of those aged 65 and over lived alone in 2008, the figure is expected to reach 37 percent by 2030.[18] In addition, the government is already suffering the effects of the huge social welfare cost of a graying population. Spending on social security, including pensions, care for the elderly, and healthcare, takes up about 55 percent of the government's total non-interest spending.[19] Japan's fiscal situation deteriorated dramatically following the government's efforts to resuscitate the economy during the 2000s, and the country's fiscal debt ballooned to 10 percent of GDP in 2012, following the 2011 tsunami and nuclear disaster.[20] Reducing that deficit may require a tightening of social security programs, which would further put the squeeze on seniors.

Naturally, Japanese people are worried about the graying of their country. The media report daily on the consequences of aging, including a shrinking working-age population, limited economic growth, cuts in tax revenues, greater expenditure on seniors, and fewer options for public policy. People have developed a sense of crisis that is evident in endless articles and letters to the editor about the aging society. The questions have become a soul-searching trope on editorial and opinion pages: What can be done to encourage Japanese women to have more children? Are women having fewer children because they must also care for the elderly? How can social security be maintained without stifling the economy?

Many outsiders see two obvious solutions to Japan's aging problem: 1) if there are too many elderly people, increase the number of births; 2) if there are too few native workers to support the aging population, let more foreign workers in. But neither of these answers is gaining any traction in Japan. Why are so many Japanese women having fewer children? And what kind of immigration will the notoriously insular Japan tolerate?

Low fertility rate

Postwar fertility rates in Japan divide nicely into three time periods: 1) 1947–57, when postwar devastation and economic hardships saw the birth rate plummet by more than half (from 4.54 to 2.04 births per woman); 2) 1957–73, a period of unprecedented economic prosperity, during which per capita income increased by about 10 percent each year, while the birth rate leveled off at about 2.00 births per woman (near the replacement level), albeit with some fluctuations; and 3) 1973–present, a period of gradual or no economic growth, during which the birth rate has steadily declined.[21] Simply put, Japan's birth rate is tied to its economy: more money, more babies.

The National Institute of Population and Social Security Research predicts that the birth rate (1.41 per woman as of 2010) will fall to around 1.35 by 2060. The country's population decline could be halted if the rate rose to the replacement rate (i.e. 2.07), but this would be an unprecedented and monumental increase. In 2005, it hit a record low of 1.26; this was followed by a gradual recovery to 1.41 in 2012. This recovery stemmed from Japan's improved economy and an increase in older women giving birth.[22] Despite these gains, there is no sign that the birth rate will reach the replacement level soon enough to stave off a crisis.

Why are Japanese women having fewer children? Delayed marriage and non-marriage are two major reasons, accounting for about half of the birth rate decline that has occurred since 1973.[23] More men and women are single, and women are postponing marriage and child-bearing. Among men, 18.9 percent are considered lifetime singles; among women the figure is 9.7 percent.[24] About a third of women in their early thirties are single, as are 47 percent of men in the same age group. Since childbearing outside marriage accounts for just over 2 percent of total births, current and past marital status is a good indicator of whether or not women will have children.

As of 2012, the typical Japanese woman gets married at the age of 29 (see chapter 2) and has her first child at around the age of 30.[25] If women marry late, they are likely to have fewer children – due to fertility problems, if for no other reason. Indeed, Japan is one of the latest-marrying and latest-childbearing nations in the world.

A rising divorce rate has also contributed to the declining births. Divorced Japanese women usually do not have any more children for both cultural and economic reasons. The divorce rate is not particularly high in Japan – about one in three marriages ends in divorce, a much lower rate than in the US – but the figure today is four times as high as it was in the 1950s.

The new economic reality of low-wage, part-time and temp work is also discouraging people from marrying. The mean wage of Japanese workers has plummeted since the 1990s. According to the government's 2011 white paper on childrearing, most men in their thirties earned 5–7 million yen in 1997 ($50,000–70,000), but only 3 million yen ($30,000) in 2007, an astonishing decline within a decade.[26]

Once people marry, the same economic pressures discourage physical intimacy. In a 2010 survey, 40.8 percent of married couples reported not having had sex in the previous month, a number that had risen from 31.9 percent in 2004, with many stating that work-related fatigue was an important factor.[27]

Interestingly, Japanese women typically say they want more children than they actually have. The ideal number of children in Japan, as expressed in surveys, has remained steady, at about 2.5 since 1974.[28] This suggests that greater governmental support for children could bear fruit.

Raising children is expensive – about $300,000 to $400,000 per child, depending on whether they go to private school. According to a 2010 survey by the National Institute of Population and Social Security Research, 60.4 percent of women cited cost as the reason they had fewer children than they wanted.[29]

The cost of raising children has led to a values debate on the 'quality versus quantity' of children. Many couples in Japan focus on quality of life for the child (usually one) they already have: they spend their money on the child's education and extracurricular activities. But others want the child to have at least one sibling, so that he or she can grow up with someone and share the burden of caring for older parents.

While financial stakes are high for parents, so are anxieties about parenting. Workplace accommodations for parents are rare, and children bring a whole suite of stresses for mothers. One survey shows that 17.4 percent of women consider the psychological and physical burden of childrearing to be the main reason for having fewer children than they want.[30] According to the same survey, 16.8 percent of women see the difficulty of balancing work and parenting as a problem, while 10.9 percent point to the lack of help from their husband. Finally, while mothers could once depend on a social network of extended family and in-laws, contemporary society has not been so accommodating, as small nuclear-family households have become the norm.

Not liking children or just stressed out?

It is not easy being a mother in Japan. In a country that strikes many visitors as surprisingly silent, mothers have to endure the complaints of neighbors who don't like noisy children running around in the courtyard. As a result, some mothers can't let their children play outside. Mothers also complain about going with their small children on crowded subways, where the commuters see them as a nuisance.

Recent controversies about baby strollers are indicative of the social difficulties of parenting in Japan. While Japanese people have a reputation for politeness, their courtesy often transforms into a passive-aggressive spectacle during the rush hour on trains. Adults silently jostle each other for the best seats; some people pretend to be asleep rather than surrender priority seats to the elderly or pregnant women. Many people do not like strollers on crowded railways, which can take up the space of four or five standing passengers. In Tokyo, strollers were actually banned on railways until 1999. Previously, parents had to fold their buggies before entering the fare gates.

With the dawn of Japan's 'barrier-free age,' in which the government urged the elimination of physical barriers for seniors, small children, and the disabled, the railway companies installed elevators at stations and lifted the ban on strollers. Since then, they have become a common sight on the rail system, much to the chagrin of business commuters.

A handful of stroller-related accidents have inspired public debate on their use on the railways. One infamous 2007 incident involved a stroller that became trapped between the train doors and that was dragged (together with the infant in it) for more than 20 yards. Men on the platform got to the baby before the buggy was smashed against a concrete wall, and no one was seriously hurt. The public reaction to this and similar accidents often pins the blame on supposedly irresponsible mothers.

In 2012, Tokyo's rail companies and local government put up 5,000 posters encouraging passengers to give some leeway to people with strollers. The poster bore a seemingly uncontroversial proposition: 'Protecting babies is everyone's concern. Please be mindful of baby carriages getting on and off the train.' But the posters generated over 1,000 complaints from commuters, ranging from 'strollers clog up narrow aisles,' to 'because of these posters, stroller users will get even more brazen.'[31] The poster has ignited online debate about buggies, on railways. Some critics argue that parents should once again be required to fold them up before boarding a train. Strollers can be bulky these days, and much criticism has focused on these 'mega' strollers and on how much space they take up. Others have even suggested that mothers with babies should be banned from public transportation, as babies are accident prone and noisy.

Understandably, pro-stroller mothers are outraged. In chat rooms, personal blogs, and the media, they have defended themselves against stereotypical perceptions that they rush onto trains without concern for the safety of their children. Some mothers shift the blame onto tight train schedules that do not accommodate stroller users at routine stops. Others have blamed malfunctioning sensor systems on doors, which sometimes fail to notify the train conductor that people are still in the doorway.

Conflict over strollers in public facilities occurs in other countries, too,[32] but the fervor over this issue in normally polite Japan is troubling. It appears to symbolize not just a concern over shared space, but a more profound irritation with babies and mothers in a stressed society. In any case, it is easy to see how Japanese women, especially in large cities, could be discouraged from having large, or even medium-sized, families. If taking one child on a subway earns such opprobrium, what would it be like to take two or three?

Older women and ninkatsu *(active pursuit of pregnancy)*

In February 2012, NHK aired a special report on pregnancy and infertility, entitled 'I want to have a baby but I cannot; shocking information on the aging ovum.' Specialists on the show explained that women are physically best prepared to have a baby in their twenties and early thirties, and after that the number of healthy eggs declines. Some participants on the show said they had not even known about the association between age and fertility.

In 2011, 24.7 percent of babies in Japan were born to women over 35, compared to only 7.1 percent in 1985.[33] Many more women over the age of 35 want children but struggle to conceive. Unfortunately, women who postpone childbirth face a number of biological and legal hurdles.

Shortly after the NHK broadcast, Hidekazu Saito of the National Center for Child Health and Development and journalist Toko Shirakawa published a well-received book, *The Pregnancy Bible*, which stresses the importance of effective planning for becoming pregnant. Coining the term *ninkatsu* (pursuit of pregnancy), Saito and Shirakawa argue that people's attitudes toward childbearing have to change as more women marry and try to have babies at a later age. 'The days that women can automatically have children are over,' writes Shirakawa. She warns that a new age has dawned in Japan – one in which having children is more difficult than ever; and she notes a 2012 report released by the National Institute of Population and Social Security Research, which estimated that one woman in five born in 1995 would remain single, while one in three would be childless.

Shirakawa asks how women can overcome the social, economic, and physical obstacles to having children in contemporary Japan. It is difficult to have a child before the age of 35, as it requires a stable job with sympathetic coworkers, flexible management, and a cooperative husband. But conception after 35 poses a totally different set of problems. As Japanese women marry older, they may resort to assisted reproductive technology, as have many women in other industrialized countries.

Perhaps no Japanese woman has been more public about these matters than veteran Liberal Democratic Party lawmaker Seiko Noda. She is the author of *I Want to Give Birth*, which documents her struggles to receive fertility treatment – and her subsequent miscarriage. Noda finally gave birth at the age of 50 to a baby boy through in-vitro fertilization (IVF) with a donor egg from the United States. It was her sixteenth IVF cycle, but her first time using a donor egg.[34] Stories like Noda's may not be newsworthy in the United States and other Western countries, but in Japan, where conservative views on maternity prevail, having a baby at 50 is eyebrow-raising. In particular, Noda's decision to use an egg donor from the United States revealed the limited options that Japanese women have in their search for motherhood. In Japan, egg donation is extremely rare. The Japan Society of Obstetrics and Gynecology (JSOG), an official organization, effectively bans its members from using donated eggs from third parties in IVF treatment, even though there are no laws regulating egg donation in Japan.

JSOG also forbids the use of surrogate mothers. Japan has no explicit laws regarding mother–child relationships in surrogate births, but under the current interpretation of the Family Registration Law incorporated into the Civil Code of Japan, the woman who physically gives birth is the legal mother. In 2005, the Osaka High Court upheld an earlier ruling that a Japanese woman in her fifties was not the legal mother of twins delivered by her American surrogate.[35] The court's reasoning was that motherhood is nurtured during pregnancy, so it is reasonable to acknowledge for the welfare of the child that the woman who gives birth is the child's mother. In 2007, the Japanese Supreme Court issued a similar ruling involving a celebrity couple, actress Aki Mukai and professional wrestler Nobuhiko Takada.[36] They were genetic parents who used a surrogate mother in the United States after Mukai had uterine cancer and a hysterectomy. The couple were open and public about their IVF treatment. After the Supreme Court's decision, they were required to legally adopt their genetic offspring to gain parenthood rights. These kinds of court decisions have severely limited the use of surrogacy in Japan.[37]

The next option, at least for women who can afford it, is to seek out assisted reproductive technology abroad. Since the simplest form of IVF, which does not involve a donated egg or surrogacy, is available in Japan at a very reasonable cost, couples who pursue IVF overseas are usually looking for donated eggs and/or surrogate mothers. The United States and India are popular destinations. California has well-established surrogacy agreements (established in *Johnson* v. *Calvert* of 1993), in contrast to some US states that ban surrogacy contracts. India is popular for gestational surrogacy because it is affordable: brokerage firms advertise that surrogate mothers in India cost one-third of those in the United States. Women who are financially strapped and concerned about skyrocketing neonatal intensive care unit costs in the United States often choose India in preference. But the Osaka High Court case ruled that women over 50 must submit pregnancy-related medical documents when they return from giving birth abroad; this makes it nearly impossible to hide the use of a surrogate for women of that age, even if the US birth certificate lists the Japanese couple as the birth parents.

While the Japanese courts maintain a conservative interpretation of the Family Registration Law, the demand for assisted reproductive technology is growing. The cost of fertility treatment in Japan, including IVF, is very reasonable compared to the United States. Greater flexibility in other matters, such as surrogacy and egg donation, would be helpful as well; but these changes seem to go against the grain of Japan's sense of order.

Coping with shoshika *(tendency to have fewer children)*

So what has the government done to address the declining birth rate? In 1989 Japan's birth rate hit the then lowest level in the country's history, with 1.57 lifetime births per woman. This was even lower than in 1966 (a *Hinoeuma* or *Bingwu* year, when superstition says that female babies are born with a bad personality). Journalists coined the phrase '1.57 Shock' to mark the birth rate crisis and solemnly announced the arrival of *shoshika-jidai*, the era of fewer children.

This was the Japanese government's wake-up call. It began to see the declining birth rate as a threat to the social welfare system, economic growth, and even the nation's identity. The government acknowledged that Japan's social and economic environment was not conducive to conceiving and raising children, and introduced policy measures to cope with the low birth rate.

In 1991, the Diet passed the Law on Childcare and Family Care Leave, which at least formally allowed both parents to take up to a year off work. In 1994 and 1999, the so-called 'Angel' and 'New Angel' plans were passed, with the aim of expanding childcare facilities to cope with large backlogs and waiting lists, and to diversify childcare programs by creating daycare and after-school facilities with extended hours closer to train stations. Then, in 1999, the Basic Law for a Gender-Equal Society was enacted, which recognized the creation of a gender-equal society as a top priority. This law defined a 'gender-equal' society as one where women and men participate in activities as equal partners. The government also created political and bureaucratic offices and councils to combat the low birth rate, including a 'Minister of Gender Equality and Family,' the first ministerial post to deal exclusively with gender equality.[38]

In 2004, a subsequent plan, the Support Plan for Children and Parenting, further addressed issues of gender equality and parent-friendly working conditions. It was meant to encourage companies to let male employees take paternity leave and receive, at the minimum, 10 percent of their normal pay. Finally, in 2010, the Democratic Party of Japan (DPJ) government started a child allowance program, under which all residents received 13,000 yen ($130) monthly allowance per child aged 15 or younger. In 2011, new legislation restricted the benefit to families below certain income thresholds, and changed the monthly amount to 15,000 yen ($150) for children under the age of three and 10,000 yen ($100) for children aged 3–15.

All these initiatives, along with countless research papers, have done little to slow the declining birth rate, or even to encourage a better environment for families. For example, just 1 percent of Japanese fathers takes advantage of paternity leave. When a Tokyo district mayor, Hironobu Narisawa, took two weeks' paternity leave in 2010, it made headlines. It was so rare – he was the first local government leader to do so – that it was newsworthy. In terms of gender equality, little progress has been made, according to international bodies such as the UN Committee on the Elimination of Discrimination against Women and the World Economic Forum. The latter ranked Japan 94th out of 134 countries in gender equality, a modest improvement from its ranking of 101st in 2009. And while the child allowance is generous, it is not enough to counter the costs of raising a child, or even of hiring a babysitter on a regular basis, so it is unclear whether or not it has had the intended impact.

Where are the immigrants?

It seems very unlikely that Japan can restore its birth rate to the replacement level of 2.07 children per family. The only way to keep the population from diminishing, then, is through immigration. Yet Japan is traditionally not an immigrant nation. As a relatively homogeneous set of islands, it has always been suspicious of immigrants. As discussed in the next chapter, even families that have lived in Japan for several generations, such as Koreans, are not automatically granted citizenship. Even including Japanese-born Korean citizens and Chinese 'special permanent residents,' non-citizens account for only about 1.7 percent of Japan's population. That is a little under a quarter of the non-citizen percentage of the 28 countries of the European Union and a fifth of the percentage in the United States. Looking at it another way, Switzerland, with its population of 8 million, has almost as many non-residents as Japan, with a population of 128 million.

There are some Japanese advocates of open immigration. Hidenori Sakanaka, a former head of the Tokyo Immigration Bureau, says Japan must accept 10 million immigrants between now and 2050, as the country 'is on the brink of collapse.' In his view, it needs 'a social revolution equal to that of the Meiji Restoration,' the 1868 transformation that ended Japan's international isolation and helped modernize the country. 'There is no way for Japan to survive but to build a society of living with immigrants and hoisting a new flag: "Immigrants Welcome."'[39]

More politicians are starting to agree. In 2009, a group of 80 conservative Liberal Democratic Party members submitted a report to Prime Minister Yasuo Fukuda, proposing an increase in the number of immigrants to 10 percent of the population in 50 years, thus adding about 10 million more foreigners. The government should not only secure immigrants, they argued, but also provide assistance with language and vocational training, and encourage the newcomers to become naturalized citizens.[40] This group's position is mirrored in a report submitted to the major political parties by Japan's mighty *Keidanren*, or Federation of Business Organizations. It argues that Japan should quickly expand its immigrant labor to offset the shrinking domestic workforce in fields such as manufacturing, construction, agriculture, and social services.[41]

In spite of these calls, the government has resisted opening up the country to foreign workers. Though Tokyo has taken several initiatives to address labor shortages in the Japanese economy, its approach on this topic has been stringent and myopic, hoping to solve a large-scale population decline while avoiding large-scale immigration.

Foreign trainee programs

In 2007, a 27-year-old Chinese farm trainee in Chiba named Cui Hongyi fatally stabbed Susumu Koshikawa, a Chiba agricultural association employee, and injured two others. It was a horrific crime, but the court acknowledged that Cui had faced labor exploitation by his Japanese employer,[42] and a manga comic portraying Cui as a slave to cruel bosses did the rounds in Japan. His employer, a hog farmer in Chiba Prefecture, paid him just 65,000 yen ($650) per month, in spite of his working long hours. Cui and his family had accumulated a serious debt in China due to the hefty fee (approximately $12,000) they had paid the people who had placed him on the farm in the first place, essentially forcing Cui into indentured servitude. When Cui complained to his Japanese employer about his salary, Koshikawa (the victim) and the employer had tried to force him to fly back to China. Cui resisted, knowing he had not earned enough money in Japan to pay off his debt. A skirmish ensued between Cui and Koshikawa. Cui lost control, grabbed a knife and stabbed Koshikawa and the others. Koichi Yasuda, a journalist who followed the murder case, reported: 'Cui didn't intend to kill anyone . . . He was just scared of not meeting his family's expectations to make money in Japan, and of not paying off the enormous debt his family had accumulated.'[43]

Cui was in Japan as part of a government-sponsored training program for foreigners from developing countries (including China), known as the Industrial Training Program (ITP), which was established in 1981. Together with the Technical Internship Program (TIP), established in 1993, ITP was ostensibly a way of helping to cultivate human resources in developing countries; in reality, both ITP and TIP were designed to supply cheap labor to struggling small and medium-size companies in Japan. After a year in ITP, trainees move on to TIP and are allowed to work for two further years at legal wage levels. Trainees, 65 percent of whom are Chinese, come to Japan in the hope of learning advanced technologies and management skills, while earning enough money to help their families back home. In 2006, some 92,846 people entered Japan on a trainee visa, 11.14 percent more than the previous year and double the number ten years before.[44] In 2011, there were 130,000 interns in TIP, the second largest group of short-term resident foreign workers in Japan.[45]

These programs have been widely criticized as ripe for abuse. Trainees and interns usually are not engaged in knowledge or skill-based tasks, but are assigned instead to onerous manual labor. Cui, for example, tended pigs from early morning until evening every day. Furthermore, because first-year trainees in ITP are legally considered 'students,' not 'workers,' they are not protected under labor laws. According to the Japan International Training Cooperation Organization, a semi-governmental agency that oversees ITP and TIP, the average monthly 'in-service training reward' received by trainees in 2009 was 65,000 yen ($650), about half of what government welfare recipients get each month. Even when ITP trainees move up to become an intern (legally treated as a worker and protected by labor laws), they earn only about 143,000 yen ($1,430).[46] Struggling Japanese companies find foreign trainees and interns an attractive source of cheap labor, and are rapidly replacing Brazilian and other foreign workers with such trainees and interns.[47]

In 2006, NHK's *Close-up Gendai* TV program reported that one Toyota subsidiary paid its trainees as little as 350 yen ($3.50) per hour. These first-year trainees were not legally allowed to work at weekends or to do overtime, but the law was often ignored. In their second year, trainees at the Toyota subsidiary moved on to TIP, became interns, and gained the legal status of 'worker,' but received just the minimum wage while being forced to work additional hours without extra pay. *Close-up Gendai* reported that the Toyota subsidiary had gone so far as to confiscate the foreign workers' passports and bank documents to prevent their escape, and even charged them 15 yen per toilet break.[48] Investigators reported similar stories of abuse of foreign trainees and interns by 23 subcontractors of Toyota Textiles and the Toyota Technology Exchange Cooperative, a textile factory within the Toyota automobile conglomerate. According to their reports, the foreign workers had scant training or legal protection.

Abuses by institutions that host foreign trainees and interns are not limited to the workplace. Investigators detailed the kind of rules the institutions imposed on them to control their behavior after work, including a ban on the use of cell phones or personal computers, a ban on participation in a labor union, a prohibition on socializing with other trainees and interns (to prevent them from exchanging information about work conditions), and a prohibition on dating and falling pregnant. Some female trainees and interns reported repeated sexual harassment and assault. The victims were too afraid to complain because their hosts could threaten to send them home before they had earned enough money to repay their fees.

Abuses of foreign trainees and interns were already being reported in the 1990s. For example, in 1999 an intermediary organization in the textile industry in Fukui Prefecture was found to have swindled Chinese interns, paying them only 10,000 yen ($100) per month.[49] The Ministry of Justice has acknowledged more than 400 cases of mistreatment in the government-sponsored trainee program so far. The *New York Times* reports government figures showing that at least 127 trainees died between 2005 and 2010 – a very high mortality rate, considering the trainees are all young people who enter the program after stringent physical tests.

Many of the deaths were reportedly attributed to *karoshi* (death from excessive work).[50] In 2010, the government acknowledged that a trainee had died from *karoshi*. This was an important acknowledgment that the foreign trainee (who was, remember, technically a student, not a worker) had in fact been engaged in overtime work, against the stated goals and rules of the program. Jiang Xiaodong, 31, from China, had started working at Fuji Denka Kogyo, a metal processing firm near Tokyo, in 2005, but had died of cardiac arrest in 2008 after working 100 hours of overtime in his last month.[51]

More trainees have resorted to the courts for damages. A Vietnamese woman in central Japan filed a suit with the Nagoya District Court against her employer, demanding payment for overtime.[52] Four female Chinese trainees sued a sewing company and a brokerage agent in Kumamoto for their unpaid overtime. These plaintiffs revealed that they were forced to work up to 15 hours a day with only a few days off each month.[53]

In 2010, a visiting UN migrant rights rapporteur recommended that the Japanese government completely scrap the program, saying it amounted to 'slavery' in some cases.[54] In 2011, the US State Department echoed the UN rapporteur in its annual *Trafficking in Persons Report*, saying that some trainees' work conditions were similar to those seen in human trafficking abuses.[55]

Some former trainees and interns state that they have benefited from their experiences in Japan, and have used them as a stepping stone to advance their career or acquire wealth in their homeland. And Mitsuru Sato, a Japanese fisheries company executive in Onagawa, Tohoku, will be remembered forever by the 20 Chinese trainees at his company whom he saved during the 2011 tsunami. Sato led them to high ground and then, once he was sure they were safe, ran back for his wife and daughter, only to be swept away by the tsunami. The Japanese and Chinese media reported this tragic incident widely and praised Sato as a hero.

But positive stories related to ITP and TIP are rare. Koichi Yasuda[56] reports that the Gifu Labor Bureau found that a staggering 90 percent of participating institutions had violated labor laws. In general, ITP and TIP have become a front for the exploitation of foreign workers who come from poverty-stricken regions for jobs that no Japanese wants to be engaged in, often in Japan's declining or dying industries.

ITP and TIP are convenient for companies that want low-paid foreign workers; but they are also good for the government. These short-term programs do not lead to permanent residency for workers. The exception is when working conditions, debt, or personal ambitions lead workers to flee their posts: since 2002, an estimated 10,000 have done so, becoming illegal workers in Japan.[57] Otherwise, ITP and TIP facilitate the import of cheap foreign labor without any violation of government policy restricting unskilled immigrants.[58]

Yasushi Inoguchi sees Japan's trainee and internship programs as based on a 'human resource development and circulation model' that helps maintain Japan's high level of homogeneity, avoids large-scale cultural and social clashes, yet secures cheap temporary labor from abroad.[59] Hiroshi Tanaka, professor emeritus at Hitotsubashi University, argues that Japan must 'admit that the country already heavily relies on foreign workers' and 'develop the system to open the door to foreign workers, while securing their human rights.'[60] To do so means abolishing ITP and TIP altogether and creating a system to provide foreign workers with a legitimate work visa.

Bring on the Brazilians

In 2009, union leader Francisco Freitas and other 'Nikkei Brazilians' (Brazilians of Japanese descent) in Hamamatsu City, home to the largest Brazilian community in Japan, were shocked to find out that the Japanese government was paying for Latin American *Nikkeijin* (people of Japanese descent) to go back to Brazil. The government was offering each Latin American *Nikkeijin* head of household up to $3,000 and each family member up to $2,000 for their airfare.

Freitas and others fumed. The government was giving a one-way ticket for Latin American *Nikkeijin* to go home, on condition that they never came back to Japan. They could not seek work in Japan again, and their privileged *Nikkeijin* visas would not be reissued.[61] The government's goal was to send the unskilled Latin American workers home, in order to alleviate Japan's rising unemployment. 'There won't be good employment opportunities for a while, so that's why we're suggesting that the Nikkei Brazilians go home,' said Jiro Kawasaki, a former health minister and an important member of a task force that devised the repatriation program.[62] To Nikkei Brazilians, the government action was a callous attempt to throw a little money at them and hope they went away. They felt dehumanized. Freitas, who had lived in Japan with his family for 12 years, felt betrayed by the country he had come to call his home.

It started in the 1990s, when Japan was faced with an industrial labor shortage. The Japanese government lured foreign labor as a cheap fix, but, fearing potential culture clashes, it gave priority to people around the world of Japanese descent, rather than inviting workers from neighboring countries such as Korea or the Philippines. In 1990, the government amended the Immigration Control and Refugee Recognition Law to allow Nikkei Brazilians and other Latin American *Nikkeijin* of up to three generations (*sansei*) to work on special Nikkei visas ('spouse-or-child visas' for second-generation *Nikkeijin*, and 'long-term' visas for the third generation). Unlike regular foreign workers, these *Nikkeijin* did not have to possess special skills and were allowed to work in any sector. It was more or less a visa for permanent residence.

It came at the perfect time for many Brazilians. Their country's economy was in a shambles with hyperinflation. Many *Nikkeijin* from Brazil flocked to Japan to take on temp (*haken*) positions in the automobile and electronics industries. In 2008, the number of Brazilians in Japan reached a peak of more than 300,000, making them the country's third-largest minority after Koreans and Chinese. Brazilian immigrants provided cheap, menial labor in factories, performing the '3K' tasks – *kitanai* (dirty), *kitsui* (physically hard), and *kiken* (dangerous) – that most Japanese didn't want to do. These *Nikkeijin* initially intended to work in Japan for a short time, but many stayed on.

After the global recession began in 2008, Japan's economic slump forced manufacturers to cut production and fire temporary workers. Unskilled workers at automotive and electronics companies were the first to be laid off, and the majority of Brazilian workers lost their jobs. With the language barrier and the arrival of new foreign competitors, especially trainees and interns from China, *Nikkeijin* have had a hard time obtaining stable jobs in Japan.[63]

Many Latin American *Nikkeijin* struggle in their daily lives because of cultural and language differences. And due to housing discrimination (encountered by many foreigners in Japan), they tend to cluster in mid-size factory towns in central Japan, often residing in company-sponsored housing or public housing developments.

Brazilian children often drop out of school because they do not understand the Japanese instructions. In general, Japanese schools struggle to support children who cannot speak Japanese, and few teachers speak Portuguese or even English. These dropout children stay at home while their parents are at work. Roughly 20 percent of school-age children from foreign migrant groups (Nikkei Brazilians, Nikkei Peruvians, and Filipinos) reportedly do not attend school at all. Japan's high-school entrance exam system does not accommodate students with weak Japanese proficiency, and so less than 30 percent of children from these migrant groups attend high school.[64] For Japanese students, the high-school attendance rate is close to 98 percent. Some children attend private Brazilian schools, but these have severe financial problems and lack subsidies from the Japanese government, while unemployed parents are often unable to pay tuition fees. Some of these Brazilian schools have closed down.

The *Nikkeijin* community suffers many social problems. Unlike Japanese citizens, who have universal health insurance, many poor Brazilian families in Japan often lack medical coverage. There are also many reports of juvenile delinquency and gang violence among Brazilian children.[65]

The 1990 *Nikkeijin* visa program was based on the false assumption that *Nikkeijin* could assimilate into Japanese society more easily than other foreigners. It was supposed to be an easy fix for the labor shortage, but it is clear now that the government failed to predict the type of problems that *Nikkeijin* workers would face in Japan, and to provide appropriate assistance for their successful integration into society.

The number of Brazilian *Nikkeijin* had slumped to 210,000 by the end of 2011. The population has fled from Japan's recession, with the government repatriation program paying for the exodus. Ironically, Brazil is in the midst of an unprecedented economic boom, and some Brazilians are going home to take advantage of it. The population of Brazilian immigrants in Japan is not likely to expand in the foreseeable future, as many manufacturers have moved their operations to other Asian countries to save on labor costs.[66]

The Japanese government turned to *Nikkeijin* to deal with the labor shortage in manufacturing, rather than recruit workers from neighboring East Asian countries, because of a strange sense of cultural compatibility that emphasized historical bloodlines over geographical and cultural proximity. And when Japan entered a recession, the government gave these same *Nikkeijin* workers money to leave the country, but only if they promised never to return.

The government's repatriation program for Latin American *Nikkeijin* reflects Japan's long-standing immigration policy, which discourages long-term immigration by unskilled laborers and accepts only foreign workers with special professional skills that native Japanese do not possess. The Ninth Basic Plan of Employment Measures, approved by the cabinet in 1999, states the three principles behind Japan's immigration policy: 1) foreign workers with professional and technical skills are accepted to help revitalize the economy and support internationalization; 2) unskilled workers are handled carefully, taking into account the impact they would have on Japan's economy and society; and 3) foreign labor is viewed as an inappropriate means of dealing with an aging population, since 'it is important to first improve the labor environment in which more of the elderly and women can actively participate.'[67]

Clearly, there is no place for unskilled Brazilian *Nikkeijin* in this policy. At the same time, the demand for cheap, unskilled labor has been persistent and at times acute, especially for small and medium-sized companies in manufacturing, textiles, agriculture, and the fishing industry.

Foreign students

Demand for unskilled labor has been on the rise in the service sector, too, and Inoguchi's 'human resource development and circulation model' is also applicable there. The government has opened a back door to foreign students in Japan, allowing them to work for up to 28 hours per week (although they frequently exceed this limit). One survey has found that about 76 percent of foreign students on a student visa are working, and a large proportion of them work in the food service industry.[68]

Many restaurants and convenience stores in major cities rely on foreign students as a source of cheap labor, as seen in Yoshinoya, a fast-food, beef-bowl restaurant chain, and Lawson and Family Mart, major convenience stores in Japan. People in the Tokyo area, in particular, are used to seeing foreign students (mostly from China) working at these places. Hiring unskilled foreign students helps keep down costs, and they are welcomed in these venues – which are usually open 24 hours a day and struggle to recruit Japanese workers on account of the low-paid, physically difficult work. Many of the students will be in line for a white-collar job when they graduate, but while in school they need money to pay for their tuition and living expenses, and so take on jobs for minimal wages.

Foreign students make up 16 percent of all foreign workers in Japan.[69] This pool of labor is expected to grow in future, as the

Education Ministry aggressively tries to increase the number of foreign students in Japan: it hopes to see the number grow from some 140,000 in 2012 to 300,000 by 2020.[70]

Nurses and caregivers

Emma Juliana has been working at a Japanese care center for the elderly for three years. 'Aren't you cold? It's been raining since morning . . . Please hold my hands, one, two, three . . . Let's go to the hallway.' She talks gently and fluently in Japanese to her old and frail client. Emma, a native Indonesian, is one of 36 foreign nurses who passed the formidable Japanese national nursing certification exam in 2012. To pass the exam she studied Japanese with a tutor every single day for three years. Her hard work eventually paid off.[71]

The most pressing demand for labor in Japan may be in nursing and care of the elderly. These are physically demanding jobs with notoriously low wages: in 2009, the average monthly wage in senior care was just 72 percent of that in any other job sector.[72] Naturally, these fields are not popular among the Japanese.

The government tried to alleviate the problem of the labor shortage in nursing and care for the elderly in what may now appear to be a typically convoluted way. In the mid-2000s, Prime Minister Junichiro Koizumi created the Economic Partnership Agreement (EPA) programs with the Philippines and Indonesia, by which hundreds of Filipino and Indonesian nurses and nursing caregivers were brought to Japan to care for the elderly. The primary objective of the EPA programs was to gain duty-free access for its exporters to the Southeast Asian market; but attracting nurses and nursing care workers was an important component.

The EPA nursing and caregiver program is seriously flawed. These Indonesian and Filipino workers can stay for only a limited time (three years for nurses and four years for caregivers) unless they pass a formidable national certification exam in the nursing or nursing

care area. Each exam requires high-level Japanese language proficiency, and the success rate among foreign nurses has been extremely
low. In 2009 – the first time foreign nurses took the national nursing
exam – nobody passed. In 2010, only three out of 254 foreign nurses
passed (a 1.18 percent success rate). In 2011, after the exam was
revised to use the English words for names of illnesses and after the
Japanese language used in the exam was simplified, a total of 47 out
of 415 passed.[73] This represents a small advance, but is still far below
what the country needs. It is also a minuscule proportion compared
to the United States, where more than 5,700 foreign-trained nurses
passed a screening exam in a recent year (though of course the fact
that Filipino nurses know English makes the American exam infi-
nitely easier).[74] Some of the foreigners who successfully passed the
exam in Japan said they had spent five hours every day on their
language studies after their regular work hours. One who passed the
2011 exam spent 12 hours a day studying Japanese for three months
prior to the exam. Many of these people had stayed in Japan to care
for the elderly after the 2011 triple disaster.[75]

With most foreign nurses and senior caregivers unable to pass the
national exam, the initial enthusiasm for foreign workers in the medical
and nursing fields has waned, and fewer Japanese institutions are
willing to accept them. These institutions, after all, have to make
considerable investments in foreign workers, including special assistance, such as hiring tutors. In 2009, 177 institutions accepted foreign
nurses and caregivers; by 2011 the number had dropped to 62.[76] The
government provides subsidies, but hosts say they are too low to really
help. This is unfortunate, since the Indonesian and Filipino nurses and
caregivers are often popular among patients and clients on account of
their professionalism and upbeat personalities.[77]

At the same time, these programs have become less attractive
to Indonesians and Filipinos. In 2011, only 58 Indonesians and
61 Filipinos applied for the 300 places designated for each country.[78]
The Japanese government is trying to improve the national exams by

incrementally changing the format and increasing the time foreign workers are allowed for the exam. But the Japanese Nursing Association opposes special arrangements for foreign examinees. It claims that any special arrangements will reduce the quality of nurses.[79] But quality may be a secondary issue for the association: it seems more concerned about declining working conditions and wages if a large number of foreign nurses take jobs in Japan.[80]

Beyond test reform, however, Japan needs to re-evaluate the program to address a bigger question: how should it deal with a rapidly aging society and a substantially reduced workforce? The government lacks any clear vision to address labor shortages in nursing and senior care. In fact, its official stance is that the introduction of foreign nurses and caregivers for the elderly is chiefly to promote bilateral economic cooperation and human exchange, *not* to promote immigration in Japan's nursing or caregiving fields. This is tantamount to saying that the program doesn't do what it does.

According to the Japanese government, there is no shortage of nurses and caregivers, since there are Japanese workers who could take these positions.[81] The government's report on the Japanese economy, released in 2010 and known as the Basic Plan of New Economic Strategies, reiterated the no-immigration stance and, rather than immigrant workers, it encourages young people, women, and the elderly to participate in the labor market.[82] However, none of these groups appears motivated to seek employment in nursing and senior care. In 2011, Japan had 1.4 million care workers – a figure that is expected to grow to 2.1–2.4 million by 2025.[83] It is unlikely that the country will be able to fill this need without relying on foreigners.

Given the world-wide shortage of nurses and caregivers, sooner or later Japan may have to compete with North American, European, and Middle Eastern countries in recruiting qualified foreign nurses and caregivers. It must assist foreign workers to pass the requisite tests, but it must also establish an infrastructure to support foreign nurses in the workplace once they pass the exams.[84] In addition, the government has to provide sufficient support to the medical institutions that host foreign workers. Of the 36 foreign caregivers who passed the national certification exam in 2012, 11 have already quit their jobs and returned to their home country.[85] Tatsumi Nakayama, the owner of a nursing home in Aomori Prefecture, regrets losing one of them. He invested 30 million yen ($300,000) in her over four years, and had been assured by a government official that she would be working for his facility once she passed the exam. However, no official contract stated how many years she was expected to work there.[86]

Despite the flaws in the EPA program, Japan signed another EPA agreement, with Vietnam in 2008, and will start accepting Vietnamese nurses and caregivers in 2014. This time, through its official development aid, it will provide a one-year Japanese-language course in Vietnam for would-be nurses, with the aim of teaching daily conversational Japanese before they arrive.[87] Whether this new tack helps Vietnamese nurses integrate into the workforce and society better than other foreign nurses before them remains to be seen.

New Nikkeijin

Since most EPA healthcare workers from the Philippines and Indonesia cannot get permanent work in Japan without passing the national exam, Japanese elderly care institutions are seeking alternatives that they hope could bring a more stable workforce to Japan. They have sought out 'New *Nikkeijin*,' the children born out of wedlock to Japanese men and Filipinas who lived in Japan in the 1980s through the early 2000s. Most of these Filipinas met their Japanese partners while working as 'hostesses' in bars on entertainer visas. Because the Japanese government revised the Immigration Control Law in 2005 to restrict the residence of foreigners on entertainment visas, many Filipinas had to return to the Philippines with their children, leaving their Japanese partners behind.

In 2008, the Japanese government amended the Immigration Law to allow Nikkei children born outside a marriage to gain Japanese citizenship if their Japanese fathers admit paternity.[88] The number of New Nikkei Filipinos is estimated to be around 30,000, including the offspring of Philippines-based Filipinas and Japanese male tourists to that country. If these Filipinos gain Japanese citizenship, they will be able to live in Japan for good, without any legal restriction; and if they are interested, they can pursue the caregiver profession. Though the legislation was passed for general human rights reasons, rather than in response to employment demands, care institutions nevertheless see these New *Nikkeijin* as having an advantage over EPA Filipino nurses and caregivers, as the former do not have to pass the onerous national nursing or caregiver exam to find permanent employment in Japan's nursing establishments.

In 2012, NHK's popular *Good Morning, Japan* news show carried a special report about a Nikkei Filipina working as a caregiver in Japan. According to the show, Norika Ando gained residence after obtaining her Japanese father's paternity acknowledgment. Ando says she moved to Japan to support her family in the Philippines and to find her father. The director of her host institution says he is eager to have more Nikkei Filipina caregivers like Ando, as his institution has chronic labor shortages – most Japanese workers quit their job within a year. One broker company introduced in this show, Career Services, says Filipinas are very popular among Japanese seniors because of their cheerful disposition.[89] *Mainichi Shimbun*, Japan's major daily newspaper, has reported that some broker companies provide language and job training to their *Nikkeijin* recruits before they move to Japan.[90]

Ando was lucky to gain her father's paternity recognition: many Nikkei Filipina and Filipino children struggle with this part of the visa. While some support groups can help them locate their fathers and obtain paternity recognition (a requirement for Japanese citizenship), the path to citizenship from there still is not easy.

The recruitment of New *Nikkeijin* from the Philippines for nursing and caregiving is similar to the government's previous efforts to recruit *Nikkeijin* from Latin America to address labor shortages in manufacturing. But the Nikkei Filipino recruitment initiative has been developed by the private sector, and has sought labor beyond the government-created EPA nursing and caregiver programs. It is a creative way to recruit workers outside Japan; but the supply is extremely limited and falls far short of the number of additional workers needed in senior care alone: at least 210,000 more caregivers needed in 2015 than in 2011; and at least 730,000 more required in 2025.[91]

What about the highly skilled?

The only group of foreign workers that is officially sought by the Japanese government are highly skilled professionals. The 1989 amendment to the Immigration Control Law mentions for the first time the importance of attracting such professionals. The aforementioned report, approved by the cabinet in 1999, also acknowledges Japan's determination to welcome professional workers. The government further intensified its 'love call' (*rabu-koru*) to foreign professionals in 2012, when it established a points-based preferential immigration system.

This new system, intended to boost Japanese technological innovation and economic growth, awards visa preference to highly skilled foreign professionals, a scheme similar to that of Canada and Australia. Under the system, foreign professionals who earn 70 points or more receive the legal status of 'highly skilled foreign professionals' and are given preferential immigration treatment. The points are based on an applicant's educational attainment, period of professional experience, promised annual salary, and research performance. The program does not give much priority to Japanese language ability; rather, it is an applicant's professional qualifications and experience that gain high points. For example, if the applicant has a PhD, she or he automatically gets 30 points; someone who is aged 39 or below and has a promised salary of 7 million yen ($70,000) a year gets 25 points.[92]

Once granted professional status, the immigrant may be accompanied to Japan even by his/her parents, as well as by the husband or wife and dependent children. The spouse will automatically receive a work permit. The applicant and his/her family also qualify for permanent residence after living in Japan for five years, rather than the typical ten years of residence required for the standard permanent residence application.

Some Japanese companies have been eager to hire more white-collar foreign workers. Globally oriented firms like Uniqlo, Rakuten, Panasonic, and Sony have targeted foreign students graduating from Japanese universities, in the hope of promoting them to managerial positions – part of a strategy to expand market share in China and elsewhere. Lawson, the second-largest convenience store chain in Japan, has been hiring foreign students since 2008, and about 30 percent of its new hires are foreigners.[93] According to a survey conducted by *Sankei Shimbun*, the majority of Japanese companies listed on the Tokyo Stock Exchange expressed strong interest in hiring foreigners.[94]

But foreign graduates of Japanese universities do not necessarily find Japanese companies that attractive. Firms usually expect foreign workers to act like Japanese and to share Japanese corporate values, such as respect for supervisors, the importance of being a team player, and endurance and perseverance – traits that foreign workers may not understand. In one not untypical incident, a Chinese worker at a Japanese company was scolded by his supervisor for missing an end-of-year department party to go instead on a ski trip with friends. Like most people outside Japan, he didn't understand why missing one company party was such a big deal; he had not yet come to understand Japan's team-building ethos.[95]

Meanwhile, new recruits receive small wages that correspond to their age, not the quality of their work. This can frustrate white-collar workers, who may find better starting salaries in other countries. The average compensation per skilled worker in Japan is 35 percent lower than in the United States and 15 percent less than in the Euro zone.[96] Finally, as with the Japanese, new foreign employees may be assigned to positions where they cannot utilize their professional skills immediately. Considering the number of foreign students studying in Japan (138,000 as of 2011),[97] the number who take on full-time employment there is relatively small – about 8,000 a year.[98]

Maximizing the value of highly skilled immigrants depends not only on policies that permit them to come and work, but also on a culture of openness and innovation that draws and maximizes talent. Some 40 percent of US Fortune 500 companies were started by immigrants or their children, including Google, Intel, AT&T, eBay, and Yahoo.[99] No other country in the world matches the US in this regard, but Japan is further behind than most.

Toward an Immigrant Country?

Immigration remains extremely unpopular in Japan, despite the economic needs of an aging society. The two bureaucratic agencies in charge of foreign workers – the Ministry of Justice, which controls the border, and the Ministry of Health, Labor, and Welfare, which sides with labor unions and opposes foreign workers – are extremely cautious about immigration. And various domestic interest groups oppose immigration outright. Most outspoken are the labor unions and occupational organizations such as the Japanese Nursing Association, which vehemently opposes the hiring of nurses from Southeast Asia. These domestic interests are afraid that immigrants will increase competition for jobs and depress the wages of Japanese workers.

The public also shares this anti-immigration sentiment. An *Asahi Shimbun* newspaper poll in 2012 asked Japanese about accepting immigrants to 'maintain economic vitality': 26 percent favored the idea, while 65 percent opposed it. Opinion polls consistently support the view that foreigners take away jobs, burden Japanese by diverting public financing, and make the country dangerous.

The Japanese are also afraid of cultural friction with foreigners. A common complaint about foreigners is that they do not follow community garbage rules. These rules are complex, and there can be as many as four or five bins for different types of recycling; but the rules are usually written in Japanese. Many foreign workers, especially low-skilled immigrants, cannot read them. Another common complaint is the noise made by foreigners who don't know about community rules.[100]

Many talented individuals in Japan are the descendants of immigrants brought to Japan (unwillingly) from the Korean Peninsula during Japan's colonial period. These include Masayoshi Son, head of the huge technology company Softbank, and Shin Kyuk-ho, president of the Lotte Group (one of the largest food and shopping groups in South Korea and Japan), as well as numerous scholars, novelists, professional soccer players, and entertainers. Yet Japanese public discourse on immigration focuses largely on the costs. There is not even consensus for bringing foreign professionals into Japan, much less unskilled workers.

Without any plans on the table to significantly increase the number of immigrants, the government is turning to other options to boost workforce participation. Family financial pressure means that the percentage of women who work is gradually ticking up, though there are far fewer career opportunities than in most developed countries. To encourage people to stay in the workforce for longer, the government decided in 2000 to gradually raise the age of eligibility for corporate pensions – from 60 to 65 by 2025.[101] As part of this initiative, companies will be required either to raise their own retirement age to 65 or to abolish mandatory retirement.

Finally, Japan is seeking to ease the economic burden of its demographics by increasing its low rates of productivity – for example, by using deregulation and tax breaks to encourage innovation. Boosting productivity in Japan will require more widespread use of information and communication technology (which, in spite of Japan's high-tech image, is among the lowest of any developed country).[102] The greater recruitment of foreign professional labor would also likely be helpful in this regard. Foreign specialists have had a big impact on technological development, education, and training in Japan, and foreign companies in the country have the highest productivity levels and job-creation rates (they doubled their hiring between 1996 and 2006). The American Chamber of Commerce in Japan – admittedly not a disinterested party – recommends 'inward globalization' for Japan to promote innovation-driven growth.

Conclusion

Japan, already the grayest nation on earth, faces a demographic time bomb unlike any other in human history. Many aspects of Japanese *wa*, and especially the desire to wall off outsiders, contribute to this. By refusing to take in immigrants, Japan has limited its exposure to many of the social challenges faced in the US and Europe, such as ethnic conflict, crime, and the burden of educating newcomers. The cost of anti-immigrant policies, though steep, has until now been manageable. However, with its population now shrinking, while its proportion of elderly continues to grow, the country may soon hit a tipping point. Unless Japan miraculously improves its lot through every other means – such as dramatically raising the birth rate, incorporating many more women and older workers into the labor force, and radically raising productivity – it may face the choice either of taking in more immigrants, or of social and economic collapse.

CHAPTER FOUR

Getting Along with the Neighbors

As an island nation with a high level of racial and ethnic homogeneity and thousands of miles of coastline to defend, Japan has always had an uncomfortable relationship with outsiders – sometimes completely closing its borders to others; at other times opening them wide with the goal of promoting the country's nationalist development and imperialist ambitions. It is hard to know whether this history is a cause of *wa* or a consequence of it; most likely cause and effect are intertwined. Japan remains a place where inside/outside distinctions are sharply drawn – whether between the in-grouped and the ostracized in a classroom, between citizens and foreign residents in Japan, or between Japanese and people in other countries. Conflict with those on the outside protects harmony among those on the inside.

Japan's current relations with its neighbors have their roots in the period from the late nineteenth century through the Second World War, when Japan brutally occupied and went to war against countries throughout the region. Following the war there was, not surprisingly, deep-seated hatred of the country throughout the region, especially in Korea and China. At the same time, Japan had experienced humiliation and defeat, its cities destroyed and its population forced into poverty. Throughout the region, there was a strong sentiment of 'never again.'

In Japan, that attitude took two very different expressions, both of them consistent in their own ways with aspects of *wa*. On the one side were the pacifists, who swore that never again would Japan be the aggressor in a war, so that it could live in harmony with itself and its neighbors. On the other side were the nationalists, who swore that never again would Japan be weak enough to be defeated, and who were dedicated to proclaiming righteousness and rebuilding the military.[1] The former universalist *wa* was at odds with the latter warrior *wa*.

As an occupied and weak country, Japan had no say over its foreign policy in the years immediately following the war. Though the occupation of Japan formally ended in 1951, the US had made sure that the new Japanese constitution included Article 9, which forbade Japan from maintaining 'land, sea, and air forces,' insisting that it 'forever renounce war as a sovereign right of the nation and the threat or use of force as a means of settling international disputes.'

For the next few decades, Japan pursued a centrist path between pacifism and nationalism. Though (through Article 9) it had officially renounced the right to build its own military, it nevertheless developed self-defense forces with limited capabilities and formed a strategic alliance with the US to come under its military and nuclear umbrella.

Japan devoted its efforts to building itself up economically; and once it started to do so, it engaged in international mercantilism, wielding its influence through trade, investment, and eventually foreign aid. During these decades, much of the region was also mired in poverty and domestic political struggle.

By the end of the 1980s, the situation had changed dramatically. Japan was now the second wealthiest country in the world and was closing in on the United States in terms of economic strength. South Korea had also gone through a miraculous period of growth, multiplying its GDP more than fifty-fold from 1962 to 1989, and emerging from dictatorship in the 1980s. China had survived the turmoil of the Maoist era and was starting its own period of rapid development. All these countries were more prepared to assert their interests internationally.

In the following decade, further changes occurred. The bursting of the bubble shook up Japan, weakening the dominant Liberal Democratic Party, which had ruled for several decades, and making room for alternative economic and political views. Meanwhile, the fall of the Soviet Union shook up international military and diplomatic affairs, with a somewhat stable bipolar era being replaced by a more unpredictable multipolar one.

Memories of war

Unlike Germany, which went through a lengthy period of self-reflection after the war, effectively leaving nationalist groups marginalized, Japan had simply set the issue aside while it focused on economic development. With the changing political and economic climate of the 1980s and 1990s, unresolved conflicts over the nature of the Second World War and Japan's international identity started to emerge. Moderate and left-leaning Japanese lawmakers increasingly spoke out to condemn the country's brutality during the war, and high-ranking legislators apologized to East Asian countries for Japan's wartime actions. The most significant apology came from Prime Minister Tomiichi Murayama, who, in 1995, issued a statement to mark the fiftieth anniversary of Japan's surrender to the Allied forces. The Murayama Statement says:

> Through its colonial rule and aggression, [Japan] caused tremendous damage and suffering to the people of many countries, particularly to those of Asian nations. In the hope that no such mistake be made in the future, I . . . express here once again my feelings of deep remorse and state my heartfelt apology.[2]

In contrast, historical revisionists argued that Japan had legitimate rights and interests in Asia during the Second World War, just like the Western powers. To these revisionists, Japan's security had been threatened by political chaos and the anti-Japanese boycott movements in China, the spread of communism there, US and European protectionist trade policies based on exclusive economic blocs, and American economic sanctions against Japan. The revisionists argued that Japan's colonies (i.e. Korea and Formosa or Taiwan) and neo-colonial region (i.e. Manchuria) had existed along with the colonial domains of European countries and the United States: China itself had been subject to European, American, and Japanese rights and interests. Arguing that Japan's actions in Asia had been nothing unique, the revisionists would ask: 'How could the Allied Powers say that Japan was the only aggressor on the Asian continent?'[3]

Struggles on these issues had been simmering for decades, for example in controversies over textbooks. In the mid-1960s, a University of Tokyo professor, Saburo Ienaga, brought a lawsuit against the Japanese Ministry of Education after it rejected his textbook manuscript, which had referred to the Japanese army's 'aggression' in China rather than using the ministry's recommended term of 'advance' into China. The ministry argued that the word 'aggression' was too negative for use in education and reflected Ienaga's personal opinion, rather than objectively depicting the war. Defiant, the professor refused to adopt the 'advance' phrase and over the years brought two more lawsuits against the ministry on other war-related terminology in his history textbook manuscripts. He claimed that the screening process infringed his right to freedom of expression. The Japanese Supreme Court eventually rejected his claim about the unconstitutionality of textbook screening, but it did accept many of his claims of illegal censorship of history textbooks. The textbook issue remained largely an internal matter until the 1980s, at which point both the governments of, and popular movements in, China and Korea started to protest over Japan's textbook policies. A particularly serious dispute broke out in 2005, when the Education Ministry approved a controversial history textbook for junior high schools. Called *Atarashii Rekishi Kyokasho* (*New History Textbook*), the book was written by right-wing Japanese scholars and downplayed atrocities committed by the Japanese Imperial Army, such as the Nanjing Massacre of 1937, the so-called 'comfort women,' and Unit 731's chemical and biological warfare experiments on live humans. By approving the textbook for junior high schools, the ministry let local governments decide on its adoption. In the event, the book was anyway adopted by less than 1 percent of all junior high schools in Japan. But it inflamed anti-Japanese protests throughout China.

Heated conflicts have also arisen over the Yasukuni Shrine. Located just outside Tokyo, it is dedicated to the 2.5 million people – including soldiers, relief workers, and even the mothers of soldiers – who died in imperial Japan's wars from 1869 to 1945. There are no actual bodies buried at Yasukuni, as it enshrines the spirits of the dead, rather than their physical remains. The Yasukuni controversy stems from events in 1978, when 14 Class A war criminals were enshrined there. They had either been hanged or had died in prison after being convicted at the International Military Tribunal for the Far East (1946–48) of crimes against peace – that is, having started a war of aggression. Even wartime Emperor Hirohito, who died in 1989, reportedly stopped visiting the shrine because he disagreed with the enshrinement of these war criminals.

After former Prime Minister Nakasone caused a rift with China in 1985 by making an official visit to Yasukuni on the anniversary of Japan's surrender, most Japanese government leaders stopped going there. However, another former prime minister, Junichiro Koizumi, stirred the pot again by visiting the shrine five times, stoking anti-Japan riots in China that raged for weeks after his 2005 visit. Since Koizumi, prime ministers have avoided Yasukuni while in office. However, other ministers and lawmakers have continued to visit, and China and South Korea have continued to protest.

'Comfort Women'

Another war wound that has been reopened in recent decades is over the 'comfort women.' Comfort women were Asian women forced to serve as sexual slaves for Japan's Imperial Army soldiers in brothels in the 1930s and 1940s. Historians estimate that as many as 200,000 women, mostly Koreans and Chinese, were forced into prostitution.[4]

As with many aspects of their Second World War behavior, Japanese officials were slow to come to terms with the evil of this tragic episode. In 1996, the education minister claimed that the comfort women were working for profit, and the following year the chief cabinet secretary claimed that Korean comfort women were just prostitutes. Finally, in 2003, then Chief Cabinet Secretary Yohei Kono issued an official statement of apology on behalf of the Japanese government. This fully acknowledged the involvement of the Japanese military in the establishment and management of brothels and in the transfer of comfort women during the Second World War, and admitted government involvement in recruiting the women.

The Kono Statement has angered Japanese revisionists, who deny any coercion of the women by Japan. Some revisionists have acknowledged that private brokers were involved in human trafficking for sexual slavery, but they refuse to accept Japan's official responsibility for forcing them into brothels. One right-wing politician, Osaka mayor and former governor, Toru Hashimoto, not only denied Japanese government responsibility, but went so far as to justify the actions, claiming: 'Anyone would understand the "comfort women" system was necessary for soldiers who were risking their lives when bullets were flying around like rain and wind . . . and they deserved some rest.'[5]

As a further sign of the rise of nationalism, Hashimoto joined with another prominent right-wing politician, former Tokyo governor Shintaro Ishihara, to form a new nationalist Japan Restoration Party in September 2012. It won 54 out of the 480 House of Representative seats in the September 2012 election, making it the country's third largest party.

Enter Abe

It was in this general context of a rise of nationalism that Prime Minister Shinzo Abe, generally considered the most hawkish Japanese prime minister since the Second World War, was elected – first in 2006 (from when he served until 2007), and then again in 2012. Abe is considered to be a 'normalist' – that is, a politician who argues that Japan should have the right to a normal defense and military role, thus overturning the limitations of Article 9 of the constitution. That in itself is not alarming – 'normalism' is a mainstream view in Japan, and is also supported by the United States, which would like the country to take on more responsibility in collective self-defense. However, Abe is considered to be a nationalist-leaning normalist, whose views on Japan's past overlap with those of historical revisionists.

For example, Abe visited the Yasukuni Shrine as prime minister in December 2013 to mark the one-year anniversary of his second premiership. After the visit, he spoke of his 'remorse' at not having visited Yasukuni during his first term as prime minister. He had earlier argued that 'It's only natural to honor the spirits of those who gave their lives for the country. Our ministers [who visit the shrine] will not cave in to any threats.'⁶ Similarly, when a group of conservative lawmakers in the Liberal Democratic Party voiced their support for revision of the Kono Statement of apology for Japan's treatment of the comfort women, Abe made international headlines during his first term as prime minister by joining them in denying that there had been any government coercion, implying somehow that these had been private brothels – or even that the women themselves were responsible.

Abe has gone beyond the topics of the Yasukuni Shrine and the comfort women to more explicitly raise questions about whether

Japan can be viewed as an aggressor in the Second World War. As he stated in April 2013: 'The definition of what constitutes aggression has yet to be established in academia or in the international community. Things that happened between nations will look differently depending on which side you view them from.'[7]

This is a typical statement from a Japanese historical revisionist. Abe was hinting that Japan's '15-Year War' (from 1930 to 1945) might look like a war of aggression from one perspective, but it could also be argued that it was a war of self-defense. Several days after his comment, his revisionist colleague Sanae Takaichi, policy chief of the ruling Liberal Democratic Party, stated bluntly: 'It was understood at that time . . . that our nation had to fight resolutely in self-defense for its own survival.' Takaichi, who made it clear that her political ideology was close to Abe's, also criticized the Murayama Statement's use of the word 'aggression.'[8] Abe himself once suggested that he was considering replacing the Murayama Statement with a more 'future-looking' 'Abe Statement,' to refine Japan's position. He has not done so, perhaps on account of mounting international pressure, particularly from the United States.

Many in the West wonder how Abe can be both an economic reformer who promotes globalization, and a nationalist who downplays Japan's war crimes. But when one understands something of Japanese history, it is not so strange. Abe's roots lie in Yamaguchi Prefecture, home of the Meiji Restoration (when the area was known as Choshu), where the very idea of Japan's national interest was born. As one journalist explains:

Much of [Abe's] political inspiration can be traced back to the mix of deep conservatism and reformist zeal of the 1860s when Yamaguchi joined three other rebellious fiefdoms to launch the Meiji Restoration that set Japan on the path to modernization . . . In Meiji times that meant learning the technological and organisational skills of the west in order to repel western colonialism.[9]

Later, Abe's grandfather, Nobusuke Kishi, served in the wartime cabinet, for which he was branded a Class A war criminal, but then went on after the war to become prime minister. Shinzo Abe has long resented what he considers to be 'victor's justice' that vilifies people like his grandfather, since in his eyes Japan was just doing in the 1930s and 1940s what the Western colonial powers were doing in much of the rest of the world.[10] By defending Japan's actions in the Second World War, Abe wants to restore the country's pride, and once again to make it a force in the world. Both nationalism and economic development are viewed as serving that purpose.

Sometimes these strains run at cross-purposes, though, as statements insulting to Japan's neighbors harm efforts at economic co-operation. In this context, as one expert put it: 'Mr. Abe has an internal struggle between his head – the pragmatic realist – and his heart. As long as his head is in control, he's OK. But if he says what he really thinks, then he gets in real trouble.'[11]

The 'internal abroad'

After the break-up of the Soviet Union, Russian leaders often spoke of the 'near abroad', former Soviet republics that border Russia and over which Russia seeks to exercise its influence. By contrast, Japan has what might be called an 'internal abroad', large groups of people who have lived in Japan for generations but are still considered outsiders. These include the *burakumin* (literally 'hamlet people'), a Japanese outcast group that has endured severe social discrimination for centuries. The group, which originated in feudal Japan in approximately the twelfth century, was placed at the very bottom of the Japanese caste system until the mid-nineteenth century. The *burakumin* lived in segregated villages and took on what were considered filthy or impure occupations dealing with death, such as slaughtering animals, tanning leather, and burying human bodies. These people were supposedly emancipated by the Meiji government in the 1870s and officially given legal status equal to other Japanese. However, social and economic discrimination against them has continued to this day.

Koreans are the other main group in the 'internal abroad.' They present a fascinating example of Japan's relationships with its neighbors, since Japanese–Korean relations entail domestic dynamics within Japan, a remarkable transnational entertainment industry and fan community, and disputes with one nation that should be an ally but is more of a rival (South Korea) and with another that is a dangerous enemy (North Korea).

Let us start with the case of Jong Te-se, an acclaimed professional soccer player. Like his parents, Jong was born in Japan, but has never received Japanese citizenship. Though a South Korean citizen, Jong developed a strong affinity with North Korea during his youth, when, like many *zainichi* (Japan-residing Koreans), he attended schools in Japan under North Korean influence (an odd phenomenon we discuss below).[12] Jong started playing soccer at elementary school, and he went on to play in (and help win) tournaments against other pro-North Korea schools in Japan. He eventually debuted in the J-League, Japan's professional soccer league, and became one of the best strikers in the country.

While still playing in the J-League, Jong obtained a North Korean passport, so that he could play for North Korea's national team while maintaining his South Korean nationality. South Korea refused his request to relinquish his South Korean citizenship, since Seoul does not recognize North Korea as a legitimate state. At the 2010 World Cup in South Africa, Jong became the poster boy for North Korea on account of his emotional response to the country's national anthem, played before a North Korea–Brazil match: the sight of his tears drew world attention. Why did a South Korean man, who had grown up in affluent and democratic Japan, choose to become a citizen of the impoverished totalitarian North – and why did he develop such strong feelings of loyalty to a country where he had never lived?

Jong's story and those of his teammates – he was one of four *zainichi* Koreans who, though born and raised in Japan, chose to play for the North Korean team in the 2010 World Cup – shed a very interesting light on the inside/outside distinction that is so crucial to Japanese *wa* and that shapes Japan's relationships with other countries and their citizens.

Japan's relationship with Korea and the Koreans represents a fascinating example of these relations. South Korea should be Japan's closest ally in East Asia. The two nations are near neighbors, only 50 miles apart at their closest point, and they share certain similarities in their languages. They are both democracies, and both among the most advanced industrial countries. They also share many cultural similarities: strongly influenced by Confucianism and Buddhism, both nations have value systems that emphasize filial piety. In fact, many cultural forms and practices in Japan were brought to Japan from China via Korea. Japan and South Korea are also US allies and face common perceived security threats, such as a nuclear North Korea and the rise of China.

At the same time, Koreans make up the second largest ethnic group in Japan itself. There are more than half a million *zainichi* who have grown up in Japan but are not Japanese citizens; about 300,000 naturalized Japanese of Korean ancestry; and 100,000 more long-term visitors to Japan from Korea who are working and studying.

In spite of all this – and despite the immense popularity of South Korean music and television in Japan – relationships between Japanese and Koreans are strained. Internationally, conflicts continue to arise between Japan and South Korea over historical issues and territorial disputes. Inside Japan, a large number of ethnic Koreans not only resist adopting Japanese citizenship, but also continue to align themselves with the tyrannical North Korean regime, Japan's number-one enemy and a country that has abducted Japan's citizens from several countries around the world and now threatens it with nuclear annihilation.

Though it has ancient roots, Japan's complex relationship with Korea springs largely from the late nineteenth century, when Tokyo began to assert control over its neighbor, sending 6,000 troops there in 1894. This culminated in the formal annexation of the country in 1910 and colonial administration of Korea by Japan until the end of the Second World War. During this time, nearly 2 million Koreans arrived in Japan. Some sought employment and educational opportunities; others were brought as forced labor to work in factories and mines during the war. Though more than half returned to Korea after the war, many hundreds of thousands remained in ethnic enclaves in Japan.

During Japan's colonial era, Koreans, most of whom were farmers from southern provinces, were exploited and paid much lower wages than their Japanese counterparts. The authorities gave them Japanese citizenship and attempted to integrate them into Japanese society through education. They were forced to use Japanese names, and inter-marriage was encouraged. Over 200,000 Koreans fought in the Japanese Imperial Army as Japanese nationals during the Second World War, and some 30,000 Koreans were killed by the atomic bomb over Hiroshima.[13]

After the war, Koreans lost their Japanese nationality, and an esti-mated 1–1.4 million of them left Japan for their homeland. Some remained in Japan for various reasons: certain privileged Koreans – those who had successful business careers in Japan – decided to stay rather than return to an impoverished homeland; others could not afford to return. During the Cold War, Korean society in Japan split into pro-North and pro-South camps. Ideologically separate, they were united in their resentment toward Japan for its continued viola-tion of the human rights of both communities of Koreans, and for its discrimination against them.

Chongryon schools

The pro-North supporters, estimated to include anywhere from 10 percent to 25 percent of *zainichi* Koreans today, are members of a pro-North organization called Chongryon or the General Association of North Korean Residents in Japan. Today Chongryon runs about 60 of the Korean schools in Japan, in contrast to the four schools run by Mindan, a pro-South organization run by the Korean Residents Union in Japan. These pro-North Chongryon schools, which range from kindergartens to high schools and a university, enroll roughly 20 percent of all Korean students in Japan.

Sonia Ryang, a professor of anthropology at the University of Iowa and a graduate of Chongryon schools herself, reports that many Chongryon students are loyal to North Korea and consider it their homeland.[14] She says it is normal for teachers and students at such schools to romanticize North Korea, for example, calling the country the 'fatherland.' For soccer player Jong Te-se, it was his mother, a former teacher at a Chongryon elementary school, who encouraged her son to get a North Korean education in order to develop ethnic pride and to learn about Korean culture and history, even though her South Korean husband wanted his son to attend a Japanese school.[15]

The Chongryon schools provide all lessons in Korean and emphasize allegiance to the North Korean regime. They even organize school trips to North Korea. Until recently, all Chongryon schools had portraits on their classroom walls of North Korea's former leader, Kim Jong-il, and his father, Kim Il-sung, the country's founding father. Chongryon schools teach students the importance of unification of the Korean Peninsula, which indirectly means the establishment of a Korean state led by the North. Many Korean students, even those with South Korean or Japanese citizenship, attend Chongryon schools primarily for an ethnic education. Some of those inevitably develop a strong sense of loyalty to North Korea and feelings of patriotism through their education.

In many ways, Chongryon schools meet the needs of ethnic Koreans in Japan, where people tend to emphasize the importance of homogeneity. Most Koreans in Japan use an alias to pass as Japanese, for fear of discrimination, harassment, or hassle. At Chongryon schools, however, students can be themselves. They don't have to worry about being singled out as a Korean, or bullied by Japanese peers. The loyalty of some Chongryon students toward North Korea should be understood in this context. Soccer player Jong Te-se's mother sees her son's tears at the 2010 World Cup as a symbol of the bitterness and pain felt by the '*zainichi* brethren.' She says she herself cried when she saw her son's tears on the stadium's large screen. She felt he had achieved his life-long dream to participate in the World Cup thanks to his determination to succeed in the face of discrimination against him and other ethnic Koreans in Japan.

How have Chongryon schools been able to operate across Japan, creating so many loyalists to North Korea? Given that most *zainichi* Korean families came from the southern regions of the Korean Peninsula – today's South Korea – *zainichi* support for Pyongyang may appear puzzling.

The North Korean lobby

Chongryon, established in 1955, is a *de facto* North Korean lobby in Japan. It incorporates organizations such as the Women's Alliance and the Youth Alliance. Japan has no diplomatic relations with North Korea, but Chongryon serves as North Korea's unofficial embassy in Japan, issuing North Korean passports to *zainichi* Koreans and managing government affairs. The top staff members of Chongryon have very close working relationships with top officials in the North Korean government, and some Chongryon leaders serve as members of Pyongyang's national assembly. Chongryon's secretive elite group, the *gakushu-gumi* (study group), is under the direct control of North Korea's Workers' Party.[16] Chongryon's news agency, the Korean News Agency, has direct links to North Korea's Korean Central News Agency.[17]

The members of Chongryon consist primarily of *zainichi* Koreans who have their nationality registered as Joseon (or Chōsen in

Japanese, meaning Korea), as opposed to those who have taken up either Japanese or South Korean nationality. The Joseon status was a legal category given to all Korean residents in Japan immediately after the Second World War, replacing the Japanese nationality they had possessed during the colonial period (1910–45). Over time, some *zainichi* have taken Japanese or South Korean nationality, but others have remained as Joseon and have supported Chongryon. Since 'Korea' does not exist as an official state, those with Joseon status are technically stateless.

From the late 1950s through the early 1970s, Chongryon expanded its schools across Japan through donations by ethnic Korean supporters. Koreans in Japan had been denied the right to an education in their own language during Japan's colonial rule of the Korean Peninsula. Even after the Second World War, Korean schools were forced to close and go underground on account of their affiliation with the League of Koreans, a short-lived communist organization established in 1946 that had close ties to the Japanese Communist Party. The organization was disbanded by the American authorities in 1952, the last year of the US occupation of Japan.

The *zainichi* dreamed of having Korean ethnic schools in Japan, to give their children the opportunity to learn the Korean language and culture and to develop ethnic pride. In the postwar period, many *zainichi* wished eventually to return home. Once Chongryon was established, the *zainichi* made generous donations to the organization, so that their children would be prepared for their return. Soon Chongryon began operating a number of schools with financial support from the North Korean government.

Chongryon performed other functions, too. From the end of the 1950s to the 1960s, it conducted a 'repatriation' program, facilitated by the Japan Red Cross and with the support of the Japanese Communist Party. This program was to send *zainichi* to North Korea, even though (as we saw above) most first-generation *zainichi* had originally come from the southern regions of the Korean Peninsula.

Lured by Chongryon's propaganda that North Korea was a 'heaven on earth,' about 93,000 *zainichi* Koreans joined the program and left for North Korea. Sadly, we now know that most of those who moved to the North have suffered extreme poverty and discrimination. Having come from Japan, a capitalist economy and former colonizer, those repatriated were placed at the bottom of the social hierarchy in the North, and have since come to rely on remittances from their *zainichi* relatives in Japan. Many of them had donated much of what they had to Chongryon before they left Japan, thinking that they would not need much money in North Korea, a 'socialist paradise,' where they expected to receive sufficient government subsidies.[18]

In the early 1960s, Chongryon created financial networks to manage *zainichi* funds. It took control of an association of credit unions that made capital available to its supporters to start businesses such as pachinko gaming parlors, bars, and restaurants. The businesses expanded rapidly during Japan's economic boom years in the 1960s through to the mid-1980s, and their owners made generous donations to Chongryon, which in turn made deposits to the credit unions. In this way, money was circulated among the pro-Chongryon businesses, Chongryon, and the credit unions. At the same time, Chongryon provided funds to the North Korean government.

Until the 1970s, Chongryon was a dominant group in the *zainichi* communities, much better organized politically, socially, and financially than its pro-South rival, Mindan. At its peak, Chongryon's membership was reported to be 500,000 out of the 600,000 *zainichi* Koreans.

But in the 1980s, Chongryon faced financial struggles. Donations to it started to slow, as many of the first-generation *zainichi* Koreans had passed away. In response to demands from North Korea's 'Great Leader' Kim Il-sung for the organization to step up its fundraising for the Pyongyang regime, Chongryon started its own businesses in the mid-1980s, creating 20 pachinko parlors and aggressively selling and buying property. The profits were funneled to North Korea and became a critical lifeline for the North.[19] However, Chongryon's business empire started to crumble in the early 1990s, when Japan's recession began, and in the following decade the Japanese authorities started to crack down on some of Chongryon's irregular financial activities.[20] The authorities started monitoring Chongryon officials in the 2000s, on suspicion of espionage, the abduction of Japanese citizens, and the smuggling of technology and missile parts to Pyongyang.[21] Revelations of Chongryon's illegal activities and the widening economic and political disparity between North and South Korea increasingly made many *zainichi* disillusioned with Chongryon. Many joined its pro-South rival, Mindan. However, the biggest blow to the pro-North *zainichi* was Pyongyang's 2002 admission (see below) that it had abducted more than a dozen Japanese citizens over the decades with the purpose of making them teach Japanese to North Korean spies, so that the spies could disguise themselves as Japanese natives. For years, Chongryon had fiercely denied allegations about North Korea's abduction of Japanese citizens, so Pyongyang's revelation shocked and angered many of its members, who had believed North Korea's official line. Today, Chongryon members represent roughly 10–25 percent of the *zainichi* Korean community, while 65 percent of *zainichi* Koreans are members of Mindan.[22]

The weakening financial and political power of Chongryon places its North Korean schools in a precarious position. More than half of them have closed (there were 161 in 1975; today there are about 60), and school enrollment has dropped from its peak of 46,000 students in the 1970s to fewer than 10,000 in recent years.

In a sign of independence from the North Korean regime, several of the schools have removed the portraits of Kim Il-sung and Kim Jong-il from their classrooms, and have changed their curriculum to place less emphasis on North Korea's political ideology and views of history. Despite these changes, many local governments, including Tokyo's, deny public funding to these schools because they have still not severed their ties with the Chongryon organization and North Korea. Furthermore, the Japanese government does not cover tuition costs for Chongryon high schools, even though it does so for all private high schools in Japan, including foreign schools. The government cites lack of progress on the issue of North Korea's abductions of Japanese citizens.[23] Chongryon officials and its supporters have criticized the Japanese government for unfairly tying innocent Chongryon students to the abduction issue. They allege that the government's refusal to provide tuition waivers for Chongryon high schools is an infringement of minority education entitlements, and they view it as part of the government's intention to eventually force the closure of all Chongryon schools.[24]

It is true that students who attend these schools often bear the brunt of official and public animosity, and are targets of harassment, verbal abuse, and even physical assault by Japanese ultra-nationalists. The situation has become worse since 17 September 2002, when Pyongyang admitted that it had abducted several Japanese citizens. It all started in the 1970s, when three young Japanese couples vanished from coastal cities on the Sea of Japan, while out on dates. The disappearances remained a mystery until 1987, when a North Korean spy was caught in Bahrain after planting a bomb on a South Korean flight, killing 115 people. Fluent in Japanese and with a fake Japanese passport, the spy had pretended to be a Japanese citizen. To Japan's shock, she confessed that she had been taught Japanese by an abductee kidnapped from Japan and taken to North Korea. Eventually North Korea admitted having abducted 13 Japanese people. It allowed five of them to return, but claimed that the others had died of illness or accidents. The Japanese government suspects that at least 17 of its citizens were abducted by North Korea – not just from Japan, but also from other countries around the world – and that several of them are still alive. Support groups believe the number abducted to be even higher. The abduction scandal enraged the Japanese people and escalated hostility towards the Chongryon movement and its schools. Since the scandal came to light, many Chongryon students have stopped wearing ethnic uniforms to school and will often commute there in groups for safety.

Polls suggest that the *zainichi* are steadily turning away from Chongryon, and many Korean youth are assimilating into Japanese society. Students at the Chongryon schools will often speak Japanese at home and with friends, once they leave school for the day. Approximately 80 percent of *zainichi* Koreans marry a Japanese partner, and an increasing number of them are taking Japanese nationality. Jong Te-se, the North Korean soccer player, is often compared with Tadanari Lee, another *zainichi* soccer player born a South Korean. Lee obtained Japanese citizenship, the first *zainichi* professional soccer player to be naturalized, and competed for Japan at the 2008 Summer Olympics.

Ethnic Koreans are thus gradually being integrated into Japanese society. At the same time, most *zainichi* can achieve this only by giving up their language and identity. Outsiders are accommodated in the 'inside group' by essentially becoming insiders, rather than by negotiating an expansion of what it means to be Japanese.

Though Koreans in Japan are increasingly assimilating, they still excite the hatred of Japanese ultra-nationalists, who regularly hold noisy protests in Tokyo's 'Korea Town' neighborhood of Shin-Okubo. The nationalists are inspired not only by the abduction scandal and North Korean nuclear threats (see below), but also by simple hatred of 'the other.' Among the objects of their protest, for example, are Japanese women who buy CDs and posters of South Korean celebrities.

While North Korea's abductions of Japanese nationals are a major stumbling block, it is North Korea's increased military power and its nuclearization that pose the real threat to Japan. Pyongyang can easily strike Japan even with conventional means: it has about 320 Rodong missiles, which have a range of 1,300 kilometers, as well as BM-25 Musudan intermediate-range missiles, with a range of 2,500 to 4,000 kilometers. Both the Rodong and the Musudan missiles typically carry a conventional warhead, but fitted with a small nuclear device they could cause catastrophic damage. North Korea has threatened to attack US bases in Japan and has warned that Japan's support for US policies could lead to Tokyo's destruction.[25]

Faced with North Korea's repeated missile tests, Japan has participated in joint research with the United States on its missile defense program, working to develop reconnaissance satellites that can detect North Korean missiles. It has focused on the sea-based Navy Theater-Wide Defense system, one of four systems within the missile defense program. By 2012, Japan had spent $12 billion on a system that includes four Aegis-class destroyers, ground-based Patriot PAC-3 missiles, and advanced radar. Meanwhile a joint Japan–US air defense headquarters has been established to connect the Japanese system to the US missile defense system in the Western Pacific.

Japan's participation in the missile defense program led to the enactment of the country's Basic Space Law in 2008, which allows space to be used for national security purposes. The focus of Japan's space program has thus shifted from commercial to military applications.

Japan may feel protected by the US–Japan security pact, which requires the United States to respond if Japan is attacked, and the Japanese may believe that US nuclear weapons will deter North Korea's attacks. But the United States wants Japan to contribute more to the security alliance, and top leaders in Japan agree that they need to do more to contain North Korea's nuclear ambitions. The constitution forbids offensive military operations, but hawkish lawmakers argue that attacking North Korean launch sites before a strike would be a pre-emptive defensive measure, within the bounds of the constitution.

The changing international security climate – with a nuclear North Korea and a China on the rise – may force Japan to rely more on American troops and to provide more initiatives to strengthen the US–Japan alliance.

K-Wave

If Japan's relationship with North Korea is clear – the country is Japan's dangerous enemy – its attitude to South Korea is more complex. On a national political level, relations are strained by disputes over islands and historical controversies over the Second World War. Yet, at the same time, the Japanese people have embraced South Korean entertainers to the point of national obsession.

Witness Noriko Iida, 52, an obsessive fan of Korean actor Bae Yong-joon, known affectionately as Yon-sama in Japan (*sama* being an extremely respectful honorific). She has seen all of his TV dramas and movies, and has visited South Korea a few times to tour shooting locations. Like many other fans, she used to go to promotional events to see the actor, and like some die-hard fans, she diligently studied Korean to feel closer to him (using a textbook that employed the scripts of her favorite television show, a mega-hit Korean soap drama). Noriko hasn't attended Yon-sama events recently, as the actor hasn't been in a movie or drama for a few years. However, she still likes him and hopes he will return to the screen. She sometimes gets together with other Yon-sama fans she has befriended to talk about his past movies and TV dramas.

At the other end of the age spectrum, Yoshiko Yamada, a 20-year-old college student, is currently passionate about K-Pop (Korean pop music). Her favorite groups include Dong Bang Shin Ki (DBSK, but also known as TVXQ) and Infiniti, and she goes to their fan get-togethers in Japan to meet the stars whenever she can afford to.

Like Noriko and Yoshiko, many Japanese women admire Korean actors and singers. The Korean Wave (K-Wave or *hallyu* in Korean) hit Japan in 2003, with the broadcast of Bae's *Winter Sonata*. This attracted more than 20 percent of prime-time viewers – the first time a Korean drama had captured such a large audience in Japan. When Bae came to Japan in November 2004, the airport was swamped by 3,500 fans rushing to have a glimpse of him. Many waited outside his hotel in Tokyo, causing stampedes, and ten women were injured after throwing themselves at his car.

What is noteworthy is that this 'love affair' has taken place between Japan (former colonizer) and South Korea (the colonized). When the South Korean media first reported on the 'Yon-sama boom' during that first visit to Japan in 2004, many Koreans could not believe it.[26] But Japanese female fans were passionate about Yon-sama, seeing him as sensitive, kind, and romantic. They elevated him to cult status, calling him a prince who had both the 'manly charisma' and 'feminine tenderness' that Japanese men lacked.[27]

The K-Wave started at a time of increasingly friendly cultural exchanges between the two nations, following South Korea's lifting of its ban on Japanese cultural imports (e.g. films and CDs) in 1998 and the two countries' co-hosting of the 2002 World Cup soccer tournament. According to numerous surveys, the Korean Wave further helped Japanese people develop positive images of South Korean culture and people for a number of years after the World Cup.[28] Indeed, Japan's new Korea Town of Shin-Okubo in Tokyo bustles with female fans trying to find their favorite stars' merchandise or experiencing authentic Korean food.

The Wave has been good for the economy, too: fans have gobbled up Korean stars' goods, including scarves, bags, accessories, cell phone straps, calendars, letter sets, photo books, memorabilia, and even Yon-sama *bento* (lunch boxes) from a restaurant that Bae owns in Tokyo. Fans have made pilgrimages to South Korea to deepen their understanding of their favorite stars. After *Winter Sonata*, Bae was called the '$2.3-billion man' for having stimulated that big a rise in economic activity between Japan and South Korea.[29]

The first Korean Wave consisted largely of film and TV shows and attracted mostly middle-aged women. A few years later, a Second Korean Wave – this time a global phenomenon – took the country by storm. It consisted of singers and pop groups such as DBSK. This Second Wave swept up millions of young fans, as Korean music hit the top spots in the Oricon charts, Japan's premier music ranking list, breaking sales records for foreign artists in Japan.

K-Pop reached its peak in 2010, since when it has not expanded its fan base in Japan.[30] Nevertheless, it remains a formidable cultural presence, especially for a country that Japan 'colonized in the first half of the last century and condescended toward in the second half,' as one journalist noted.[31] Could this mean that Japan is ready to reach out more respectfully to its neighbors?

Disputed islands: Japan and South Korea

Unfortunately, Japan's hunger for K-Pop has not overcome the political wrangles bound up with the historical and territorial disputes between it and its neighbor. Relations between the two countries deteriorate whenever questions arise over Japan's colonization of the Korean Peninsula in the first half of the twentieth century. The two nations also dispute ownership of a group of islets called Dokdo (in Korean) or Takeshima (in Japanese).

Akie Abe, the wife of nationalist Prime Minister Shinzo Abe, is a big K-Wave fan. In 2013, she was criticized harshly by the Japanese right wing for a Facebook post praising a popular Korean musical, *Caffeine*. In the view of her critics, she had acted carelessly, disregarding Japan's problems with South Korea over history.[32]

K-Wave stars also occasionally find themselves in the crossfire over sensitive historical or territorial issues between the two countries. For example, some Koreans insist that K-Wave celebrities should vocally support Korea's territorial claims. In 2005, Bae Yong-joon was questioned about his stance on the Dokdo/Takeshima issue during a press conference to promote his newly released movie. He dodged the question at the time, but later felt pressured to voice his view of the territorial dispute on his blog. This included one sentence that was rapidly removed from his statement: 'Dokdo is the territory of the Republic of Korea.' Although the intention of his overall message stressed the importance of bilateral understanding and cooperation with Japan, that short sentence on the islets is what caught the attention of fans in both countries.

Tensions boiled over in the summer of 2012, when Korean popular actor Song Il-gook, together with patriotic singer Kim Jang-hoon, took part in a 220 kilometer relay swim to Dokdo/Takeshima to assert South Korea's territorial sovereignty. Song swam his leg on 15 August, the anniversary of Korea's independence from Japanese colonial occupation. This followed South Korean President Lee Myung-bak's visit to one of the islets on 10 August that year, the first visit by the nation's top leader. Furthermore, President Lee commented a few days later that if Japan's Emperor Akihito were to visit South Korea, he should apologize to Koreans for Japan's wartime atrocities. The president's actions and comments were viewed in both countries as a way of winning domestic support amid financial scandals involving his staff and his brother. Though President Lee caused a furor in Japan, Song's swim added fuel to the fire.

Japan's TV stations reacted swiftly and postponed indefinitely the airing of two Korean dramas, *Man Called God* and *Homicides*, both of which featured Song as the main character. Fuji TV also pulled Korean actress Gu Hye-sun's Taiwanese drama *My Perfect Darling* (the actress had reportedly said in an interview with the Korean media, 'Dokdo is Korean territory'). Perhaps the biggest disappointment to Japanese K-Pop fans was that Korean singers were dropped from the hugely popular New Year's music program on Japan's public station NHK in 2012, on account of what the broadcaster called consideration of Japanese 'public opinion.'[33]

Following Song's relay swim, some Japanese tabloids tapped into the nationalist fervor. *Yukan Fuji* listed eight South Korean entertainer 'offenders' who had publicly made 'anti-Japanese remarks' on the territorial dispute. The worst 'offender' was actor Bae Yong-joon (Yon-sama), with his blog statement that South Korea had sovereignty over the disputed islets. The newspaper's list also included Song and the popular female group Girls' Generation, which in 2008 had performed a song that claimed Dokdo/Takeshima for South Korea. Other tabloids such as *Shukan Shincho*, popular among Japanese men, blamed Japanese middle-aged female K-Wave fans for having financially enriched South Korea and for having contributed to 'harming Japan.'

K-Wave stars are naturally concerned about their Japanese audience's reaction to the their statements on political issues. Although some Korean entertainers do have limited audiences in the US and Europe (and some, like PSY, have soared to international stardom), the K-Wave industry still depends on the Japanese market for 60–70 percent of its overseas yield. It is thus understandably sensitive to Japan's reactions to Korean stars' patriotic remarks.

After Song's relay swim, Korean girl band KARA skillfully dealt with a question about the group's stance on the Dokdo/Takeshima dispute at a press conference in Japan, thus succeeding in maintaining peace with its Japanese fans. But while the band may have dodged a bullet in the Japanese press, it caught the ricochet in South Korea, where internet users chastised the band for not supporting Korea's sovereignty. These netizens recalled a 2010 stumble by one of the group's members when she pronounced the Korean national dish *kimchi* (vegetable pickles) in the Japanese manner – *kimuchi* (with a 'u') – when she was on a Japanese TV show. The controversy was over more than a slip of the tongue: the Japanese *kimuchi* imitation had been outperforming the authentic Korean *kimchi* in Southeast Asian markets, and patriotic Koreans were incensed over the success of the Japanese version. Netizens lashed out at KARA for being unpatriotic back then, and then carried it over into a condemnation of KARA's evasive remarks on the disputed territories.

The Dokdo/Takeshima controversy, which has heated up over the past decade, may be one factor in the slowdown of the K-Wave industry. Surveys of K-Wave fans show some of them abandoning their Korean favorites. But loyal fans manage to separate their favorite pop stars from bilateral political issues.[34]

Disputed islands: Japan and China

Unfortunately for Japan, it faces another – and far more dangerous – island conflict with Asia's most powerful country, China.

China historically had a large impact on Japanese culture, language, and society; but from the sixteenth to the nineteenth centuries, the two countries drifted apart, as China was weakened by foreign invasion and Japan focused on forging its own independence. Japan occupied Taiwan from 1895 to 1945, but without engendering as much hostility as in South Korea. Today, Japan and Taiwan have close relations and little or no animosity.

Japan's relationships with China are different. The Japanese invasion and occupation of much of eastern China from 1937–45 was particularly brutal, and conflicts over wartime issues – such as comfort women, depictions of the war in Japanese textbooks, and visits to the Yasukuni Shrine – are sources of great tension between the countries. At the same time, as China becomes wealthier and stronger, it is starting to flex its muscles in the region, taking more aggressive stances over island disputes that Japan considered already settled.

In 2012, relations between Japan and China hit rock bottom over some islands in the East China Sea, called the Senkaku by the Japanese and the Diaoyu by the Chinese. A dispute flared when Japan nationalized three of the five Senkaku/Diaoyu islands, following a bid by right-wing Tokyo Governor Shintaro Ishihara to purchase them from their private Japanese owners. Prompted by Ishihara's announcement that he wished to build a port on one of the islands, the national government, under the leadership of the Democratic Party of Japan, bought the islands, in the hope that that would calm Japanese nationalist fervor.

But its hopes for that were dashed, and at the same time it failed to anticipate China's response. Anti-Japan protests flared in nearly a hundred cities across China, some of them turning into violent riots. The Japanese media repeatedly broadcast images of young Chinese destroying Japanese restaurants, retail store Aeon, a Toyota dealer in Qingdao, and Panasonic factories in Qingdao and Suzhou. The protests peaked on 18 September, the national anniversary of the 1931 Mukden Incident, which marked the beginning of Japan's invasion of Manchuria.

During and shortly after the demonstrations, many Japanese companies suspended their operations in China. The riots gave Japanese companies conducting or considering expanding their business in China some pause for thought. Business leaders voiced caution about making investments in China, and plans to make inroads into Chinese markets were put on hold. A Reuters poll from September 2012 showed about 41 percent of Japanese firms saw the escalating territorial dispute affecting their business plans in China, and some even considered closing their offices in the country and seeking opportunities elsewhere.[35] Public TV station NHK reported that some Japanese companies, already struggling with China's rising wages, were preparing to exit the Chinese market quickly, and predicted that more companies would follow suit.[36]

The demonstrations eventually died down, and trade and investment resumed. However, a new conflict arose in 2013, when China declared a 'maritime air defense zone' over the islands. It demanded that any aircraft flying over the zone should identify itself to the Beijing authorities, and it threatened unspecified defensive measures against any that did not comply. This was seen by both Japan and the United States as a dangerous escalation of the island dispute. It remains unclear how it will be resolved. The ongoing conflicts over the islands show that Japan's difficult relations with China stem not only from historical interpretations of the Pacific War, but also from twenty-first-century competition for offshore territory, sea lanes, and natural resources.

In an attempt to assert its territorial claim and to shape Japanese children's views, the Japanese government has revised the national teaching manuals, which provide guidelines for teachers. The new manuals make it clear that secondary students should be taught that the disputed islands are an integral part of Japan's territory.[37]

The changing power structure in East Asia, and especially China's rapid rise and North Korea's nuclear threat, emphasize the importance of national security in Japan. That raises two questions: how can Japan maintain and strengthen its security reliance on the United States, and to what extent does the country need to develop its own military capacity and alliances?

Despite its dependence on the US to cope with China, Japan has done much to carve out a role for itself in East Asia. Under DPJ leadership, the country initially attempted to gain some autonomy from the United States by suggesting in 2009 the creation of an East Asian Community. But this idea proved short lived, because its initiator, Prime Minister Yukio Hatoyama, stepped down the following year.

Tokyo's policy in East Asia has altered significantly over the past couple of decades in response to a changing international environment, and particularly rising Chinese military power. Mostly this has involved important, small or medium-scale incremental change within the existing constitutional framework: more than 60 major national defense measures have been put in place since 1991,[38] such as the introduction or revision of 41 laws and the signing of 12 treaties and joint statements. Most of the changes reflect Japan's desire to play a more active role in international security, by undertaking greater responsibility in the US–Japan security alliance.

The US–Japan security alliance

After the Second World War, as we have noted, Japan's postwar constitution forbade it from using force as a means to settle international conflict. Since then, apart from its own limited self-defense forces, Japan's security has been ensured by the US military – a formal US–Japan security alliance was created on the very day that Japan regained its sovereignty in 1952. The US security umbrella served

Japan well for decades, as the country could devote its resources to economic and social improvement. Japan depended on American protection, particularly its nuclear umbrella, without having to develop its own full-fledged military. It in turn served the US, which had a major ally in the region and a location for its military bases.

But in recent decades the alliance has faced some strains. On the one hand, the US has demanded that Tokyo shoulder more of the burden of collective security. Much to America's irritation, Japan cannot provide military assistance to its allies, even if an ally is under attack. On the other hand, the large and continuing US military presence in the country has been an ongoing source of conflict, especially in Okinawa, where the large majority of US bases and military personnel are to be found.

Okinawa

Okinawa is the poorest prefecture in Japan and is heavily burdened by US bases. With only 0.6 percent of Japan's land area, it hosts approximately 75 percent of the US forces' facilities in Japan. These facilities take up nearly 20 percent of the island of Okinawa, the main island in the prefecture. The US maintains about 27,000 personnel, including 15,000 marines, and Okinawa is host to the largest US military base in East Asia, the Kadena Air Base.

The history of Okinawa reflects Japan's imperial past and America's Cold War policy. Before its annexation in 1879, this was the independent Ryukyu Kingdom. Toward the end of the Second World War, Japan made Okinawa its southern bastion to slow down the Allies' advances on the main islands of Japan. A quarter of the civilian population was killed in the 1945 Battle of Okinawa – the last and the biggest of the Pacific battles of the war. During it, Okinawans were prohibited from surrendering to the Allied forces and many were coerced by the Japanese military into committing suicide, rather than be taken captive, in order to maintain the country's honor. This tragic battle left lasting scars on many Okinawans, who do not trust the Japanese government and feel that Okinawa has sacrificed too much for the mainland of Japan. A 2007 attempt to rewrite a history textbook by whitewashing the 1945 Battle of Okinawa further infuriated the locals and led to mass protests.

While the 1951 San Francisco Peace Treaty restored Japanese sovereignty, America actually held on to Okinawa. While on the mainland 28 April is a day for commemorating the restoration of Japan's sovereignty, to Okinawans it has traditionally been a 'day of infamy', a day that symbolizes Okinawa's continual hardships under US occupation. In 2013, for the first time the Japanese government hosted a ceremony there to mark the 1952 restoration of sovereignty – something that provoked the ire of Okinawans.

In the late 1940s and into the 1950s, despite farm owners' protests, the Americans forcibly seized land on which to build military facilities. Some landowners called off their protests after receiving assurances that they would continue to own the land and would benefit from significant increases in rent payments from the Japanese government.[39] Others, however, have continued to protest against the US bases.

From the 1950s through to the early 1970s, the US bases in Okinawa were used to fight America's Asian wars, serving as supply depots and airfields for conflicts – first on the Korean Peninsula, and then in Vietnam. The US even stationed nuclear weapons at an army ammunition depot in the northern part of Okinawa Island. Because of their experience of atomic bombs, the Japanese are said to be 'nuclear allergic.' So throughout the 1960s, the US concealed the nuclear weapons in Okinawa. It was only in 1969, when the US and Japan were negotiating for the return of Okinawa, that President Richard Nixon admitted to Prime Minister Eisaku Sato that US bases in Okinawa were housing American nuclear weapons. Nixon and Sato then secretly agreed that, even after Okinawa reverted to Japan, the US could continue to store nuclear weapons at the bases in times of emergency, as determined by the US 'with prior consultation of Japan.'[40]

The US has never consulted Japan about nuclear weapons, which allows Tokyo to maintain plausible denial that American nuclear weapons are being brought into the country – crucial, as Sato had promised that Okinawa would be returned without nuclear weapons (*kaku-naki henkan*), even if it hosted US military bases. He also violated his earlier proclamation of the 'three non-nuclear principles' for Japan (non-production, non-possession, and non-introduction of nuclear weapons), for which he earned his Nobel Peace Prize in 1974. Okinawa reverted to Japan in 1972, on the basis of the secret Nixon–Sato deal.

Another US base in Okinawa, the US Marine Corps Air Station Futenma (the Futenma Base) in Ginowan City, continues to be a thorny issue for the US and Japan. Local residents and politicians in Ginowan City have always complained about the base – established at the end of the Second World War to transport troops, supplies, and ammunition for the planned attack on mainland Japan – because of problems with noise from aircraft and other base operations, accidents associated with US military training and exercises, and violent crimes committed by US service members. In 1996, the US and Japan agreed to relocate the Futenma Base after the rape the previous year of a 12-year-old Okinawan girl by three marines stationed there. The rape enraged Okinawans and led to months of protests against the US bases. After intensive negotiation, the US agreed to move the Futenma Base facilities out of Ginowan City to a new location elsewhere in Okinawa.

The base was to be moved to an offshore location in Nago City's Henoko district, where US Camp Schwab is also located. But Henoko is the site of a coral reef and is home to the dugong, an endangered marine mammal. The original idea was to relocate the base to Henoko within five to seven years of the 1996 agreement. But local opposition has continually stalled the plan. In 2006 the two governments announced another agreement (known as the 'Roadmap for Realignment Implementation') to transfer nearly half of the 18,000 marines in Okinawa and their dependents to Guam, contingent upon the Futenma relocation, but this has been delayed as well.

Residents of Henoko and elsewhere in Okinawa have opposed the Futenma transfer *within the prefecture* (*kennai-iten*). A 1997 referendum conducted by Nago City showed that more than half of voters opposed the plan. This resistance has proved persistent: a poll of Nago residents conducted in 2009, more than a decade later, recorded about 70 percent of Okinawans continuing to oppose the Henoko relocation plan.

The Futenma issue was complicated by Prime Minister Yukio Hatoyama of the Democratic Party of Japan, which came to power in 2009. Hatoyama had made the relocation of the Futenma Base a major election campaign promise. Once his party won and Hatoyama became prime minister, to the delight of Okinawans he called for its relocation 'at least out of Okinawa.' This angered both American officials and members of the Japanese defense establishment, since it contradicted the earlier US–Japanese agreement to relocate within Okinawa. In the face of strong American pressure, the prime minister eventually retracted his proposal, enraging many people in Okinawa.

The Abe government, in power since 2012, regards progress on Futenma as an important step toward strengthening Japan's relations with the US. For the Japanese government, the US military presence on Okinawa has taken on fresh significance now that Japan faces increased tension with China over the disputed Senkaku/Diaoyu Islands in the nearby East China Sea (see above).

In 2013 Abe succeeded in clearing what may be the last legal hurdle to the relocation of the US airbase, by obtaining a landfill permit from Okinawa Governor Hirokazu Nakaima to construct a new runway off the coast of Henoko.[41] Whether this will lead to the new runway and facilities finally being built, or whether there will be further delays is unclear, as community organizations and local politicians continue to mobilize against any relocation within Okinawa.

Some Okinawans earn a living from the US bases by working in US facilities. Others are the US bases' private landlords and can collect rent: unlike the main islands of Japan, where 87 percent of US bases are on national property, about 76 percent of the American bases in Okinawa are located on private land. There are about 3,000 landowners for the Futenma Base alone, and more than 40,000 for all bases and installations in Okinawa.[42] Yet the opponents of US bases outnumber their supporters. Various anti-base movements have emerged in Okinawa over the decades, engaging environmentalists, minority rights activists, women's rights activists, and union workers. These protesters have even formed human chains around the bases to demand the withdrawal of US troops from Okinawa.

Okinawans' resentment of the bases is directed at the Japanese government and the Japanese people, whom they consider to be insensitive to Okinawa's plight. Protests over the bases are in fact protests against central government and the Japanese people outside Okinawa. Japanese administrations have spent billions of yen in an effort to gain Okinawa's support for the continued presence of the US bases; but no amount of money has been able to buy the hearts of many Okinawans. The locals view the mainland Japanese as Nimbies, who only value the US protection of Japan if it is not in their backyard. Two aspects of inside/outside boundaries thus come into conflict. On the one hand, the US presence in Japan helps protect the broader nation from outside attack. On the other, the sizeable presence of US bases and military personnel in Okinawa is a serious irritant to the local population. Not surprisingly, the former issue – protecting the nation from attack – has taken precedence. But the latter issue is not likely to go away.

Collective self-defense

Another irritant in US–Japan relations is Japan's inability – due to the strict interpretation of the constitution – to cooperate fully with the United States in military affairs. The nub of the problem is that Japan cannot engage in collective self-defense: any action using Japanese armed forces to protect another state is banned, but Washington is obliged to defend Japan under the US–Japan Mutual Security Treaty. The Japanese government claims that, while Article 51 of the UN Charter gives Japan the right to defend itself, it cannot defend *other* nations because of Article 9 of the Japanese constitution. In the government's view, Article 9 allows the use of force only for the nation's own self-defense, not to assist other states. In this sense, America is obligated to defend Japan when it gets into trouble, but Japan makes no promises to defend the US.

Former US Deputy Secretary of State Richard Armitage, one of the most respected former US diplomats in Japan, says the self-imposed prohibition on collective self-defense is an impediment to US–Japan cooperation.[43] His view is most famously known through the 'Armitage Report,' a white paper published in 2000 by a study group under his leadership. His new publication, the 2012 'Armitage–Nye Report,' uses stronger language to urge Japan to take action:

> The United States needs a strong Japan no less than Japan needs a strong United States . . . For Japan to remain standing shoulder-to-shoulder with the United States, she will need to move forward with us.[44]

The 2012 report again urges Japan to expand the scope of security responsibilities to include defense of the United States.

Many Japanese leaders, including Prime Minister Abe, favor a lifting of the ban. During Abe's first term as prime minister, an official government panel argued that Japan should exercise the right to collective self-defense in four specific cases: 1) to destroy a ballistic missile flying over Japan – for example, from North Korea to the United States; 2) to defend American military ships engaged in joint operations with Japan's maritime self-defense forces (SDF) on the high seas; 3) to defend allies in UN peacekeeping operations; and 4) to provide logistical support for UN troops using force.[45] These acts are currently prohibited under the strict interpretation of Article 9. But any change toward a more flexible military could heighten tensions with China and South Korea, which worry about Japan's militarization. Given lingering concerns over its imperial past, Japan has yet to convince the skeptics that exercising the right to collective self-defense would help the country contribute more proactively to international stability.

Japan has made important, though limited, changes to its security policy since the 1990s. Perhaps the most significant has allowed the Japanese government to send the SDF abroad to support US troops in combat operations. Assisted by Foreign Ministry officials, the Japanese government has taken a series of steps to establish precedents for this power. First, in 1995, the government fought to expand the 1976 National Defense Program Outline (NDPO) to allow the SDF to support US troops in 'situations in the surrounding areas' of Japan. Prior to the NDPO, the Japanese government had only deployed the SDF overseas for mine-sweeping operations (from 1991) and UN peacekeeping operations (starting in 1992). The 1996 US–Japan Joint Declaration on Security, signed by Bill Clinton and Japanese Prime Minister Hashimoto Ryutaro, incorporated the 'surrounding areas' concept. In 1999, the government adopted new US–Japan Defense Guidelines, which stipulate Japan's role in providing rear-area support to US forces in operations in 'surrounding areas.'[46]

When the 'War on Terror' began after the September 11th, 2001 attacks on the US, the government extended the notion of rear-area logistical support to locations beyond the 'surrounding areas' of Japan. The 2001 passage of the Anti-Terrorism Special Measures Law allowed the SDF to deploy to the Indian Ocean to provide logistical support to US-led operations in Afghanistan. Japan then adopted the Iraq Special Measures Law in 2003 to deploy the SDF to Iraq for reconstruction work. The government made these changes despite public opposition. For example, only 19 percent of respondents in a 2003 public opinion poll approved of the SDF dispatch to Iraq, while 38 percent disapproved.[47] With these laws as precedents, the SDF can take part in most non-combatant overseas activities under one law or another.[48]

To the United States, these are positive changes, but are still a long way from the kind of flexibility that military strategists would like to see. Japan's security policy remains severely circumscribed by Article 9 of the constitution. Prime Minister Abe and other pro-US lawmakers want to revise the constitution to allow for a more proactive security policy. They are starting by addressing the process of amending the constitution, and have attempted to lower the procedural hurdle to revise Article 9 – from a two-thirds majority in both chambers of parliament to a simple majority vote in each.

While the United States would like Japan to revise Article 9, doing so will be seen as a threat by its Asian neighbors. As international relations expert G. John Ikenberry points out, Japan projects itself in a highly contradictory manner: a militant bully that evinces no remorse for past atrocities, and yet generously contributes money to the international community for the promotion of peace, prosperity, and the protection of human rights.[49] Obviously, it is in Japan's interests to promote the latter image internationally; but the former is constantly brought to the minds of Asians whenever Japanese revisionists shout that Japan did nothing wrong during the war.

As a result, the Japanese projection of power abroad is paradoxical, if not downright schizophrenic: Japan presents itself as a soft diplomatic power that has learned from its imperialistic mistakes, even as it denies those mistakes and strives to remilitarize.

Conclusion

After the Second World War, Japan's military ambitions were crushed and the country channeled its energies into economic development. In foreign policy, as in many other areas, consensus ruled. Japanese foreign policy in the 1950s through to the 1980s – a policy that enjoyed broad support – has been described as 'yen diplomacy'. Within both the political arena and the broader population, there was widespread recognition of the fact that an active military role was neither desirable nor possible; instead Japan could make its influence felt through its growing economic clout.

Political and economic change in Japan, East Asia, and the world made 'yen diplomacy' no longer possible. The growing strength of China and the military threat from North Korea emphasized the need for Japan to increase its defense capability. An overstretched US sought military commitment from Tokyo not only to defend Japan, but also to support other international campaigns.

This new context has created an opening for 'normalists' – those who want to break the bonds of the postwar constitution and develop normal military capacity. However, they are walking a tightrope that reaches to the heart of Japanese identity in the postwar era. Can Japan remilitarize but still live peacefully with the international community? Or are we seeing a re-emergence of the warrior *wa*, which brutalized East Asia last century and could do so again? To most of the world, the latter seems unlikely, but revisionist efforts in Japan to assert the righteousness of Tokyo's Second World War aggression do little to allay the fears of Japan's neighbors.

In the meantime, Japan has had an often tense but evolving relationship with the largest group of foreigners in its midst – the sizeable Korean community. After decades of living apart from the mainstream, allied to a government that is Tokyo's enemy, Koreans are now gradually assimilating, though often at the cost of their language and identity (not unlike the experience of immigrant communities in many other countries).

Tokyo's relations with its neighbors and with foreign residents help us add some nuance to our understanding of Japanese culture and its influence. They confirm a central aspect of *wa* – sharp and often conflicted inside/outside boundaries. They also help us understand that consensus does not mean unanimity: within a broad consensus on Japanese foreign policy, there has always been a variety of views. Finally, cultural expressions evolve over time: we have seen Japan's militarism in the first half of last century; its aversion to militarism in the second half; and an awkward approach toward establishment of a 'normal' armed forces and defense policy at the beginning of the new millennium. In international relations, as in other areas, culture shapes the way in which the Japanese conduct their affairs, but does not simplistically determine policy or behavior.

CHAPTER FIVE

Meltdown

What must be admitted – very painfully – is that this was a disaster 'Made in Japan.' Its fundamental causes are to be found in the ingrained conventions of Japanese culture: our reflexive obedience; our reluctance to question authority; our devotion to 'sticking with the program'; our groupism; and our insularity.

Had other Japanese been in the shoes of those who bear responsibility for this accident, the result may well have been the same.[1]

When Kiyoshi Kurokawa, the chairman of the special commission investigating the Fukushima nuclear accident, wrote these words in the commission report's English preface, they caused quite a stir. Ex-president of the Science Council of Japan and a former advisor to Abe, Kurokawa is one of the most prominent scientific leaders in the country. The commission he chaired was set up by the National Diet of Japan, the country's legislature, to examine the causes of the Fukushima accident, and it was the first independent public investigatory commission in Japanese history.[2] Its report was eagerly awaited by people in Japan and throughout the world.

Kurokawa's words were not without controversy. Some wondered why they were only issued in a separate 'message from the chairman,' rather than in the actual report issued in the name of the committee. Others pointed out that this commentary was only in the preface to the English version of the report, not the Japanese. Finally, and most substantively, Kurokawa was accused of attempting to deflect blame from those responsible. As Columbia University professor and Japan expert Gerald Curtis wrote, 'to pin the blame on culture is the ultimate cop-out. If culture explains behaviour, then no one has to take responsibility.'[3]

Two main question arise from the triple tragedy – and especially from the nuclear meltdown. Was it a reflection of Japanese culture? And what impact will the event and its aftermath have on Japan?

To begin to answer these questions, we have to go back in time some 60 years, to when Japan first started down the path of nuclear power.

Nuclear Japan

It may seem odd that the first and only country devastated by nuclear weapons so quickly turned to nuclear energy after the war. But by the 1950s, the economy was starting to ramp up and it was clear that the resource-poor country would need energy. Japan had no oil, was running out of coal, and liquefied natural gas was not yet available.[4] Nuclear energy appealed to Japan's interest in advanced technology, and it also represented an enormous business opportunity for the country's power reactor vendors, such as Toshiba and Mitsubishi.

Japan's investment in nuclear energy began in 1954, and the first commercial reactor was launched in 1966.[5] The turn to nuclear power accelerated after the oil crisis of 1973, and, in the decades that followed, 54 nuclear plants were opened. Up until the Fukushima disaster, these plants generated about 30 percent of the nation's energy. An anti-nuclear energy protest movement, made up of environmentalists, leftists, and nuclear bomb survivors, ebbed and flowed over the decades; but, for the most part, the Japanese government succeeded in changing the discourse in favor of 'good nuclear power,' as distinct from 'bad nuclear weapons.'

Green Japan

Though nuclear power was launched in Japan before anybody had ever heard of global warming, this phenomenon eventually came to play an important role in Japan's environmental policy. As early as 1994, the OECD applauded Japan for decoupling economic development and air pollution, as the nation's air quality actually improved while the economy thrived.[6] Another OECD report, this time from 2002, concluded that Japan's 'mix of instruments used to implement environmental policy is highly effective' and that 'regulations are strict, well enforced and based on strong monitoring capacities.'[7]

Respect for the environment is taught both in Japanese schools and at home, with a special emphasis on not being wasteful. Japanese children learn, for example, not to waste food and are taught to eat every last grain of rice in their bowl. If they leave any, they may be chided with '*mottainai*' ('don't be wasteful' or 'what a waste') by an adult. Given the country's lack of natural resources and frequent natural disasters, as well as the poverty and food shortages experienced during and after the Second World War, it is understandable that people in Japan, especially the older generations, should have a keen sense of vulnerability and thus emphasize the concept of *mottainai*. Author Mariko Shinju took up this concept and wrote a bestselling children's book featuring *Mottainai Basan* (Mottainai Grandma), a fussy grandmother who scolds children for wasting food and other things. Shinju wrote this book because her four-year-old son did not understand why he had to finish all the food on his plate.[8]

The Japanese people honor the concept of *mottainai* through the three Rs of environmentalism: reduce, reuse, and recycle.[9] With a popular consensus in favor of conservation, Japan is able to implement one of the most rigorous and effective recycling programs in the world. Though the precise details of the scheme vary from region to region, throughout the country Japanese citizens painstakingly separate their garbage into many different containers.

For example, in Shinjuku, Tokyo – as explained not only in Japanese, but also in English on a special website for foreign residents – all garbage must be recycled into five separate bins: for recyclable paper; plastic containers and wrapping; combustible rubbish; metal, ceramic, and glass items; and 'glass bottles, cans, plastic bottles, spray cans, cassette gas cylinders, and dry-cell batteries.'[10] The result is dramatic. Whereas in the US, a full 70 percent of waste ends up in landfills, in Japan the figure is only 16 percent.[11]

Not surprisingly, Japan has paid much more attention to its greenhouse gas emissions than has the United States. In 2010, for example, its carbon dioxide emissions per person were well under half those of the United States.[12] Partly due to the population density of the country (but also to the cost of energy and environmental consciousness in Japan), people live in smaller houses, drive smaller cars, use more public transportation, and otherwise conserve their resources much better than in the United States.

Producing 30 percent of its energy from low-carbon nuclear sources also had a huge effect on reducing greenhouse gas emissions. Nuclear energy was a winning formula in Japan – as long as the plants could be operated safely, which could never be guaranteed in this, the most earthquake- and tsunami-prone country on earth.

Japan's Chernobyl

There had been a few small nuclear accidents in Japan from the 1970s through the 1990s, but nothing that could have prepared the country for 11 March 2011, when an earthquake measuring 9.0 on the Richter scale struck northeast Japan. This was the biggest earthquake in Japanese history and the fifth largest earthquake in recorded history.

In itself, the earthquake was disaster enough, but it also triggered huge tsunami waves, which engulfed the Tohoku region of Japan and killed more than 20,000 people. News reports showed horrific footage of cars racing away from the shore along highways, only to be swallowed up in the water. And still that wasn't the end of the disaster.

Fukushima Daiichi nuclear power plant had six reactors. The earthquake and tsunami seriously damaged four of them. First, the quake stopped power from flowing to the plant from the grid; then the floods disabled all but one of the plant's emergency diesel generators. Without power, the reactors could not cool the fuel rods, which led to core meltdowns of three of the six reactors.[13] This was the first time in the history of nuclear power that there were simultaneous multiple core meltdowns.

Fukushima became Japan's Chernobyl. Both accidents rated level 7 on the International Nuclear and Radiological Event Scale, the worst rating possible. By comparison, the 1979 Three Mile Island disaster in the United States was level 5.

The first week

The Fukushima plant uses what nuclear engineers call 'boiling water reactors,' designed in the 1960s. A boiling water reactor is essentially a nuclear tea kettle. It heats up water in the core to create steam; that steam pressure drives a turbine, which generates electricity. The reactor usually uses water to cool the fuel rods to the ideal temperature: hot enough to maintain the necessary pressure, but cool enough to prevent the pressure from cracking apart the infrastructure.

Perhaps it helps to imagine a tea kettle, where the source of heat is located inside the kettle, boiling the water surrounding it. Imagine that the spout of the kettle is plugged. The heat and pressure generated would start the kettle rumbling, as the steam frantically sought to escape. If you didn't unblock the spout and pour the boiling water into your teacup, the pressure would eventually become so intense that the kettle would blow open, cracking and sending hot water spurting all over the kitchen.

This is similar to the situation at the Fukushima Daiichi plant, except that the plant required a steady supply of cool, fresh water. When the station blackout cut all of the station's cooling systems, the plant manager, Masao Yoshida, was faced with a major problem: how to get water into the reactor, in order to stop the 'tea kettle' from cracking.

Reactor Units 1, 2, and 3 were operating when the earthquake hit the plant. As they were designed to, they automatically shut down when the power failed. But stopping the reactors did not stop heat being generated by radioactive decay. The reactors needed to be cooled down, but the emergency diesel generators that were supposed to do this had been flooded by the tsunami.

Reactor Units 4, 5, and 6 had been shut down for routine maintenance. Unit 6's diesel generator, which survived the tsunami, was rigged to supply power to Unit 5. But Unit 4 was a different story. Though technically offline, it still had more than 1,500 spent fuel rods stored in a pool that required a steady flow of coolant water. Without a power supply, no water was cycling through, and the water in the pool had started to evaporate.

Units 1 through 4 were in crisis. Unit 1's short-term emergency cooling system failed to kick in. At Units 2 and 3, engineers tried to use some short-term backup cooling systems that did not require an outside power supply, but eventually even these failed. With the collapse of these cooling systems, Units 1, 2, and 3 all overheated, while Unit 4 had its own crisis with spent fuel rods boiling through a limited tank of water.[14]

The world watched in horror as Tokyo Electric Power Company (TEPCO) workers and contractors struggled to cool the reactors. Every step forward spawned a new crisis, as hydrogen explosions blew the tops off Units 1, 3, and 4 and damaged even more equipment, further complicating strategies and hampering the efforts to bring the plant back under control.[15]

Within five hours of the earthquake, Prime Minister Naoto Kan declared a nuclear emergency at Fukushima Daiichi. About ten hours after the earthquake, Unit 1 started melting down, and the following day a hydrogen explosion destroyed the reactor's building. After that, a horrific chain of events made it even more difficult for workers to cool the reactors. As well as Unit 1, Units 2 and 3 both suffered melt-downs: Unit 3 had a meltdown on 13 March and a hydrogen explosion on 14 March; Unit 2 had a meltdown on 14 March.[16]

Fukushima Daiichi plant operators saw a grim fate ahead of them. If they lost control of the temperature and pressure inside a containment vessel or a spent-fuel pool, it would spew enormous amounts of nuclear substances into the air. If that happened, no one would be able to come close enough to stop it. This would spur an almost apocalyptic chain of consequences as the other reactors at Fukushima Daiichi succumbed to the same fate. Six spewing nuclear reactors would be a nightmare; but Fukushima Daini, another TEPCO-owned nuclear power plant only 10 kilometers away, was vulnerable to this chain reaction. According to a doomsday scenario, TEPCO could lose control of all six reactors at Fukushima Daiichi and four at Fukushima Daini.[17] With ten reactors scattering radioactive particles into the air so close to Tokyo, the science fiction horror of countless manga comics seemed all too realistic: an abandoned, irradiated Tokyo.

Yoshida, who was tasked with preventing this scenario, also feared the worst. He told hundreds of TEPCO workers and contractors to evacuate Fukushima Daiichi, leaving behind only about 70 essential staff, later known (inaccurately) as the 'Fukushima 50.'[18] Yoshida subsequently said he had given up hope of surviving the Unit 2 crisis. He had imagined that about 10 out of the 70 would have to remain at Fukushima Daiichi, fighting to the death.[19]

The chair of the Japan Atomic Energy Commission, Shunsuke Kondo, ran a computer simulation that predicted the worst-case scenario: more than a thousand spent fuel rods would overheat, pumping vast amounts of nuclear radiation into the air; 30 million residents of the Tokyo metropolitan area would have to be evacuated; and a third of Japan, including Tokyo, would become completely uninhabitable.[20]

Unit 2

Unit 2 was the most dangerous of the reactors, and in the end it released the largest amount of radioactive substances. Though it did not suffer a hydrogen explosion of its own,[21] it was directly between the explosions at Units 1 and 3. The first explosion at Unit 1 damaged fire engines and hoses placed at the site to inject seawater into Unit 2, thus delaying that injection. The Unit 3 explosion also damaged a mechanism that regulated the venting valves at Unit 2, which were crucial for that unit's depressurization.[22]

As the pressure within Unit 2's containment vessel rose, workers had to depressurize it, otherwise any water they tried to pump in would immediately be blown back out. They tried to open one of the safety relief valves, but could not. Meanwhile, coolant water was evaporating rapidly.[23] The workers tried to vent the primary containment vessel directly to the outside, but the pipes had been damaged by the earthquake. The pressure vessel was running out of water, and the fuel rods were becoming exposed.[24]

Finally there was the sound of an explosion from Unit 2: the melted core had cracked the suppression chamber in the containment vessel. This allowed a large amount of radioactive material to leak out, but seems to have avoided a total catastrophe at Unit 2.[25] What exactly did happen to Unit 2 is still under investigation, and it is unclear how badly the reactor was damaged.

Unit 4

Although Unit 4 was offline when the tsunami hit, it nonetheless spiraled into a separate crisis. The reactor had no fuel rods in the containment vessel, but more than 1,500 spent fuel rods were stored in a pool of water inside the reactor. When the cooling cycle stopped, these rods started to use up a supply of water that was not being replaced as it evaporated. Once the reactor roof was destroyed in a hydrogen explosion, the spent-fuel pool was completely exposed to the outside. If the remaining water evaporated, the rods would release enormous amounts of radiation into the air. To make matters worse, it was impossible for the operators to gauge the water level in the spent-fuel pool, and they could not easily observe the rods.

The US government was extremely worried about Unit 4. Gregory Jaczko, US Nuclear Regulatory Commission chairman, testified to Congress on 16 March, one day after the hydrogen explosion at Unit 4, that the water in the pool must have run out as the rods over-heated.[26] This spawned fears of Tokyo being turned into a ghost town.

Miraculously, Unit 4 had enough water to keep the rods cool for several days. But the coolant was running out as fire trucks from Tokyo – deploying 80ft ladders – pumped water into the spent-fuel pool at Unit 4. Later, SDF helicopters dropped water on Unit 4 and Unit 3.

Heroism and oversights

The workers at Daiichi faced extremely hazardous conditions. They had to work around the clock, so they were exhausted, and they had only rice balls and instant noodles to eat. Measuring equipment was destroyed, so operators struggled to discern the status of the reactors. And without power, they worked in the dark. Pairs of workers would run into a radioactive area together so that one could hold a flash-light while the other took meter readings.[27] According to one worker: 'It was surreal. It was like a war zone.'[28]

They stayed on at their posts, even though many did not know what had become of their loved ones after the tsunami. Such heroism was not confined to the 'Fukushima 50': workers who had evacuated to Fukushima Daini nuclear plant also returned to Daiichi to join the rescue operation.

Through intense efforts and with the assistance of firefighters and SDF members, Yoshida and the plant workers eventually succeeded in securing a stable water supply for the reactors and in restoring electricity by the end of March. This was a key turning point in the battle to stop the nuclear meltdown. Nearly nine months later, in mid-December 2011, the government announced that the reactors had finally reached the stable cool state of 'cold shutdown.'[29]

According to Ryusho Kadota, the author of *The Man Who Stared Down Death*, a book about Yoshida's handling of the Fukushima crisis, 'Yoshida saved Japan' by doing what he thought was right.

Soon after, Yoshida died of esophageal cancer at the age of 58.[30] He had earned the respect of plant workers as an unusually caring boss who was totally committed to his work. At his funeral, people who risked their lives during the Fukushima crisis said they had done so because of him; under his leadership they had even been prepared to die saving Fukushima.

However, Yoshida's admirable leadership during the crisis is only one aspect of his legacy. He was also one of the TEPCO leaders who ignored its own 2008 study, which warned that an earthquake measuring 8.3 (equivalent to the Meiji Sanriku earthquake of 1896) in the Tohoku region could create a massive tsunami that would disable Fukushima Daiichi. At the time of this report, Yoshida was head of the nuclear facilities management division at TEPCO, but even after he became plant manager, he failed to address the danger.

While Yoshida's actions at Fukushima Daiichi were undoubtedly heroic, an honest appraisal of the situation reveals that he was one of the many players entangled in a web of oversights that led to the worst nuclear accident since the 1986 Chernobyl disaster.[31]

What went wrong?

The Fukushima crisis was sparked by an unprecedented natural disaster. But the National Diet's Nuclear Accident Independent Investigation Commission (NAIIC, or *Kokkai Jiko-cho*), mentioned at the beginning of this chapter, argued that it was a human disaster. Its report insists that the primary cause of the disaster was TEPCO's poor contingency planning and Japan's lax regulatory system, and suggests that the effects of the disaster could have been mitigated by a more effective human response. Many pitfalls, including communication breakdowns and equipment failures, complicated the onsite operation.[32]

TEPCO's poor contingency planning

On the human side of the disaster, much of the blame lies with TEPCO, the owner and operator of Fukushima Daiichi. As mentioned above, back in 2008 its own studies found that the power station was threatened by floods, and acknowledged the possibility of tsunami waves up to 15 meters in height.[33] But TEPCO's top officials dismissed the report as unrealistic – it would, after all, have been a disaster of historic proportions. They assumed that waves could reach no higher than 5.7 meters, and TEPCO clung to its 6-meter wall at Fukushima Daiichi. Of course, the waves from the 11 March tsunami were of historic proportions: reaching nearly 15 meters at the plant, they were more than twice the size TEPCO had ever imagined. The tragedy is that TEPCO not only conducted its own study, but also had a third party study the possibility of large tsunamis, in response to a call from Japan's nuclear regulator, the Nuclear and Industrial Safety Agency (NISA). And yet TEPCO failed to act on the study findings and deliberately postponed taking the necessary decisions on measures against large tsunamis.

Because TEPCO never imagined that tsunami waves could top the 6-meter sea wall, the company did not anticipate the total loss of the plant's normal power supply (from the power grid) and its backup power (the diesel generators). In fact, the backup generators were housed in the plant's basements – almost guaranteed to be the first place to flood.

After the crisis, the company dodged responsibility, to the growing annoyance of the general public. TEPCO's argument hinged on the unprecedented scale of the tsunami, which it claimed no one could have predicted. It repeatedly used the term *soteigai* (unforeseen) to defend its unpreparedness. The company acknowledged that the plant had failed to withstand the *soteigai* tsunami, but touted the apparent success of handling the earthquake: three of the six reactors with fuel meltdowns had shut down automatically, as they were designed to. But the rest fell victim to what the media called a 'once in a millennium' tsunami. That was *soteigai*, beyond the scope of emergency planning,[34] and TEPCO claimed that it could not possibly have planned for it.

The special commission disagreed. It argued that the earthquake had damaged the reactors and safety equipment to the point of crisis even before the tsunami. NAIIC suggested that TEPCO was dodging responsibility for the disaster by putting all the blame on the tsunami, rather than on the quake. The commission found that the company (and the government's regulatory agencies) had failed to meet basic safety requirements; not least, the company had failed to assess the probability of a disaster and to minimize potential collateral damage. The commission's report concluded that TEPCO management had deliberately avoided taking action.

Another government-initiated independent committee – the Investigation Committee on the Accident at the Fukushima Nuclear Power Stations of Tokyo Electric Power Company (or the Government Investigation Committee (*Seifu Jiko-cho*)) – echoed NAIIC in criticizing the company's use of the term *soteigai*. This panel argued that running a nuclear power plant required those responsible for the plant to anticipate every possible crisis.

Soon, the Government Investigation Committee turned to semantics. They looked at the term *soteigai* and saw two meanings. One is where a disaster is unimaginable to humankind, even with the most advanced knowledge and experience. The second is legalistic: compromising on emergency preparedness for financial reasons, by restricting preparedness to scenarios that are thought to be more likely. TEPCO had adopted the second definition, assuming that it was acceptable to take a minimalist approach to things that could not reasonably be considered urgent. 'TEPCO lacked a sense of urgency and imagination toward major tsunami,' stated the committee.[35] Another investigation panel initiated by journalists and academics – the Public Investigation Commission (*Minkan Jiko-cho*) – agreed that TEPCO should have worked harder to foresee the unforeseeable.

As one might imagine, all this arguing about semantics was not merely an academic exercise. Indeed, it meant that lawyers and money were involved. TEPCO was trying to claim that Japan's nuclear damage law applied to the Fukushima disaster.[36] If it did, the company could not be held liable for compensation: the law states that any nuclear damage incurred in a grave natural disaster 'of exceptional character' is exempt. TEPCO claimed that the tsunami was 'an extraordinary natural disaster' and so it was not responsible for compensation.

Nobody was convinced. TEPCO was eventually forced to cover compensation for the victims, and was also to be temporarily nationalized in exchange for bailout funds. But the debate reflects the mentality of the company's top executives, such as Chairman Tsunehisa Katsumata, that TEPCO was blameless and that the company itself was a scapegoat for the government's own failures. In particular, Katsumata and other TEPCO leaders blamed Prime Minister Kan for the exacerbated crisis, since, in their eyes, the prime minister had meddled in the operations at Fukushima Daiichi and sowed confusion (see below).[37]

Finally, 19 months after the earthquake and tsunami, TEPCO acknowledged its faults in accident preparation. This was after it had given up on the nuclear damage compensation law and after it had been nationalized. TEPCO's internal reform task force stated that the company had been aware of the need for safety improvements before the crisis, but had failed to take action.

There is little doubt that the nuclear disaster was exacerbated by TEPCO's false belief in safety (or *anzen shinwa*, 'myth of safety'). It simply did not believe that a severe nuclear accident could happen, and its nuclear plant operations had been based on this false sense of security. The company did not train workers or contractors at Fukushima Daiichi (or at its other nuclear power plants) to handle a nuclear crisis with multiple failures. The employees did not even have a useful emergency manual to follow. Had they undergone rigorous safety and emergency training at TEPCO, they could have dealt with the crisis more effectively. Indeed, serious human errors took place throughout the crisis; for example, the temporary coolant systems were halted, which contributed to the meltdowns.[38]

The motives behind TEPCO's promotion of the safety myth were strange, and yet pragmatic. For one thing, the company worried that training for severe accidents might suggest the possibility of severe accidents. In other words, workers and residents near nuclear plants may have been upset by the very notion of disasters that they needed to prepare for. TEPCO worried that drills or worst-case-scenario planning could lead to the rise of anti-nuclear sentiment, which could get in the way of plant operation and construction bids. It also feared the prospect of litigation if it admitted to the possibility of a severe accident.[39]

TEPCO also had a history of covering up accidents.[40] In 1978, it had a 'criticality' (uncontrolled nuclear fission) incident at Fukushima Daiichi, which the company hid until 2007.[41] In 2002, falsified safety inspections came to light when an American whistleblower, Kei Sugaoka, a General Electric onsite inspector at TEPCO's three plants (including Fukushima Daiichi, yet again) reported that the company was hiding evidence of cracks in the containment vessels of its nuclear reactors. TEPCO denied the allegation and refused to cooperate fully with the government's investigation. Sugaoka provided further evidence to NISA, which eventually revealed to the public that TEPCO had hidden 29 cracks in the vessels of 13 of its 17 reactors. The company finally admitted the cover-up. Following NISA's revelation, TEPCO temporarily shut down all of its reactors for inspection, and its chairman, president, and vice-president all resigned (though all of them were given advisory positions in the company).[42] TEPCO failed to make any significant reforms.

Who's on first?

At the time of the earthquake and tsunami on 11 March 2011, TEPCO President Masataka Shimizu was out of town, sightseeing with his wife in Nara. He could not get back to TEPCO's Tokyo headquarters until the following day. The company's chairman, Tsunehisa Katsumata, was away on a business trip to China and was not aware of Shimizu's schedule. The absence of the top two executives slowed the decision-making process at TEPCO. Managing Executive Officer Akio Komori assumed command of TEPCO's initial response to the nuclear disaster. But with the company's rigid hierarchies, Komori was still required to ask Shimizu and Katsumata for permission to implement decisions, despite the urgency of the crisis. His hands were bound by red tape, as he had to assess, and then re-explain, problems such as reactor ventilation and seawater injections, both of which would have significant consequences. Komori's consultation with the two top executives required additional time during the initial time-sensitive critical response period.[43]

Meanwhile, TEPCO was deferential to the prime minister's office to the point of withholding information that might upset the office. On paper, the primary decision-making authority rested with the onsite Daiichi plant manager, Yoshida. But TEPCO thought instructions and requests from the prime minister should take priority.

Thus, for example, Ichiro Takekuro, a former TEPCO executive vice-president in charge of nuclear operations, told Yoshida to stop pouring seawater into Unit 1. Takekuro, who was in the prime minister's office at the time, felt that the prime minister's 'mood' was against the seawater injection, even though Takekuro knew the operation was absolutely necessary to cool the reactor. In fact, Prime Minister Kan never told anybody to stop the seawater injection; Takekuro had merely sensed from 'the atmosphere' that Kan wanted it stopped, despite the urgent need for it. Luckily, Yoshida ignored Takekuro.[44] But this tale shows that respect for hierarchy was so rigid that even a nuclear expert would suggest the opposite of what was scientifically necessary, if he felt a higher authority wanted it that way.[45]

TEPCO headquarters was supposed to provide useful technical advice to the plant operators. But really it only confused everybody, especially over the venting operation at Unit 2. Headquarters did not fully understand the detailed structure of its own reactor or the configuration of the vent line.[46] It was also powerless to provide assistance to Yoshida: he repeatedly asked for more technicians and equipment, but his pleas were often ignored.[47]

The company made a series of foolish mistakes. When Fukushima Daiichi lost power, Yoshida wanted to restore electricity using mobile generators. TEPCO ordered these, but their arrival at the plant was delayed by traffic jams and obstructed roads. When they did finally arrive, it turned out that the voltage they produced was incompatible. It took 40 workers at the plant to install and connect a one-tonne transformer and to establish a temporary electricity generator cable for Unit 1. Six minutes after it had been installed, a hydrogen explosion at the unit destroyed the cable.[48]

Yoshida asked for 12V (volt) batteries to operate some emergency equipment. TEPCO ordered hundreds of useless 2V batteries instead. When it ordered 1,000 12V batteries, it couldn't get them delivered to Fukushima Daiichi until 14 March – three days after Yoshida's request and a day after the Unit 3 meltdown.[49] On 13 March, the

operators at Unit 3 desperately needed 120V batteries to open a valve
and depressurize the reactor. Frustrated by TEPCO's ineptitude,
Daiichi workers drove to another city to buy ten 12V batteries (to
make 120 volts) but found only eight. Eventually, the onsite workers
took 12V batteries from their own cars.[50] But by then it was too late
to prevent a meltdown at Unit 3, as the reactor had been without a
coolant system for too long.

Atsufumi Yoshizawa, a senior official in charge of procurement at
TEPCO at the time, said that TEPCO had failed to deliver the 12V
batteries quickly because the company had had many requests for
equipment after the earthquake and could not prioritize Fukushima
Daiichi's request. He explained that time constraints meant that the
procurement department could not prioritize requests, and instead
put orders together on a first-come, first-served basis.[51] It was clear
that TEPCO was not prepared for a crisis of this magnitude.

Another serious fault with TEPCO lay in its reluctance to share
information with the government and the public. By law, TEPCO
was responsible for providing information to the government regulator, NISA. Though the regulator did not function properly during
the crisis (see below), TEPCO avoided direct communication with
the prime minister's office. TEPCO expert Takekuro, who was
stationed at the prime minister's office, could not obtain adequate
information from TEPCO and could not assist the prime minister
effectively.[52]

Within 24 hours of the earthquake and tsunami, Prime Minister
Kan was already extremely frustrated with TEPCO. When Yoshida
requested the emergency mobile generators and batteries for
Fukushima Daiichi, the prime minister's office ordered Japan's
self-defense forces to assist in delivering the generators, but TEPCO
never explained why they were not used (because they had the wrong
voltage). The prime minister's office was thus left in the dark as to
why the plant could not restore power to cool the reactors.[53]
Meanwhile, the US government was getting frustrated with its

Japanese counterpart, and thought Japan was concealing information. In fact, TEPCO was simply refusing to provide information to the prime minister's office.

The prime minister's office developed an acute distrust of TEPCO. On 12 March, Unit 1 urgently needed 'wet venting' – that is, venting steam through water in the suppression chamber in order to prevent an explosion in the containment vessel. But the prime minister could not get any information from TEPCO headquarters about the status of the reactor. When no information was forthcoming from TEPCO as to whether or not it had started the venting operation, an extremely irritated Prime Minister Kan took the bold step of traveling in person to Fukushima Daiichi. Kan was satisfied after his talk with Yoshida during his short trip to the nuclear plant, and was impressed by Yoshida's determination to save the reactor, even by forming a 'suicide corps' (*kesshitai*), if necessary, to conduct the venting operation.

On 14 March, Kan heard from members of his own Nuclear Emergency Response Headquarters (NERH) that TEPCO President Shimizu had asked permission to withdraw all TEPCO workers from the Fukushima Daiichi plant. This was refused. Shimizu visited the prime minister's office at 4 a.m. on 15 March and agreed that TEPCO would not withdraw; but Kan had lost all faith in him. As he did a couple of days earlier with Fukushima Daiichi, the prime minister went to see TEPCO's other decision-makers in person early in the morning of 15 March, and instructed them not to withdraw from the plant. 'Japan could be ruined if the situation stays as it is,' he exploded. He reiterated that if TEPCO abandoned the Fukushima plant, the reactors would collapse and massive amounts of radioactive substances would be released: 'It will be twice or three times worse than Chernobyl, and you know what that means!'[54]

Kan later said that he struggled to cope with the lack of information from TEPCO and the absence of trustworthy and reliable experts. 'We were on a cliff-edge situation,' he said.[55] Deputy Chief

Cabinet Secretary Tetsuro Fukuyama, who accompanied the prime minister to TEPCO, was surprised that the company's headquarters lacked any sense of urgency. Some workers abandoned what they were doing to catch a glimpse of the prime minister, and Fukuyama had to order them back to work. One TEPCO employee later said that Kan's visit had demoralized workers at the headquarters, as they had been expecting words of encouragement.[56]

Most of the public have been mystified by the lack of information shared with the prime minister. But Naoto Kan was, by all accounts, an intimidating man. TEPCO executive Takekuro said the prime minister's office needed something like boric acid to calm him down.[57] A politician's short temper should never influence decision-making in a crisis, but fear of Kan's outbursts frequently slowed down communication among timid staffers and advisors. Workers were terrified of being publicly chastised by the prime minister.[58]

Kan also liked to micromanage technical matters and used to challenge people with detailed questions, often getting angry when they could not answer him. Intimidated bureaucrats were so afraid of him that they reacted like Japanese students afraid of a teacher, stalling for time so that they could be perfectly prepared when they answered. This is fine in a classroom, but not during a nuclear crisis, when there needed to be a rapid flow of communication. Nonetheless, people around him hesitated to explain things to him on account of their thin skins.[59] Notably, it was Yoshida, the head of the Fukushima plant, who ultimately earned Kan's trust as the most knowledgeable player in the crisis. After Kan's visit, however, TEPCO headquarters began sharing information with the government, through the establishment of a joint command center.[60]

Meanwhile, TEPCO Chairman Tsunehisa Katsumata never once visited Fukushima to meet with victims after the accident. Despite everything that had happened, he demanded a government bailout, so that the company could remain solvent, while refusing any government intervention in the company's future management.[61]

Lax regulatory system

The Fukushima crisis highlighted the fact that TEPCO and other Japanese utilities were subject to lax oversight. The task of oversight fell within the purview of Japan's now defunct nuclear regulator, NISA, which was ultimately just as responsible for the Fukushima disaster as TEPCO.

NISA was a faulty organization from the start. Though charged with regulating the nuclear industry, it usually took the industry's side. Part of the problem was simply the agency's pedigree. It came under the jurisdiction of the Agency for Natural Resources and Energy, which itself is under the umbrella of the Ministry of Economy, Trade, and Industry (METI). These two organizations are major pro-nuclear advocates within the Japanese bureaucracy. Most of NISA's personnel started out with METI, and many officials used to rotate between METI (charged with promoting nuclear energy) and NISA (charged with regulating nuclear energy).

To make this relationship even cozier, retiring regulators often ended up with lucrative positions at nuclear-related companies that they had been regulating. This practice, called *amakudari* ('descent from heaven') encouraged regulators to tiptoe around utilities, lest they be deprived of future opportunities in the industry. As the largest electrical utility in Japan, TEPCO was a plum post for METI and NISA officials. The *New York Times* reports that from 1959 to 2010 four former top METI officials filled the position of vice-president at TEPCO. In fact, the company's vice-presidency is known as METI's 'reserved seat.' Besides the vice-presidential seat, many retiring METI officials take advisory positions at TEPCO.[62]

NISA's lack of neutrality and independence was partially due to lack of expertise. Many top leaders at the agency lacked the nuclear science education required to regulate the industry independently. Its inspections were not rigorous, because its regulators simply were not trained or educated enough to conduct such inspections: 'NISA regulators were dumb and we lucked out,' said one utility employee at a conference on nuclear energy.[63]

Because of the organization's lack of expertise, NISA often took on retired or active engineers and safety experts from within the nuclear industry. This practice, known as *amaagari* ('ascent to heaven'), often led to conflicts of interest. NISA became too dependent on experts who were unlikely to criticize their former employers. As a result, it insisted on only the safety standards that utilities such as TEPCO could actually afford.[64] When utilities had accidents at nuclear power plants, NISA focused the bulk of its energy on persuading local residents of the 'safety' of the plants.

The agency never provided training for local residents, either. Matching TEPCO's internal concerns, it feared that training would only inspire anxiety about the risk of disasters, in turn triggering anti-nuclear sentiment that could interfere with plant operations or lead to litigation. Like TEPCO, NISA felt the need to emphasize nuclear safety in order to gain public support for the operations.[65]

This led to an ironic strategy of sabotaging stronger nuclear safety standards in an effort to reassure communities that nuclear power was safe. In 2006, the Cabinet Office's Nuclear Safety Commission (NSC) was in the process of revising its emergency plans for nuclear accidents, and suggested using safety standards proposed by the International Atomic Energy Agency (IAEA). But NISA opposed the IAEA guidelines – especially one that designated emergency evacuation zones for nuclear accidents. The NISA director at the time, Kenkichi Hirose, explained why his agency was opposed to it: 'The nation has finally put away its fear of nuclear accidents, the first time since the [1999 Japan Nuclear Fuel Conversion Co. (JCO)] nuclear accident at Tokaimura ... Why do we need to "wake a sleeping child"?'[66]

Hirose's reference is to a nuclear accident at the Tokaimura nuclear plant, when untrained workers of the JCO brought together too much high-level enriched uranium, sparking an uncontrolled nuclear chain reaction. Two of the workers died from radiation exposure, and the incident raised public anxiety about nuclear power. Worrying that establishing evacuation zones would make the public uneasy, NISA resisted the IAEA guidelines. In a letter to the NSC, it argued: 'Japan's nuclear disaster management has no particular problem and changes are not necessary.'[67] In the end, the NSC did not adopt the guidelines.[68]

NISA also ignored warnings by safety inspectors at the US Atomic Energy Commission (AEC) that General Electric reactors of the type Fukushima Daiichi employed were liable to explode and release radiation in the event of a meltdown. The AEC had issued such warnings as early as 1972, but NISA neglected to take any action to address this concern.[69]

NISA's response to the Fukushima nuclear crisis was a deplorable continuation of its irresponsibility. The organization's director, Nobuaki Terasaka, was by no means a nuclear expert, having obtained the position with only a bachelor's degree in economics. When he could not answer Prime Minister Kan's basic question about where Fukushima Daiichi kept its emergency diesel generators, he responded to Kan's chastisement by abandoning his responsibility for monitoring the plant during the crisis. Instead, he sent NISA Vice-Director Eiji Hiraoka, who was about as knowledgeable as Terasaka himself.[70]

Four NISA officials at Fukushima Daiichi fled the site in fear. When ordered to return, they provided a modicum of assistance to the plant operators who were racing to restore power and find cooling water. Then they left again. At the Fukushima Prefectural Office, 50 kilometers away from the plant, they finally abandoned their responsibility as regulators. With these officials gone, NISA had no onsite monitoring or communication either with the prime minister's office or with TEPCO.[71]

NISA also botched the evacuation around the plant. The System for Prediction of Environmental Emergency Dose Information (SPEEDI) is a computer-simulated forecast that models how radiation might spread. The Ministry of Education, Culture, Sports, Science, and Technology (MEXT) gave the information to NISA early on, but the regulator never provided it to Prime Minister Kan's Nuclear Emergency Response Headquarters.[72] Of course, the ministry could have provided the same information to the prime minister's office, but it was NISA's Emergency Response Center that was ultimately responsible for sharing information.

Without any guidance about radiation risks, residents near Fukushima fled north on the advice of town officials, who believed the winter winds would blow the radiation south. Many moved to Nagadoro district, whose residents, including small children, stayed in the district for about two months. As it turned out, however, the Fukushima winds were blowing north, directly over Nagadoro. The SPEEDI models showed high levels of radiation in Nagadoro, and NISA officials knew it; but they never shared that knowledge with the prime minister or the public.

Why didn't NISA share the information with the prime minister? There is speculation that its director, Nobuaki Terasaka, who abrogated his responsibility to collaborate with the prime minister's office, did so to avoid any further confrontations with the prime minister's office.[73]

NISA is not the only tentacle of the nuclear bureaucracy that failed. The Cabinet Office's Nuclear Safety Commission failed to critique safety inspections conducted by NISA. It could not argue with the decisions made by NISA, because they were backed by the powerful METI. And the NSC was hardly an independent organization anyway: when it was drafting its 2006 seismic design guidelines, most of its recommendations came from experts within the nuclear industry, and a member of the panel who opposed the pro-utility guidelines resigned in protest.[74] The NSC never considered an extended station blackout at Fukushima Daiichi,[75] or a scenario of nuclear meltdown due to power failure. The NSC never even provided a manual to follow during this kind of crisis.[76]

After the meltdown, the problems of the existing regulatory structure became clear. In 2012, NISA and the NSC were replaced by the Nuclear Regulation Authority (NRA). Supervision for the NRA was transferred from METI, the ministry responsible for promoting the industry, to the less sympathetic Ministry of the Environment. Presumably cutting ties to METI and the nuclear industry should lead to a more independent NRA.

The radioactive ghost towns of Fukushima

The Japanese government first established an evacuation zone in a radius of 2 kilometers from Fukushima Daiichi on 11 March, expanding it to 10 kilometers on 12 March, and to 20 kilometers later that same day. As the crisis deepened, on 15 March the government further announced that territory between 20 kilometers and 30 kilometers from the plant was designated an 'indoors-only zone,' but ten days later it issued a voluntary evacuation order for residents within that radius as well.[77]

A month after the accident, Fukushima residents learned that radiation levels outside the 30-kilometers radius were still very high. The radioactive materials were not spreading in concentric circles: some places northwest of the evacuation zone were more contaminated than certain places inside it. Soon, a mandatory evacuation order from the national government instructed the residents of these outlier areas to leave.

Iitate, a quiet village that was home to just 6,200 people, is 35 kilometers from Fukushima Daiichi. It took in people from neighboring villages inside the evacuation zone. National officials told the Iitate villagers not to worry about radiation, and so, as Iitate was not in the evacuation zone, the anxious residents tried to remain hopeful.

On 15–16 March, however, Iitate found itself right where the winds from Fukushima Daiichi were blowing, carrying with them radioactive substances at the height of the crisis. It was snowing over Iitate, and the falling flakes brought the radioactive elements to the ground.

In April, panic ran through Iitate: the whole village was subject to the national government's 'all village evacuation' order. The residents were ordered to leave by the end of May, but the government provided no directions about where to go or how to get help. At a meeting with the village's mayor, residents worried about their crops, farmland, and cattle. The mayor, who had not much more information to go on than the villagers, was inundated with panicky questions about the effects of radiation exposure on the health of the villagers and their children. Without answers, frustrated residents broke down in tears at the meeting, having no idea what to do with their lives. Many had hoped that their children and grandchildren would inherit the farms; the evacuation disrupted not just their lives but an entire lineage of ancestral traditions.[78]

Iitate villagers abandoned their homes, their cattle, vegetable crops, farmlands, and pets. Three hundred cows in the village had to be slaughtered. Unemployed villagers who had lived off their land found themselves jobless in small apartments. Some elderly residents refused to leave, despite the government order, while young people fled in fear.[79]

Iitate, like other areas near Fukushima, was divided into three zones: 1) a zone safe for short visits or daytime work (where the annual radiation level was expected to be less than 20 millisieverts (mSv)), 2) a visitation-only zone (between 20 and 50 mSv); and 3) a no-entry zone where, without a special permit, all visits were forbidden for five years (more than 50 mSv). In Iitate, the Nagadoro district fell into the no-entry category. Together with a few towns and villages right by the Fukushima Daiichi plant, the district became an uninhabitable area, sharing the fate of Ukraine's Pripyat.

What is most notable, however, is what did not happen: there were no riots and no violent looting. Although the town was in the midst of a blackout and an evacuation, news reports showed long lines of people calmly waiting at gas stations. Even the notorious Japanese mafia, the *yakuza*, contributed to relief and repair efforts.[80] Here we see the much lauded Japanese trait of privileging harmony in a crisis: a double-edged sword, with calm, collective responsibility on the one hand, and on the other a paralysis in the face of emergency. It was the latter edge of this sword that was tragically revealed behind the scenes of the emergency evacuations.

Early on, the SPEEDI models had indicated the direction of the wind that was carrying the plant's radiation, and revealed that Nagadoro was threatened by high levels of radiation. Within a week of the crisis breaking, MEXT officials had measured the radiation level in Nagadoro. But with bureaucrats reluctant to release the information to the prime minister or the public for fear of causing panic, residents were not informed of the results for a month. While the government hesitated to issue an evacuation order for Nagadoro, its residents were exposed to radiation.[81]

Many of those residents – who now live outside Iitate as evacuees – are angry. But instead of taking to the streets, they have gone to court. Realizing that they were seriously exposed to radioactive materials for a month or more (since their evacuation took time), nearly 200 of them have demanded compensation from TEPCO for psychological damage: they are worried about their own health and that of the children in the district. The young people will have to live with the anxiety of radiation exposure and possible future health problems. As farmers, they had never benefited from the nuclear business and had not been employed by TEPCO, but they would have to bear the burden of the company's mistakes.

In 2013, the residents brought their suit before a government mediation agency that handles claims arising from the Fukushima nuclear accident. The mediation agency proposed that TEPCO should give 500,000 yen ($5,000) to each resident, plus an additional 500,000 yen to each pregnant woman and every child under the age of 18. TEPCO rejected the settlement, arguing that there was no scientific evidence to indicate any increased risk of cancer for Nagadoro residents.[82]

'An unspeakable rage'

With angry street protests and violent outbursts nowhere to be seen in Fukushima, one might be tempted to dismiss evacuees as docile and resigned to their fate. But in fact their anger has turned inward.

Hamako Watanabe, a 58-year-old evacuee, set herself on fire in the summer of 2011, having become despondent after the accident. She and her husband, Makio, had lost their home and their jobs at a chicken factory. Their sons had lived with them, but they moved to another city when they were evacuated. Hamako constantly worried about money and cried incessantly.

After her suicide, Makio filed a lawsuit against TEPCO, blaming the company for his wife's death. He claimed that TEPCO had been too slow to restore the lives of affected residents. Makio wanted TEPCO to compensate people and treat them as victims not of a natural disaster, but of a man-made accident. In his view, that would expedite the compensation process. Watanabe demanded justice and an apology: 'I feel an unspeakable rage.'[83]

Some have turned to alcohol. Moriaki Sato, a 60-year-old single evacuee from Okuma town, died of a heart attack in 2012. He had been living in temporary housing for evacuees. Despite the disaster, he had never given up his dream of building a house in Okuma, where he would invite his elderly mother to come and live with him. But his dream was dashed in December 2012, when most of Okuma became a no-entry zone. Realizing that he might never be able to return to the town, he started drinking heavily. He was found dead in his apartment, but only after three days. His room was still full of the smell of alcohol.[84]

It is impossible to pin down how many people have died indirectly from the nuclear accident at Fukushima. According to data released in May 2013 by the Reconstruction Agency (established in 2012 to work on the reconstruction of the affected areas), there have been 2,688 *shinsai kanren-shi* (deaths related to the March 2011 disaster) – that is, any death caused by extreme physical and/or mental fatigue connected to evacuation, job loss, or the loss or separation of family members.[85] Of all these deaths, 1,383 occurred in Fukushima, and more than 90 percent were senior citizens who were not strong enough to withstand the physical and mental challenges. Most deaths took place within six months of the disaster, but 147 deaths (129 of which occurred in Fukushima) came up to a year later. Nobody has yet died from direct radiation exposure, and it is unclear if anybody will. But it is expected that the number of *shinsai kanren-shi* will rise, as evacuees from the no-entry zones continue to succumb to depression.[86]

In August 2013, in Japan as a whole, there were nearly 300,000 people classed as evacuees following the triple disaster. Fukushima accounted for the largest number of them – almost 150,000, of whom about 88,000 had been forced to move specifically because of the nuclear accident. About 92,000 evacuees had remained in Fukushima, while 52,000 had left the prefecture.[87]

Even people who were not in the evacuation zones left Fukushima soon after the crisis. Many went to the Tokyo area; others to Osaka. Still others chose prefectures further away from Fukushima, such as Okinawa.

Those evacuees from the Fukushima disaster who are prohibited from returning home for five years or more have received (or will receive) a lump sum of 6 million yen ($60,000) per person to cover the entire period. Those who cannot return for two to four years can choose to receive either a one-off sum of 2.4 million yen ($24,000) or a monthly payment of 100,000 yen ($1,000) per person. Residents who can return home after decontamination work is completed will receive 100,000 yen ($1,000) per month per person until they do return. But many evacuees feel the money is insufficient compensation for their hardships.[88]

Farmers

Hisashi Tarukawa, 64, was an organic cabbage grower in Sukagawa City, Fukushima Prefecture, about 80 kilometers from Fukushima Daiichi. Having worked for 30 years in the organic farming business, he was a proud farmer who boasted of using his own leaf mold to improve the soil. His cabbage was served to children at local schools for lunch.

On the morning of 11 March 2011, his 7,500 cabbages were harvested. While his house and barn were damaged in the earthquake, his cabbages survived. Also his farm was well away from the shore and was spared by the tsunami. It seemed like a stroke of luck.

But on 21 March, Tarukawa learned that the government had imposed restrictions on the shipping of spinach grown in Fukushima. Now nervous, he focused on preparing his cabbage and tried to get ready to ship it as soon as he could. But on 23 March, a new government restriction was imposed on Fukushima-grown cabbage. Devastated at the waste of a year's labor and despairing that he might never be able to sell his cabbages again, Tarukawa hanged himself from a tree in his field.[89]

Tarukawa's son made headlines when he demanded not only that TEPCO compensate his family for his father's death, but also that TEPCO officials come to light incense at his father's funeral. Finally, in 2013, TEPCO agreed an out-of-court settlement to compensate the family, admitting that the nuclear disaster had contributed to his death.

Fukushima was once Japan's fourth largest source of rice, but since the disaster, fields throughout the no-entry zone have been abandoned. Even in places far removed from the evacuation zones, farmers cannot see a future in the land. Even after the government declared food from the region to be safe and lifted the ban on its sale, consumers shied away from Fukushima produce. Farmers face *fuhyo higai*, financial damage caused by a bad reputation.

Fukushima farmers who live outside the no-entry zone but still face high radiation levels in the soil have demanded greater help from the government. At a meeting in 2013 with TEPCO and government officials to discuss compensation, farmers expressed their outrage. They argued that they used to be proud farmers who grew safe, top-rated produce. They maintained that the main problem was not (as one official claimed) the *fuhyo higai* of Fukushima foodstuffs, but the fact that there actually was radiation in their produce, and no matter how hard they worked to decontaminate their soil, it was not going away.

'Even if we clear the minimum regulatory threshold of contamination levels . . . we don't want to sell produce contaminated with radiation. Would you feed contaminated vegetables to your child? Answer my question! Would you do so?' shouted an angry farmer at a couple of officials.[90]

Hidekazu Hirai, a 68-year-old Tokyo resident, is urging older people to eat Fukushima rice, in order to help the prefecture's farmers struggling with *fuhyo higai*. As he says, 'The elderly must eat Fukushima rice.' Compared with young people, the elderly are supposed to be less prone to the harmful health effects of radiation, which tend to accumulate over time. Hirai's campaign has actually resulted in the sale of thousands of kilograms of Fukushima rice; but that is a long way off the 240,000 tonnes of annual rice production in the prefecture.[91]

Fishermen

Some fishermen near Fukushima still wake up early and head out to sea in boats equipped with nets to catch sole, sea bream, and sardines. But these fish will not end up on sushi conveyor belts or in tin cans. Instead, the catch will be tested to determine radiation levels.

Commercial fishing off the Fukushima coast has been largely banned since 3/11. But members of one municipal fisheries association – those who haven't given up fishing – have restarted their catches on an exper-imental basis, and the Fukushima prefectural government has been monitoring the safety of the fish by measuring radiation (e.g. cesium) levels inside different species of fish caught near Fukushima. Fish with less than 100Bq/kg (becquerels per kilogram) is considered safe, and Fukushima Governor Yuhei Sato is eager to use these measurements to prove the safety of the Fukushima coastline's fish and shellfish species.[92] But fisheries in Fukushima face numerous challenges. Fish caught on the sea bottom, such as cod, have reportedly had radiation levels higher than 100Bq/kg.

TEPCO admitted in 2013 that contaminated water had leaked out, and that 300 tonnes of contaminated groundwater had been released into the ocean – an accident rated as a level 3 serious inci-dent on the IAEA radiological scale. Even though the Japanese government and TEPCO say the contaminated water does not extend outside the bay area, this was terrible news that temporarily halted the experimental program. Another fisheries association that was set to conduct experimental fishing temporarily postponed its opera-tion. And even if the fish are scientifically proven to be safe, there are plenty of skeptical consumers inside and outside Japan who would be wary of anything labeled 'produce of Fukushima.'

South Korea has banned imports of fish from Japan's 600-mile northeastern coastal line, stretching to Chiba Prefecture near Tokyo, 'regardless of whether they are contaminated or not.'[93] Most seafood products that Japanese consumers purchase are already from over-seas, and the Fukushima contamination problem will accelerate Japan's dependence on foreign fish. Meanwhile, the fishing industry in Fukushima and other prefectures nearby is pretty much doomed.

Future of TEPCO

In the summer of 2012, the Japanese government bailed out TEPCO with 1 trillion yen ($10 billion). The government had to keep the utility company from collapsing, so that it could deal with the billions of dollars in compensation claims and the decommissioning of at least four of the Fukushima Daiichi plant's six reactors. The bailout was a burden on the government, which itself faced a huge fiscal deficit. Under the rescue plan, TEPCO was made liable for compensation, decontamination, and decommissioning of the crippled reactors. The utility was required to use its revenue to pay for decommissioning, but for compensation claims and decontamination, it was allowed to borrow up to 5 trillion yen ($50 billion) from the Nuclear Damage Liability Facilitation Corporation (NDLFC), an independent supervisory body established after the Fukushima disaster to help TEPCO with compensation (that is, the government's credit line for compensating victims).

TEPCO is no longer the same TEPCO as before, at least legally and from a management perspective. With the bailout, the company has been nationalized and the government has acquired majority voting rights at TEPCO to influence the utility's decision-making process. Management of the company has been given to the NDLFC. The government has decided not to cap TEPCO's payment to victims, despite repeated appeals by the company's (now ex-) chairman, Tsunehisa Katsumata, for it to do so. Also, TEPCO has been forced to change its top leaders to make a new start. The new president, Naomi Hirose, was managing director at the utility responsible for compensation for Fukushima nuclear victims, and the new chairman, Kazuhiko Shimokobe, was an active member of the NDLFC.[94] Due to the lengthy time needed for TEPCO to restore its credibility and raise money on the corporate bond market, the company is expected to remain nationalized for some 20 years.[95]

The decommissioning of the reactors at Fukushima Daiichi will, it is estimated, take four decades. The process has already been complicated by the increased amount of contaminated water at the plant site – 350,000 tonnes as of September 2013. There is a lot of natural groundwater in the plant area, and when it runs underneath the plant it becomes contaminated. TEPCO has to figure out how to stop leaks and how to store all that contaminated water safely.[96]

With TEPCO nationalized, the Japanese taxpayer is now paying most of the compensation bill for the nuclear disaster. The utility has cut its costs by selling its properties and cutting salaries, but it has taken losses of more than $25 billion. For example, because of concerns for nuclear safety, TEPCO has not succeeded in winning local support to restart its Kashiwazaki Kariwa nuclear power plant in Niigata Prefecture, which would save the utility about $1 billion every month in terms of fuel costs.[97]

Given TEPCO's accumulating debts, some Japanese lawmakers have pushed to liquidate it; but that is a minority view in Japanese political circles. The company may in fact be too big to fail. Its bankruptcy would have a major impact on the Japanese bond market as a whole. To extend TEPCO's life, the government is willing to pour money into the utility, at the same time as strengthening the authority that monitors it. To contain the leaks and decontaminate water at Fukushima Daiichi, the government has announced that it is ready to spend about half a billion dollars.[98] It seems that every time Fukushima Daiichi has a problem, the government will have no choice but to pour money into it.

The corporate management of TEPCO has changed, but has its corporate culture? One of the major problems during the Fukushima crisis of March 2011 was the utility's reluctance to share information with the government and the public. The revelation of contaminated water leaks came late – two months after the utility found the problem. The new regulatory agency, the NRA, was also irritated with TEPCO. The NRA's chief, Shunichi Tanaka, complained that TEPCO had misled the public by providing poor information and needlessly obfuscating the facts. For example, it had announced that it had found radiation levels of 2,200mSv per hour near tanks with contaminated water. But Tanaka said it made no sense to use the millisievert unit to describe water contamination, which is typically measured in becquerels. 'It's like describing how much something weighs by using centimeters,' he complained.[99]

The legacy of Fukushima

TEPCO's future is the future of Japan's utility sector. Ten regional utilities, including TEPCO, enjoy energy monopolies and dominate the market for both electricity generation and transmission. As a result, Japanese residential consumers pay nearly twice as much as Americans. Reformers demand the break-up of these monopolies, arguing for the market to be opened up to new firms. They say it is ultimately necessary to separate generation from transmission. Such reforms would promote efficiency and reduce costs. The government is interested in liberalizing the utility sector, and new laws may be passed in the Diet to do just that. It also wants to divide the utilities into power generation and power transmission companies by 2020.

In the wake of Fukushima, Japan began shutting down all nuclear reactors, causing huge power shortages. The Japanese, who are used to limiting the use of air conditioning in summer to lower energy costs and protect the environment, did so to extremes in summer 2011 when much of the nation's power supply was shut down. By early 2014, the proportion of Japan's electricity generated by nuclear power had fallen from 30 percent to zero.[100]

In the long run, Japan needs more energy, either from nuclear power or from other sources. Environmental activists call for greater use of natural sources of energy. However, renewable sources such as solar and wind power account for less than 2 percent of Japan's energy, and, as in other countries, serious obstacles exist to ramping those numbers up. To date Japan has largely resorted to importing natural gas. But with a weakening yen, the cost of imported energy continues to rise. In addition, natural gas and other carbon-based sources of energy are worse for the environment.

After successfully reducing its carbon emissions by an average of 9.2 percent each year from 2008 to 2011, Japan increased its emissions by 3.9 percent in the year ending 31 March 2013, due mainly to the shift from nuclear to carbon-based energy sources.[101] Then, in November 2013, it announced that it would dramatically change its target for greenhouse gas emissions: whereas the previous government had promised, before the Fukushima crisis, to cut emissions by 25 percent between 1990 and 2020, the new target envisaged an increase of 3 percent in emissions over that same period.[102] While the previous target had been regarded as unrealistic, this change in it was so large that it cast a shadow over international negotiations on a global climate change pact.

Given Japan's tragic nuclear history – from Hiroshima and Nagasaki to Fukushima – anti-nuclear sentiment in the country runs deep; yet the elites would like to return to nuclear power. Japan expert Richard Samuels divides perspectives on 3/11 into two main narratives: that of the 'nuclear village' and that of the 'black swans.'[103] The nuclear village narrative considers the root of the problem to be villainous collusion between people in industry and government, egged on by people in academia and the media, to illicitly capture energy policy in Japan and push it in an unsafe direction. Critics attack the cozy relationship between private-sector groups (such as the Japan Atomic Industrial Forum) that consort with the government to set policy, with no consideration for transparency or control. One magazine cited by Samuels described how 'the government and TEPCO became one and, like a bulldozer, pushed nuclear power forward.' Those who advance the 'nuclear village' narrative argue for this government–industry collusion to be broken, so that the country can move forward to a nuclear-free future. In support of this view, a 2013 anti-nuclear protest attracted 60,000 protesters to the Diet in Tokyo. Some of them held up placards that read 'Unevolved Apes Want Nukes!' The group gathered 8 million signatures to a petition denouncing government plans to return to nuclear power.[104]

In contrast, the 'black swans' narrative seizes on the extreme rarity of an event such as 3/11. According to Samuels, there are actually two separate groups pushing this narrative. The *business as usual* crowd emphasizes *soteigai* and thus tries to deflect blame. From this perspective, nobody was to blame, and the country just needs to get back post-haste to nuclear power. In contrast, the *realist* crowd readily acknowledges mistakes made by the nuclear power industry, but argues for a gradual return to a safer variant of nuclear power as a cool-headed and rational policy. This stands in opposition to the emotional response of either totally shunning nuclear power or embracing it uncritically, as was the case in the past, when insufficient safety precautions were in place.

The future of nuclear power has become one of the key issues debated in local elections. In the February 2014 Tokyo gubernatorial race, two of the leading candidates ran on anti-nuclear platforms. Aside from the main leftist candidate, attorney Kenji Ustonomiya, there was also (more surprisingly) Morihoro Hosokawa, a former prime minister. Hosokawa was backed in his campaign by an even more unlikely political figure – charismatic former Prime Minister Junichiro Koizumi of the Liberal Democratic Party (LDP), who, during his time as premier (2001–06), worked in tandem with the pro-nuclear Abe. Hosokawa and Koizumi vigorously campaigned together to try to turn the gubernatorial election into a referendum on the future of nuclear power.[105]

Although Hosokawa and Ustonomiya were defeated by Yoichi Masuzoe – a former health and welfare minister who came out in support of nuclear power and who was backed by the Abe-led LDP – the activism of prominent figures like Koizumi illustrates that opposition to nuclear power has become a mainstream political issue.[106]

Conclusion

An event such as Fukushima has many causes. One of the largest earthquakes in human history, a historically large tsunami, and major design flaws all played their role. While the size of the earthquake and tsunami were not expected, given Japanese history they were certainly not outside the realms of possibility. Taking simple, prudent measures in advance – such as moving diesel generators and other emergency power sources to higher ground on the plant site – could have done much to prevent or contain a meltdown.[107] The too cozy relationship between government and the regulators, made possible by the 'ascents to' and 'descents from Heaven', no doubt helped make possible a myriad of bad decisions that allowed the crisis to occur. The regulators hardly spent any time regulating. By relying on the expertise and opinion of utilities, they promoted special interests – particularly TEPCO's interests – at the expense of the public's. This is the ultimate insider's game, with those on the outside – those who might dare to employ independent expertise and actually do some regulating – prevented from getting in on the act.

Once the accident had occurred, the bureaucracy hindered a fast and effective response. Bureaucratic sabotage caused the delay in sharing the SPEEDI information, preventing Nagadoro residents from evacuating in a timely manner. Nobody in the bureaucracy wanted to be the bearer of 'bad news' of radiation to the public or the prime minister. Also, TEPCO officials were at times overly deferential to what they thought the prime minister *might* want, thus delaying actions that they knew were warranted to manage the crisis (e.g. seawater injection).

That is why, rather than preventing the crisis at Fukushima, Japan's regulatory structure actually contributed to it. The regulators rubber-stamped rather than regulated, and then layers of bureaucratic oversight added red tape to critical response times. The situation is similar to other breakdowns we have seen in Japanese society (think of the Olympus scandal), where a slew of companies have encouraged business practices that covered up shocking mismanagement, and where a web of cooperation and collusion has resulted in major crises.

In the end, the 'nuclear village' and the 'black swan' narratives are not necessarily incompatible. This was a once-in-a-millennium event; yet it was an event that would not have been so catastrophic if it had not been for the collusion of the nuclear village. This suggests that the crisis was, at least in part, 'made in Japan,' but that solutions involving future use of nuclear power can also be 'made in Japan,' *if* more democratic and less corrupt forms of regulation are implemented. That, however, is a big if.

CHAPTER SIX

What We Learned at Lunch

It is 6 a.m. and Kenji, 15 years old, is waking up for school.

He will have a bowl of rice or a piece of toast for breakfast, and he'll find a *bento* (lunch box) prepared by his mother, who rose an hour earlier. He will dress as he always does: in a deep-blue school uniform, its design borrowed from Prussian academies. His school-issued book bag crammed with unfinished homework and his clothes for his sports club, he cycles from his family's apartment to the train station, ready for a half-hour commute.

Kenji lives in Kyushu, where early-morning extracurricular classes are still the norm. His teachers are already there, waiting for him, long before the school day – or their workday – officially begins.

During homeroom, he will meet with his homeroom (form) teacher, Mr. Tanagawa. Kenji will probably spend his three years of high school with the same teacher and the same classmates. Mr. Tanagawa gives him some good-natured ribbing about the length of his hair; if it gets too long, he'll receive a sterner scolding at the uniform and manner inspection later in the week.

His school has six regular periods, with ten-minute breaks in between and 45 minutes for lunch. For the most part, Kenji and his classmates stay in a single room, with the teachers coming to them.

At the start of each class, all 40 of the students stand in unison and bow to the teacher; at the end of class, it's the same. During the class, the students listen attentively, occasionally taking notes and rarely asking questions. However, when a student does not understand a task, he will readily turn to a neighbor and ask for an explanation; this student will explain the task or concept as he or she understands it. A friend asks Kenji if he has understood the third problem; Kenji explains it to him as best he can. The class instructor sees this and doesn't mind; likewise, he knows that Kenji would probably sit in silence if he was asked to give the answer out loud to the class.

Kenji eats lunch in the same room, though he does have the option of using the cafeteria. Sometime around the fifth period, he starts feeling drowsy – a combination of the dense, carbohydrate-laden *bento* and mental exhaustion. A teacher wanders around the room and gently taps the back of his head to wake him up. After the sixth period, Kenji joins in the school-wide cleaning. For 20 minutes the school students scrub the floor with sponges, sweep their classrooms, and clean the windows. In Kenji's school, as in many others, gentle music is broadcast over the loudspeakers during cleaning time.

When they finish, it is 4:15 p.m., the end of the official school day. But Kenji goes to one more lesson, another extracurricular class that meets twice a week. He tries to pay attention, taking notes as the teacher lectures him, but occasionally he dozes.

Despite his exhaustion, Kenji has baseball practice – his role in the team is the defining social aspect of his life, and so he will join the team for a 5km run at 5 p.m.; then catching practice until 6 p.m.; then half an hour of batting practice; and then a practice game until 7 p.m. That is when the students have to leave to go home, because the school closes. The teachers will stay behind with some of them (for guidance or disciplinary reasons), or catch up on paperwork until 9 p.m.

Kenji, however, will head to a nearby cram school for an hour of instruction in passing the university entrance exam. He is at the top of his mid-level high school, but his future is far from certain. With some extra help, he can pass the exam to a mid-level university.

At 9 p.m. Kenji takes his train home, another half-hour commute. He settles into his room to finish his homework assignments, falling asleep at his desk around midnight.

Not every student in Japan is as committed to his studies and sports as Kenji; and not all teachers work until late in the evening. But there are many Japanese like Kenji and his teachers, and the norms of commitment to schooling in Japan are quite different from those in the United States.

A collectivist system

Japan's education system has long been the envy of the world. Some 95 percent of all junior high-school students go on to attend high school; in 2011, 96 percent of high-school students graduated,[1] and nearly three-quarters went on to some kind of post-secondary education. Japan's students and adults score among the highest in the world on many educational measures, with girls doing just as well as boys in science and mathematics. Every year, a greater percentage of students list reading – and discussing books – as a pleasurable activity than in almost any other country.

The Japanese system of primary and secondary education consists of six years of elementary school (6–12), three years of junior high (12–15), and three years of high school (15–18). Elementary (primary) and middle school (junior high school) are compulsory, and everyone follows the same curriculum. High school is voluntary, but 98 percent of 15-year-olds enroll in it.[2] High schools vary in type: about three-quarters of students enroll in general academic high schools, and about a quarter choose specialized schools that focus on subjects such as nursing, home economics, agriculture, or fisheries. Among the general academic high schools there is also a wide range: some are very difficult to get into and cater for students who are seeking to enter elite universities; others are of a more average or basic level.

Students spend most of their time in school. Legions of children in school uniforms can be seen in front of convenience stores late at night, when club activities and extracurricular classes end. As our model student illustrates, students and teachers enjoy a unique relationship that often mirrors, if not replaces, the relationship of the family in the West.

Teachers in Japan are among the hardest-working educators in the world. According to the OECD, they work for 1,883 hours per year, placing them third among the 36 OECD reporting nations.[3] Yet paradoxically, teachers in Japan spend less time actually delivering lessons than in any other OECD country: only 27 percent of those 1,883 hours are actually spent teaching (in the US, the figure is 69 percent). As a result, the total number of teaching hours in Japanese schools is, at 510 hours per teacher per year, 23 percent below the OECD average. The average class size in Japan (32.7) is more than 40 percent larger than in the United States (23.2) or on average in the OECD countries (23.3).

This discrepancy in long working hours vs. low classroom instructional hours is explained by a number of factors. Part of it is due to the role of teachers in Japan: they are expected to take a special interest in the lives of their homeroom students, working with them as a guidance counselor, discipline enforcer, role model, and educator. For example, elementary school teachers spend a fair amount of time supervising their students as they clean up the classroom, sweep the hallway, and serve lunch.

Part of it is also due to the collective attention to detailed instructional planning in Japan. In the United States, teaching is largely viewed as a solitary activity. Teachers' work time, beyond teaching, is thus largely devoted to their individual grading and preparation. However, in Japan, teaching is viewed as a highly cooperative activity. Classroom teachers, especially in grades 1–9, spend a great deal of time on 'lesson study.'[4] In this activity, teachers meet for several hours a week, first to identify a lesson goal to focus on, then to conduct a small number of lessons that explore this goal, and finally to reflect on the process, including by producing written reports.

For example, a group of elementary school teachers, after carefully reviewing their students' work, may decide on a topic such as 'promoting students' ability to think on their own, invent, and learn from each other.'[5] They could then set specific goals to foster this through instruction in mathematics, Japanese language, and even physical education. The teachers could then draw up a three-year plan for working toward these goals, including researching and preparing sample lessons designed to help achieve the goals; teaching the sample lessons in real classrooms, while other teachers look on; coming together to discuss the lessons, based on what was observed; refining the lessons; and then teaching and discussing them again, and issuing final reports. A fascinating and detailed example of this process, with photographs and sample lessons, is provided by Makoto Yoshida. It illustrates how teachers at a Japanese elementary school developed approaches for their students to use tiles, cubes, and other manipulatives to develop both their mathematics and their Japanese language skills.[6]

Japan has a reputation in the US for focusing on rote learning, and that is certainly the case in some subjects. A great deal of time is spent memorizing and practicing the thousands of individual *kanji* (Chinese characters) that students must master to become literate in Japanese, and history is also taught largely by having the students memorize events and dates, rather than through critical analysis. Rote teaching especially plagues English instruction, as is discussed below. However, the teaching of math in Japan is quite conceptual, compared to the United States, where the focus is instead largely on algorithms and procedures – a study has shown that in 96 percent of US math lessons students practice a procedure, compared to only 46 percent of lessons in Japan. By contrast, in only 1 percent of US math lessons do students formulate the procedures themselves, as compared to 44 percent in Japan. Furthermore, none of the video-taped US lessons showed instances of deductive thinking, compared to 61 percent of Japanese lessons.[7] Of course, the fact that so many Japanese students practice their skills and procedures in private schools, after the end of the school day, may free up their math teachers in school to focus more on concepts.

A comparative study of videotaped science lessons found similar cross-national differences, with Japanese instruction focusing far more consistently than science teaching in the US on developing conceptual understanding (through, for example, the use of evaluation of evidence).[8] The teaching of both math and science in Japan achieves much better results than in the United States – at least as reflected in international test results – and activities such as lesson study are among the many factors that contribute to this. Though there certainly are other contributory factors: less poverty in Japan, more total study hours in and out of school, and a greater emphasis on education within the home.

In the United States, classroom instruction – especially in courses such as math and science – is highly stratified, due to ability tracking. That is not the case in the Japanese system: secondary students keep to one desk in their homeroom (form class), which is visited by a different teacher for each subject. Typically, the same students are assigned to a group with a single homeroom teacher, and they then stay together for each subject. So all students have the same schedule.

The homeroom teacher is tasked with making the group dynamic comfortable, as well as with providing instruction in a given subject. The group will eat lunch together, attend school trips together, and serve as a team during class sports matches. An effective homeroom teacher guides the students through any interpersonal spats and mediates in conflicts within the group.

This homeroom tradition is coupled with deliberate social-engineering efforts by the Ministry of Education (MEXT). While it is primarily local and municipal government that funds education, MEXT has managed to impose rigid standards by earmarking grants tied to certain behaviors and outcomes within schools. These strict guidelines give it significant leverage in establishing a national curriculum with little local variation: local schools can choose text-books, for example, but only from a limited range of those approved by MEXT. The same applies to teacher certification processes and daily school activities and courses.

MEXT's goal is full equality for students within the system, regardless of income or geography – even if it means that Japan has historically had one of the lowest ratings for school autonomy in the world.[9] But MEXT is also tasked with molding students into an image reflecting the desired national character. To this end, its 'Student Guidance Outline' (*Seito shido teiyo*) offers instructions for teachers to 'develop practical and healthy attitudes' among students, through classroom and extracurricular activities.[10] One example is the school lunch program.

It's more than just a lunch

School lunch in Japan provides an excellent case study into how Japan views education: not merely as a tool for training future Japanese workers, but also as a tool for teaching Japanese values and culture. MEXT's goals for school lunch include the following four principles:[11]

1. To foster proper understanding of food and desirable eating habits.
2. To foster pleasant social habits and contribute to the enjoyment of school life.
3. To improve physical health and nutrition.
4. To foster and guide a correct knowledge of production, consumption, and distribution of food.

These principles are outlined in great detail, and include specific points such as 'to learn the correct way to hold, align (or lay out) dining ware; to follow the proper posture (sitting and eating) and master basic manners when eating,' and 'To deepen human relations while dining.' The guidelines note that 'students should not have any picky habits and also understand the importance of chewing one's food properly.' The government also mandates that students develop the skills to 'cheerfully and peacefully' promote conversation during mealtime.[12] These principles are based on the Basic Act on Food Education 2005, which seeks to promote *shokuiku* (food education) and teach not only nutrition and health, but also the importance of Japanese traditional food and good citizen behavior/civic values.[13]

A typical lunch period in elementary or middle school is an exercise in student responsibility and interdependence. Every pupil must perform some kind of lunch duty on a rotating basis. A 'lunch committee' is assigned to collect meals from the school kitchen or a special wagon in the hallway, while other students stay behind to tidy and prepare the classroom. Desks are placed together and cleaned, the floor is swept, and utensils handed around. The committee returns with the lunch trays and ladles out soup, with teachers stressing proper portion control. Once the meals are served, every student is silent until it is time to eat, marked by the student committee's cry of *Itadakimasu!* (literally, 'I humbly receive'; figuratively, *bon appétit*).

Elementary school students are encouraged (but not generally pressured) to eat everything that is served to them. This tendency has come under considerable scrutiny in the wake of the death of students with food allergies, and now it seems only the strictest teachers enforce it.[14] Nevertheless, it is the social norm to finish all that is on one's plate – and to eat up, as any delay may postpone the students' entrance into recess periods.

Japanese students are thus taught how to eat; but that is just a small part of a national cultural consciousness instilled into students about food. They are also likely to receive lectures on the origins of the food. For example, if students in Kyushu eat *dojo* (an eel-like fish) with their lunch, they may be told about Yanagawa City, which is known for that fish. They may also be exposed to international cultures through being served, and hearing explanations about, foreign foods, albeit typically prepared in a somewhat 'Japanized' style.

Students in elementary school also encounter a tradition that will stay with them throughout their teenage years: cleaning time. They are required to organize the cleaning of their classrooms after lunch, after school, or sometimes both. This teaches a mixture of self-reliance and interdependence, as again, any dawdling by any member of the class has severe repercussions (postponed club activities, for example).[15]

Moral education to develop nationally valued character traits is widespread in Japanese compulsory education, and not merely in the lunchroom: it permeates Japanese education – often literally, as many schools deliberately throw open windows in winter to encourage perseverance through hardship. MEXT's guidelines promote team-building, group work, and other ethical and moral components.

This moral education forms part of the unique relationship between student and teacher in Japan. In some cases, when a mis-behaving student is caught by the police, they will notify the home-room teacher of the school, rather than the parents. Schools regularly send homeroom teachers to visit parents at home, thus extending the role of the teacher into areas traditionally reserved elsewhere for social workers. This relationship is also said to drive some of the educational outcomes of Japanese schools: students are not necessarily entertained in class, and nor do they speak out; but because of their personal connection with their teachers, as well as their goal of preparing well for high school and college entrance exams, they are motivated to perform and engage with the ideas the teacher presents.

With this national directive focused early in the educational process, students leave their compulsory education for high school, which can often be a big change. In high schools that are oriented toward preparation for college, there is strong pressure to achieve academically, and students must find a balance between personal success and the support of their peers.

School spirit, school bullies

In high school, the educational drive for unity shifts toward an individual focus on achievement. Nonetheless, group unity is encouraged, and enormous time is set aside for sports days or culture days and/or class matches. These events are designed to forge the character of the students, no less so than the school lunches described above.

Preparation for a sports day event at a high school on Kyushu, for example, has students spending hours a day learning how to form human pyramids. The students are assigned tasks within the group, based on their abilities – from the kids at the bottom of the pyramid to the leader, who orchestrates the event for the public. The students work in the heat for a week or more to learn to perform these acrobatic feats, which will be displayed once and then forgotten.

Sports days encourage group formation and a strong sense of finding one's place within the hierarchy of the school, a model lesson for a broader socialization within society. Students usually know their place by the time they start at high school, having passed or failed various entrance exams since middle school to end up where they are.

Other tasks left to the students include, once again, the school cleaning time – a period of about 20 minutes, during which students are assigned tasks such as rubbish disposal, mopping and sponging the floors, and cleaning the toilets. This is also character development, encouraging pride in the school and personal responsibility for its appearance.

In every case, the school's central social unit, the homeroom, is required to participate fully. Individual students within the group are required to set aside their own lack of interest to make sure the group succeeds at its task – be that cleaning the school's toilets or building a human pyramid in the blazing summer heat.

School uniforms are another source of group cohesion and identity. Not only are secondary students required to wear uniforms, but many schools have strict rules on hair styles, brands of socks, or the wearing of makeup. Schools may send photographs of students home to parents with descriptions of acceptable hair styles, noting even the degree at which a girl's ponytail can be angled. Frequent uniform checks are conducted to ensure that students follow the rules.

There is no doubt that decades of this kind of character building have had a positive impact on modern Japan. The product of this education system was particularly visible in the aftermath of the triple disasters of 2011, when the world's media reported – not without some shock – stranded victims waiting patiently in the debris, or the famed 'Fukushima 50' who remained working in the failed and highly radioactive Fukushima nuclear power plant at great risk to their personal health (see chapter 5).[16] Even at the national level, the reaction was marked by communal sacrifice, including self-imposed blackouts to reduce the need for controlled power outages by overstressed power plants.[17]

Japan enjoys one of the lowest homicide and assault rates in the developed world. The National Police Agency actually keeps records of how many juveniles received 'police guidance' for underage smoking (roughly 600,000 in 2006).[18] Social behavior outside school is also controlled by school uniform, which marks out any student engaging not only in illegal behavior, but in anything approaching rowdiness. A typical complaint to a school is that students on trains hang from the passenger grips of the subway car; some schools even receive reports if a student is walking while distractedly texting.

But the emphasis on group harmony in school events and class-rooms has a dark side. In 2012, nearly 70,000 cases of bullying were reported in Japan, and legal cases arose from almost 4,000 of those incidents, according to the legal affairs bureau. In 2013, the national police noted that the number of police investigations, while still small, had nearly doubled over the previous year, and was at its highest for 25 years: 511 students had been arrested or taken into custody for actions related to bullying.[19]

Bullying has a hold on the Japanese imagination, but it is hard to know exactly how large the problem is, relative to other countries, as there is no internationally accepted definition of bullying, nor any single standard for reporting it.[20] Japan is not necessarily creating an epidemic of victims; it may be that there is an epidemic of bullies.

Japanese bullying takes a different form from its Western counter-part, because it follows the group-cohesion emphasis of the Japanese education system. Bullying is translated as *ijime* in Japanese, but *ijime* implies a group dynamic – some 80 percent of violence in these inci-dents is collective.[21]

For example, one student was ridiculed and tortured for months by a group of bullies who 'pantsed' and beat him, pressured him to shop-lift for them, forced him to eat dead bees, and even made him 'prac-tice' committing suicide. That student, 13 years old, killed himself, sparking huge national concern over the way the affair had been handled. Teachers had been alerted, but the students concerned had received only verbal warnings, and some teachers even reportedly laughed as the bullies tried to choke the victim.[22] In another case – one that dates from much earlier, but that still resonates today – a student who had been badly bullied for months came to class to find the desks transformed into memorials, with incense and condolence cards mocking him, as if he were already dead. One of the cards had been signed by four of the student's teachers, including his 57-year-old homeroom teacher. The student committed suicide two months later.[23]

A *Mainichi Shimbun* survey found that 70 percent of teachers simply did not have time to address bullying, which accounts for the lack of school response.[24] However, many teachers are worried about losing control of the class, where the relationship between students and teacher is the top priority. They are often evaluated on the basis of their classroom management skills, and reports of bullying can harm a teacher's long-term prospects.[25]

The structure of education in Japan – with its group emphasis, large classrooms, and uniformity – sometimes fosters a culture that silences outlying members. In the words of one Japanese researcher, schools are 'untouchable communities,' where students are 'forced to follow the pack, to think the way everyone else is thinking.'[26]

Some well-intentioned teachers worry that identifying a situation as bullying can damage the victim's ability to adjust to the situation. Telling a student he is being bullied undermines a crucial defense mechanism of denial – a denial that also maintains harmony in the classroom – so the belief goes. If everyone assumes that everyone is OK with the joke, nobody feels uncomfortable.

Generally, behavioral problems in Japanese schools are dealt with by finding group consensus in the homeroom. If a student misbehaves, there is a class discussion during homeroom, with the student present, to talk about how to resolve the problem. This reinforces the social cost of poor behavior. It usually works: students are addressed in a way that is part condemnation and part earnest effort to help them tackle the 'problem' at the root of the behavior. This leads to a tremendous sense of personal accountability in Japan, which carries through into adulthood – precisely the goal of MEXT's interest in character education.

It all starts in pre-school, where children who seem a bit 'cranky' are often made to feel different from those that are happy: a pre-school teacher may ignore a sad child, hoping that the indirect pressure of the group will encourage him to come back to play; or the teacher may even point him out as 'strange' and 'peculiar' in order to ramp up the social pressure for conformity.[27]

High-school students interviewed about bullying see it as a necessary tool to force students to adapt to social norms. Here is one exchange with a researcher, Tamaki Mino:

> **Akiko:** We tried to talk to the person being isolated when our teacher told us to do so. But she didn't really respond to us. If she could be a bit more cooperative, like try to join in or talk to us, then I think things can get better.
>
> **Tamaki:** You mean, she won't be bullied if she changes her attitude?
>
> **Akiko:** Yes, because that's why she is being rejected . . . actually it's like she is rejecting being with us. If she wants to be a part, she's got to change herself.[28]

The persistence of bullying in Japan has continued to gather national and even international attention. Legislation that calls for zero tolerance of bullying came into force in Japan in September 2013, though exactly how it will be implemented is unclear.[29] In addition, a national task force has developed a proposal to include moral education as an official required subject, again with a major goal of tackling bullying.[30] Finally, at the suggestion of Japanese music producer Kosaku Yamada, American folk musician Peter Yarrow (of Peter, Paul, and Mary fame) wrote and produced an anti-bullying song and album, 'Never Give Up,' that draws on the words of the Dalai Lama. He traveled to Japan in November 2013 to release the album and publicly perform songs from the record.[31]

Testing, testing

At the high-school level, each school typically runs two types of entrance tests. One is a simplified exam, geared specifically to students who have been recommended to the school; it often consists of an essay and an interview. These students are usually the top performers in their junior high, or have personalities well suited to specific high-school cultures. The other type is the general entrance exam, which is sat by students across the prefecture on the same day once a year. Students decide which school they want to attend, and then take the exam at that location, where the local staff of teachers grades it.

The entire process is very secretive. Teachers are not allowed to leave the building while grading of the general exam is going on, and cell phones and internet communications may be restricted. Any discrepancy in start time or even in the order of test administration can have major repercussions for the school and students – up to and including having the results declared null and void. The goal is to ensure that every student takes the same test with as little variation as possible, in order to guarantee a level playing field for everyone.

If students achieve the score a school sets – a selective high school might set the bar at 80 percent – they may be allowed to enter that school, or they may have to move on to another round of selection, such as an interview test, a sports or performance exam, or some other specialized school exam.

The reputation of the best high schools hinges on how many graduates go on to their preferred university: the schools and even the media tout how many of their leavers are admitted to the University of Tokyo and other elite colleges. So the most powerful force in shaping the curriculum for high schools is actually the next round of gatekeepers: those who design and score the university entrance exams. But testing anxiety starts considerably earlier, as junior high schools are in turn keen to prepare their pupils to pass the tests offered by the more exclusive high schools in the area. Thus even junior high-school students feel the trickle-down impact of the university entrance exam.

With up to three students competing for each desk in the first-year homeroom of a high school, many students end up taking the entrance test at a school that refuses them. These students are in a bind: they cannot take the test at another school, or transfer their results, because schools administer and determine intake in the same two-day span. Those students who do not succeed in getting into the public school of their choice thus often have to go to private schools, which are both more expensive and of lower quality.

The final 'exam hell' is the one that rewards talented high-school students: Japan's basic university entrance exam – the Center Test – is administered on a single day in spring, at a cost to each candidate of 12,000 to 18,000 yen ($120 to $180). The Center Test is mostly multiple choice, and covers Japanese, mathematics, science (three branches, from which students choose one or two), a foreign language (frequently English, Korean, or Chinese) and social studies (six subjects, from which students again choose one or two). The Center Test is offered just once a year. Most selective universities then set their own entrance examination a month after the Center Test, specialized by department.

For decades, the media have cheered or lambasted the entrance exam process as a national event. It is filled with pomp and ritual: thousands of students descend into shrines and temples to receive special pencils, and line up for blocks around the universities. Meanwhile the media report on the stress experienced by the candidates and on the competition. But things have changed in Japan. While top scores are still needed to secure a place at an elite university, demographic changes mean there is now less competition for slots at non-elite schools.[32] As Japan's student population has fallen, so colleges have relaxed their standards and now select from a smaller pool of applicants to fill the same number of places. A 2008 survey by the Promotion and Mutual Aid Corporation for Private Schools of Japan found that nearly half of the 565 private universities surveyed had so few applicants that they could not reach their desired student quotas. Today, 90 percent of students who apply end up in some form of tertiary education. In fact, a larger proportion of students than ever is enrolling in universities, whose quotas have not changed since the 1990s. Rather than cut departments or teachers, the colleges have simply widened the net for entrants – a trend particularly noticeable at mid- to low-level universities. Kotoro Takahashi, a MEXT official, admitted in 2012 that while the population of 18-year-olds had plunged to 1.2 million (from 2 million in 1991), the number of first-year students accepted by universities had remained the same for 20 years, at 500,000 to 600,000.[33] This decline in the university applicant pool has led to widespread hand-wringing about declining test scores.

Those who fail to get a place at their top-choice college generally spend a year cramming, so that they can try again the following year; these are the so-called *ronin* – a name once given to rogue samurai, but now applied to rogue examinees. However, the *ronin* are not really rejected students: they could easily attend another college, but they elect to spend an extra year preparing to retake the exam so that they can go to their first choice.

'Exam hell' may seem like a confounding ritual to outside observers; but it remains entrenched in Japan for a number of reasons – not least because it has reinforced a cultural belief that success rewards hard work, rather than good luck or innate intelligence. This *growth mindset* (as it is known by psychologists) is much more conducive to success than the *fixed mindset* that unmalleable traits (such as intelligence or talent) determine life's outcomes.[34]

These high-stakes tests also reinforce the lesson that a student's results are the product of his or her community's support: the students take the test, but they are supported by a network of family, friends, teachers, and private tutors. This creates a collective expectation of success, which drives students to perform. The focus on hard work and perseverance is built into the Japanese education system at every turn, with tests and exams becoming 'teachable moments' about the triumph of perseverance over adversity. As with many rites of passage, the exam system is accepted not so much out of tradition and a stubborn reliance on old methods, but rather because of its usefulness in teaching broader lessons about the traits that are valued within Japanese society – a natural extension of the Japanese educational system's moral training.

Cramming into the night

There is an inbuilt contradiction in all of this: students share homerooms for years, but they must also compete with one another to enter the top universities. This conflict is at odds with the social emphasis of middle and high school. Japanese students are often left struggling to reconcile these competing instincts – to enter a university, not only do they need the top scores from their school, but they also need to win speech or science contests, gain math awards, or secure places as student leaders. This focus on the individual is what drives the cram school, or *juku*, industry.

With the egalitarian norms espoused by MEXT often at variance with the intense competition for student achievement, parents worry that their children lack the advantages they need to secure a place at a top university or high school. With teachers hesitant to provide extra advantages to gifted students within their own school, a niche industry has emerged: there are now up to 50,000 cram schools throughout Japan, catering to almost 2 million students.

These are private, after-school (often late-night) classes geared toward the materials and strategies that are useful for entrance exams. There is a mock exam (at both the junior-high and the high-school level) so that students can get a better idea of the school/college they are most likely to get into. Such cram schools are widespread in other Asian countries, too, most notably in Korea.

Japanese students might attend *juku* between one and five evenings a week, often until 9 p.m. It is common to find pupils asleep in class at school: the schedule of club activities, extracurricular classes, *juku*, and homework sadly foreshadows the exhausting work life that lies ahead of most students.

Cram schools range from national chains that have huge advertising budgets and whose premises are located in shopping malls and office buildings, to the basements of local residents, whose businesses are sustained exclusively by the recommendations of former students. These schools registered a boom just at the same time as Japan did. They rose in popularity throughout the 1970s, as many left-wing campus protesters of the 1960s found themselves dogged by background checks in their search for a career. Coming from top universities, many of them became tutors and (later) *juku* operators. Today, 21 *juku* conglomerates are big enough to trade on the stock exchange.

In 2007, nearly a quarter of primary-school and half of middle-school students were enrolled in a cram school.[35] The typical cost can be as high as 40,000 yen ($400) a month, which contrasts sharply with MEXT's ideals of a level playing field, where students are free to achieve on the basis of skill, rather than economic background. Parents who earn a good salary can more easily afford to send their children regularly to these cram schools than can parents who may struggle even to pay for a private high school.

According to a 2008 MEXT survey of parents and children, many parents (39 percent) see *juku* as a way of helping their children review their school lessons, while 23 percent see it as a way of preparing specifically for exams.[36] Twice as much is spent on middle-school students as on primary-school students: 43 percent of the parents of middle-school-aged children see *juku* as extra preparation for the high-school entrance exams, and nearly a quarter expressed the fear that middle school alone 'could not adequately prepare students for school entrance exams.' Most of these middle-school students – 88 percent – take English classes at *juku*, possibly to supplement the substandard English taught at schools (see below). Math was the second most common course.

In the exam crush, however, one benefit of *juku* is often overlooked: a third of parents send their children to cram schools because they do not trust their children to study of their own accord. In essence, *juku* forces the students to finish their regular homework. Parents reported that they sent their middle-school children to cram schools because they have trouble studying alone (33 percent) or at home (32 percent).[37]

Despite their reputation abroad as 'sweat shops of education,' nearly half of the students surveyed said they liked *juku*, particularly because of the smaller class sizes (sometimes even individual tuition), because they received more attention from the teachers (who were also easier to understand), and because the classes covered topics that are not covered in the compulsory education.[38] Among the students who did not like *juku*, the quality of the instruction barely registered as a factor – the leading problem (cited by 70 percent) was that they were too exhausted afterwards.

Are the classes effective? Surveys indicate that they are: on average, students perform 25 percentage points better in tests when spending on *juku* tops 50,000 yen per month ($500). Unfortunately, only 5 percent of households that earn less than 2 million yen ($20,000) a year spend even 20,000 yen ($200) per month – a statistic that sends the egalitarianism of MEXT into a tailspin.

While *juku* seem to be dedicated to the individualistic side of the Japanese drive to achieve, the schools also reflect a broader lack of egalitarianism – one that has many educators and politicians worried about low-income students and the potential achievement gap. *Juku* are widespread, but they are not universal: attendance ranges from 39 percent of public elementary pupils to 75 percent of public middle-school students and 38 percent of public high-school students, according to a 2002 survey.[39]

For example, in contrast to Kenji, the student from a middle-class family whom we met at the beginning of this chapter, let us consider another boy, Yusuke, who lives in the same city, but whose father is a short-term manual laborer working on construction projects. His family's finances limited his opportunities for exam preparation, and he was unable to gain admission to a good public high school, so his parents instead enrolled him in a private school. His father has spells of unemployment, and so, to help out financially, Yusuke works some 15 hours a week after school at a convenience store. This is against school rules, but Yusuke works in secret; most of his earnings go on school fees, uniform, textbooks, and supplies. His after-school work prevents Yusuke from attending cram school (which further limits his future educational opportunities) and from participating in any sports or culture clubs (which limits his social acceptance).

Yusuke is far from alone. Though Japan has far less income or educational inequality than the US, pupils from low-income families still suffer educational disadvantages.[40] Whereas students from families with an income of less than $40,000 per year are as likely to embark on a four-year university course as they are to join the workforce straight from school, those from families with an income of more than $100,000 per year are 11 times as likely to go to university as they are to join the labor market.[41] University graduates, in turn, are more likely to be offered regular employment than are high-school graduates; they then earn higher incomes, and so can send their own children to *juku*.

MEXT has taken steps to address the economic inequalities in education. In 2010, the government made public high-school tuition free and began offering subsidies of between 118,800 yen and 237,600 yen ($1,188 to $2,376) per family, depending on household income, to assist with the cost of tuition at private schools.[42] This all helps, but it does nothing to cover the cost of cram school.

Also in the interests of equity, MEXT frequently rotates teachers, so as to ensure that the best ones are not concentrated in high-performing schools. Each March, just two weeks before the start of the new school year, some teachers from each school are randomly reassigned to other schools within the prefecture. For teachers, it is stressful – not only because of the change in commute and routine, but also because they have a close bond with the students: many homeroom teachers are responsible for the same 30 to 40 students for all three years of their high-school education. Though the system has many downsides, it does avoid the problem found in the United States, where low-performing schools have difficulty in attracting talented staff.

Measuring up to the world

Whatever the strengths and weaknesses of its school system, Japan has achieved outstanding results. It pays a great deal of attention to how it performs on international tests. An earlier effort at reform called *yutori kyoiku* (relaxed education), which sought to ease the pressure on Japanese youth by cutting school hours and reducing the curricular content to be covered, fell out of favor when Japan dropped a few places in the international rankings.[43]

Recent test score results give Japan much to be proud of. On the most recent versions of the Program for International Student Assessment (PISA), Japan showed solid gains in all areas. In fact, excluding scores for individual cities or city-states (e.g. Shanghai, Hong Kong, Singapore), Japanese students performed best in the world in science and reading, and second best (after South Korea) in math.[44] Along the same lines, a recent OECD survey of adult literacy skills shows that Japan has the highest rates of adult literacy and numeracy of all the developed countries.[45] These studies confirm that, according to these important measures, Japan has arguably the best educational system in the world.

Yet, in spite of its high test scores, in recent decades Japan has floundered economically, compared to other East Asian countries such as China, Korea, and Singapore. There are many reasons for this, of course, but some of them stem from weaknesses in the Japanese education system – particularly in regards to English and technology.

'Bangup Maxpower It's a Wide World!'

There is a small niche group of internet fanatics who eagerly share evidence of 'Engrish,' cases of poorly worded malapropisms or totally incomprehensible English, boldly emblazoned across Japanese products or worn with pride on T-shirts and handbags. Products with strange or even politically incorrect names reach a level of popularity incomprehensible to English native speakers: a milk tea product called 'Pungency,' a canned coffee called 'Black Boss,' T-shirts with curse words. One need not be an 'Engrish' cultist to appreciate T-shirt slogans like these, to be found on any Tokyo street:

'LACKED HAVE TO LIFE IN ME WHEN SUCH A THING'
'LOOK FOR LOVE BY THE GROPING'
'THE GOD OF SURFING HAS GOTTEN OFF IN ME'
'BANGUP MAXPOWER IT'S A WIDE WORLD!'

The joke, as it plays out on forums of native English speakers, is that the Japanese can't speak English, and are fooled into buying absurd products out of some naïve desire to indulge in foreign cultural goods. The irony, of course, also extends to the legion of Westerners who wear tattoos of *kanji* symbols with incomprehensible meanings. However, the joke stings more in Japan, because of its notorious struggles with teaching and learning the English language.

Despite Japan's top test scores in other subjects, English has remained an embarrassing topic. In 2012, the Educational Testing Service (which creates and administers the international Test of English as a Foreign Language, or TOEFL), ranked Japan second from bottom of the Asian countries, just ahead of Cambodia.[46] In the oral section of the TOEFL test, Japan ranked second from bottom *in the entire world*. On the one hand, such comparisons are rather unfair on Japan, since a broader section of its population takes the TOEFL test than in many other countries. At the same time, they are indicative of the general low level of English in the country, and will come as no surprise to anyone who has tried to ask directions in English in a Japanese city, even within earshot of a major university or financial center. As a British professor in Kyoto put it, English remains for most Japanese an 'alien' language, suitable for fashion decoration but not for functional communication.[47]

The reasons for substandard English learning in Japan are complex, with linguistic, cultural, and pedagogical factors all playing a role. The substantial linguistic differences between Japanese and English are important, but the problem is not insurmountable, as is evidenced by the comparatively better performance in English of nations such as China and South Korea. Many Japanese teachers of English have limited expertise in the language, which thus contributes to a vicious cycle: without good English teachers, Japanese students cannot learn English well, and the next generation of English teachers is thus similarly underprepared.

The exam-driven nature of Japanese education is certainly a major factor as well. As with much of the education system, university exam preparation weighs heavily on teachers and students, and remains extremely influential in the sphere of English language education. This means that teachers focus their energy on the kind of language that appears in the exams.

Examination English, being a product of the academic environment, tends to be mired in the bizarre world of academic writing and jargon. This creates a very tall order for a non-native speaker. Consider this passage, from the Kurume University Medical School entrance examination. The first half is provided to the student – typically a 17-year-old high-school student whose native language is Japanese. The words below the passage must be rearranged to form the missing portion of the sentence:

In recent years, theories of paradoxical consequences have been strongly influenced by game theory, which indeed is . . . an hour.

a) its name
b) while
c) away many
d) often true to
e) in providing puzzles
f) enough to
g) intriguing

The answer? 'In recent years, theories of paradoxical consequences have been strongly influenced by game theory, which indeed is often true to its name in providing puzzles intriguing enough to while away many an hour' (d, a, e, g, f, b, c).

This sentence strikes many English teachers (and native speakers) as clumsy, stilted, and unlike anything people ever write or say. Its stilted nature, however, is par for the course in English sample essays and materials in Japan. The examination is designed to determine which future medical students will be best positioned to read and write for international academic journals. The burden then shifts down to the English instructors at secondary schools to prepare students to answer this kind of odd question, and this comes at the expense of communication skills. In spite of regulations from MEXT to the contrary, most English lessons in Japanese schools are taught in Japanese and focus on narrow and stilted points of grammar and vocabulary. Typical lessons discuss points such as:

- the difference between 'I will' and 'I shall'
- the difference between 'until the rain stops' and 'until the rain will stop'
- the difference between 'he is a tall man' and 'what a tall man he is'
- the differences between lie-lay-lain and lay-laid-laid.

Some of these are technically valid points to learn in English, but still they are relatively unimportant (how many native speakers of

English can correctly conjugate and distinguish 'lie' and 'lay'?). Others are absurdities (does anyone ever say 'until the rain will stop'?). None are really important in a country where few secondary students can understand and answer simply questions such as 'Where are you from?' or 'How old are you?' Instead of teaching students how to communicate in English using these (and other) important terms, phrases, and sentences –through things like pair work, group work dialogues, songs, video, and conversation – class time in Japan is devoted to the most tedious explanation in Japanese of these linguistic points, and grammatically transposing sentences – for example, from 'I happened to see her in the train yesterday' to 'it was in the train that I happened to see her yesterday.'

Japanese classroom instruction in some subjects relies on asking students to follow precise steps in a prescribed order. This is certainly the case with *kanji*, the Chinese characters used in writing Japanese, where each character is assigned a precise stroke order. This practice of discrete steps extends into various situations in school, from athletics to the aforementioned human-pyramid building during sports day. *Kyudo*, or archery training, for example, depends on practicing individual steps – students might practice how to walk up to the bow for months, before moving on to holding it. Likewise, tea ceremony, calligraphy, origami, and other traditional arts emphasized in schools require a careful attention to small detail and instructions carried out in a precise order.

Unfortunately, this methodology is often carried into English language education as well, with simple sentences being drawn on blackboards with all the markings of a complicated theorem. English is taught not as a means to a communicative end, but as a series of rules, with endless exceptions that must be memorized and followed through. As a result, students struggle with active communication, because they are trying to construct a sentence using the discrete building blocks of language, rather than striving to be understood. The sentence 'Dog is walking across the street' would likely be marked fully wrong by many Japanese English teachers, simply because the 'A' is missing before 'dog'. Students therefore become conditioned to strive for perfect sentences at the expense of communication, rather than forming an imperfect sentence. One American teacher complained that teaching English in an environment so unreceptive to authentic communication was 'like planting seeds in concrete.'[48] Another long-term foreign teacher became so frustrated with the influence of bad English tests on instruction that he wrote a novel about it called *The Tale That Wags*.[49]

Pedagogical problems intersect with broad sociocultural factors, including the relative ethnic and linguistic homogeneity of the country, Japan's isolation as an island nation, and social norms against speaking up or sticking out. For all of these reasons, Japanese young people are very risk-averse when it comes to trying out and learning foreign languages: they appear much less motivated than young people in Europe (or even other Asian countries) to try to use English in authentic communication, no matter how many hours a week they work on memorizing odd phrases for exams. Lack of motivation to learn English (as well as fear of losing out within the rigid Japanese educational and hiring system – see chapter 1) is also reflected in the small and decreasing number of Japanese who study abroad.

Problems with English teaching are widely recognized in Japan, and the government has taken a number of steps to try to address these, including through reform of college entrance English language exams. This has proved a knotty problem. The national Center Test discussed earlier is designed centrally and has gradually been improved, following input from experts in language teaching and testing. However, scores of private colleges throughout the country also offer their own entrance exams (and thus their own English tests), and they often have little incentive or expertise to change them. And sometimes when colleges have attempted to do so, they have encountered resistance from local schools and *juku* that are used to the old system. Inertia wins out, the exams stay, and language instruction suffers.

The Abe government has been emphasizing educational reform, especially in the area of English language teaching, to try to make the Japanese more competitive in the global marketplace. As part of that effort, a Liberal Democratic Party advisory panel has now called for the international TOEFL test to be mandatory for entrance exams to public universities.[50] If this change were to be made, it could have a positive long-term impact, as TOEFL is more geared to real-life communication skills than are the current English language entrance exams in Japan. However, the proposal has had a mixed reception, with some arguing that the test is so difficult for most Japanese that it would have little use as a mechanism for ranking college applicants.[51] It is also unclear whether private universities would follow the lead in such an initiative.

Abe has also called for a tripling of funding for the Japanese Exchange and Teaching (JET) Programme, which brings several thousand native English speakers from the US, UK, Australia and elsewhere to teach in classrooms alongside native Japanese teachers, as 'assistant language teachers.' The JET programme has been widely criticized in Japan, on account of both its cost and its limited effectiveness. Some teachers in the program complain that they are little more than 'human tape players,' simply mouthing English expressions without an opportunity to teach communication. Nevertheless the JET assistant language teachers are often the only teachers in a school who can hold an unstilted English conversation, and the Abe government hopes that they can contribute to improved English communication skills.

Aside from government investment in English education, a push from the private sector to incentivize English has been gathering some steam (and some resistance). The online retailer Rakuten announced in 2010 that any corporate officer who was not proficient in English would be replaced.[52] The company immediately switched its cafeteria menu to English and announced that English would be the mandatory language for executive meetings and internal memos.

Work time was set aside for poor speakers to study, and employees are given longer to prepare English-language versions of internal documents. Rakuten, being an online business, adopted the measure as a way of becoming a true online retailer with an online culture, speaking the language of the web rather than limiting itself to the Japanese market. An English-language culture could appeal to talented marketing executives in the 27 countries to which Rakuten hopes to expand by the end of the decade. Uniqlo, a casual clothing store that has been aggressively expanding overseas, has similarly embraced the idea of holding meetings in English.

This kind of corporate shift, if adopted with even half the zeal of Rakuten, could pressure the universities to change their approach to English in the entrance exam, perhaps shifting the focus from parsing academic jargon, and instead emphasizing a more dynamic, communicative approach that would be useful in conducting business meetings with international partners.

Fax to the future – Japan's technological weakness

With its obsession with mobile phones, its huge video screens blasting out at intersections, and its successful robotics industry, Japan is viewed as a world leader in new technologies. However, in many ways it is losing its competitive edge. Today's centers of digital innovation are to be found in Silicon Valley, Sweden, Tel Aviv, and Seoul rather than in Tokyo. Even the once-proud Sony lost some $6.4 billion in the fiscal year ending 31 March 2012 and has a market value now just one-ninth that of Samsung, and less than one-twentieth that of Apple.

Those seeking the roots of Japan's demise as a tech leader might start by examining its schools. Unlike Korea, Singapore, and the United States, each of which has large numbers of computers (and increasingly iPads, Samsung Galaxies, or other tablets) in schools and active policy debates on the role of educational technology, computers are rarely found in Japanese classrooms and are seldom discussed. A typical Japanese school simply has one computer laboratory, where secondary students may go a few times a week for a technology lesson, which will focus on how to use basic office software. Teachers may or may not have a computer in their office, and for many schools, tight email security rules encourage a heavy reliance on outdated fax machines for inter-office communications.

As for the classroom, though, nary a computer is to be found, either for teacher presentations, teacher record keeping, or any kind of student work or integration into the curriculum. Questions addressed to math, science, history, Japanese, or English teachers in Japan about the role of technology will typically result in a confused look and a suggestion that the questioner should seek out the computer teacher, who is the only one able to answer the question. Indeed, questions to principals on the same topic receive a similar response.

Some observers will probably say 'good for Japan!', believing that schools should focus on the basics rather than on high-tech tools. However, the limited use of technology in Japanese schools has contributed to low levels of technology skills among Japanese adults – especially young adults, as evidenced by the OECD study mentioned above. Some 12.9 percent of Japanese young people aged 16–24 declined to use the computer in the testing, the highest percentage in the OECD. And of young Japanese adults who took the technology skills test, 10.5 percent had a failing score, more than twice the rate of any other OECD country.[53] Thus nearly a quarter of young adults were unable to demonstrate even the most basic familiarity with computers. Consistent with this, adults in Japan (aged 16–54) use technology both at home and at work less than in any other OECD country.[54] This, in turn, undoubtedly contributes to the country's low level of productivity – only two-thirds that of the United States and well under the OECD average.[55] Limited technological ability also reinforces and amplifies the deficiencies in English, since the global use of online communications is invaluable both for mastering English and for deploying it to business and scholarly ends.

Of course, the relationship between educational technology in schools and the use of technology by adults goes both ways: not only does lack of technology in schools result in low adult skills, but lack of knowledge of technology among adults – including educators – influences educational technology policies and practices. Finally, limited technology in the workplace reduces the market demand for these skills. Moreover, while Japan has maintained its 1950s'-style classroom organization, other Asian countries, such as Korea and Singapore, have leveraged greater integration of technology in schools (and indeed industry) in successful pursuit of their economic goals.

As with English language reform, the improved use of technology in instruction is strongly supported by the Abe government. Yet the social and cultural norms of the Japanese educational system – norms that emphasize order, discipline, tradition, and moral character – run counter to this. Taking that into account – and bearing in mind the limited skills on display among teachers and administrators across the country, their attitude toward the use of technology in education, and their knowledge of it – it will likely be a long time before the effort pays off.

Higher(?) education

The hectic life of the typical secondary student in Japan – filled as it is with a long day of studies at school and then *juku* in a frantic attempt to prepare for the life-altering college entrance exam – gives way to a much more relaxed experience of higher education. Japanese students have a reputation for coasting through college, since so much of their future is determined not by what they do at university, but by which university they go to.

One foreign scholar, Brian McVeigh, went so far as to write a book called *Japanese Higher Education as a Myth*, in which he pondered why so many students 'pretend-study' and so many faculty 'pretend-teach.'[56] Few Japanese would use these terms, but most would agree with the basic premise that Japanese higher education is seriously lacking in quality. A Japanese scholar, citing surveys which show that three-quarters of Japanese college students spend less than three hours per week on homework or study, concluded that 'Japanese universities have become places in which no learning goes on outside the classroom.'[57] Other recent reports suggest that little learning goes on *inside* the classroom either. Japanese students welcome their university years, which have been called a 'time-out between entrance exams and employment.' As one female freshman explained, 'The purpose of Japan's *daigaku* [university] is to sell time to young people.'[58]

Kariya Takehiko, a professor at Oxford University and a pre-eminent international scholar on the sociology of Japanese education, suggests that the problem of low quality stems from broad structural problems in Japanese higher education.[59] Basically, in trying to rapidly expand Japanese higher education in the postwar era, the country faced a 'trilemma' between maintaining high standards, expanding access in order to equalize opportunity, and keeping the fiscal burden on the state sustainable. By encouraging the growth of affordable private universities, Japan was able to meet the second and third conditions of this trilemma, while failing at the first. Nearly 90 percent of Japan's colleges and universities are private, and, with little state funding, they are forced to compete for students in order to remain in business.[60] This creates a fast-food type of educational experience, with large lecture courses, little attention to quality, and low standards.

The demand side for education also influences educational reform, as is discussed by Takehiko in his blistering critique entitled 'Higher Education and the Japanese Disease.'[61] He explains that Japanese firms traditionally provide lengthy on-the-job training. In recruitment, they emphasize cooperation, teamwork, and train-ability, rather than advanced skills or knowledge. Since studiousness, intelligence, and speed of understanding are believed to be measured by university entrance exams, employers pay much more attention to the type of university attended than to what a student accomplished there. That creates little incentive for improvement in university teaching and learning.

Though students don't spend much time cracking the books, they do keep themselves busy, with two major outlets being sports and clubs. For example, Waseda University, a large private institution in the center of Tokyo, features hundreds of student clubs: music, sports, nature, comedy, drama, broadcasting, languages, social issues, computers, manga and anime, horse racing, literature, crafts, arts, and dozens of other areas.[62] There are eight different clubs for classical music fans; seven different clubs for nature lovers; and twenty clubs on politics and economics. For food aficionados, clubs include the 'Bagel Community,' 'Ramen Noodle Study Group,' 'Sweet Bun Study Group,' 'Italian Wine Study Group,' and ten others. A vast infrastructure, from printed guides to specialized search engines, exists to help students identify clubs of interest. Altogether, a typical student in Japan spends more than three hours per day attending club activities and playing sports – or more than twice as long as they reportedly spend on their studies.

Once students enter their third year of college, their focus shifts elsewhere: securing their careers. It is easiest to understand the university-to-career path in Japan by contrasting it with the United States. The pathway is quite flexible in the US: people can enter college as 18-year-olds, straight from high school, or as 38-year-olds, after two decades in a career or raising children. They can begin in a community college and then transfer to a university, change majors several times, or drift in and out of college for years before graduating. As long as they finish with the right degree in a field with sufficient demand, American students – however flexible their path through college – have a fighting chance of securing a job.

By contrast, Japanese students typically have only two or three 'cracks at the bat.' The first major hurdle for a Japanese boy or girl is getting into the right university straight from high school. That is the critical event that will shape their future opportunity to land a life-time permanent position. However, with the economy no longer expanding as it did in the postwar period, getting into a good university is no longer sufficient: students need to go through a dreaded and demeaning process known as *shukatsu* (job hunting) in the summer of their third year of study.

As satirized in a beautiful but biting animated gem on YouTube called 'Recruit Rhapsody,'[63] students spend week after week rushing to company seminars and other events, in a desperate attempt to secure an interview and a job offer. Those who are unable to get a position that summer have been known to ask their professors to fail them the following year, so that they can extend their studies for one more year, and thus have one more shot at getting a stable permanent job offer before they graduate. Once they do graduate, their status changes from *shinsotsu* (newly graduating) to *kisotsu* (previously graduated), with the latter group discriminated against in the job market (see chapter 1). Thus graduates who are unable to secure employment up to and during their critical last year of university studies may well be relegated to a lifetime of temporary, part-time, and poorly paid work.

Not surprisingly, the shortcomings in Japanese higher education have spurred efforts at reform. In 2004, Japan carried out what was called the 'Big Bang' – large-scale deregulation, which was viewed at the time as the most important higher education reform in more than a century. Its national universities, which account for less than 20 percent of the students in higher education but receive some 80 percent of the higher education national budget, were turned into independent agencies, and their faculty were no longer national civil servants with guaranteed jobs for life.[64] These universities were given much greater authority to hire and fire, set their own budgets, review their academic programs, and adjust staff pay. The reforms brought about a far more decentralized educational system – but they did not result in any dramatic improvement in educational quality.

More recent reform efforts have focused on globalization, as the Abe government has sought to discard the 'Japanese universities for nurturing Japanese' mentality. It has pledged financial support in an attempt to double the number of Japanese studying abroad, and recent reports suggest that the downward trend in overseas study is being reversed.[65] Abe has also vowed to increase the number of internationally competitive universities in Japan: currently only the University of Tokyo is considered a world elite university. He has called for eight additional national universities to be raised to the elite level through the recruitment of top-notch researchers and instructors from around the world.[66] Simultaneously, he is pushing universities to step up the 'Global 30' program, which aims to recruit 300,000 international students to study in the country.[67]

As part of this effort, 13 Japanese universities now offer one or more degree programs in English.[68] Programs such as Waseda University's School of International Liberal Studies and the International University of Japan's Graduate School of International Management – both of which offer full degree programs in English – draw a mix of international and Japanese students and are attractive to employers. Akita International University, in the north of Japan, and Ritsumeikan Asia Pacific University (APU), in the south, are making ambitious attempts to offer curricula in English, or in a combination of English and Japanese. Half of APU's student body are foreigners, coming from 83 countries, and more than 95 percent of its graduates are successfully employed upon graduation, often by large international corporations such as Mitsubishi, Sony, and Fujitsu.[69] Yet in spite of these success stories, Global 30 overall has progressed slowly, only raising the number of foreign students from about 124,000 (when the initiative was launched in 2008) to 137,750 in 2012.[70]

Recent debates over the university calendar highlight how difficult it will be to break with tradition in Japan. Currently the Japanese academic year begins in early April and ends in mid-March, with breaks in summer, winter, and spring. The University of Tokyo did discuss proposals to adopt a traditional Western academic calendar, based on a September to June schedule. The idea behind the proposal was to facilitate easier student and faculty interchange with major universities in the United States and Europe. After lengthy discussions that lasted for year, and a great deal of resistance from Japanese corporations – which preferred a single graduation timeline for recruitment purposes, rather than having to interview and hire students graduating on different timelines – the proposal was rejected. Instead a minor change was instituted: the April start date was retained, but the summer vacation was lengthened. In the Japanese university system, as in primary and secondary education, tradition holds powerful sway.

The culture of scientific research

The paradox of harmony in Japanese education extends beyond undergraduate education to Japan's status in academic research. In spite of having a highly educated population that excels in math and science, only one Nobel Prize in science was awarded to a Japanese in the 1990s. By contrast, 44 were awarded to people living in the United States during that decade, the great majority of whom were Americans. This phenomenon has been analyzed by Richard Nisbett, one of the world's leading authorities on culture and cognition.[71] He quickly dismisses simplistic explanations, such as differences in scientific funding, pointing out that Japan spends twice as much on basic research as Germany, which gained five Nobel Prizes in the 1990s.

Instead, Nisbett points to several aspects of Japanese culture (compared to Western culture) that shape scientific research, including a greater respect for elders, which leads more research money to go to older, no-longer-productive scientists; a smaller premium on individual achievement and personal ambition; and, perhaps most interestingly, less willingness to debate and disagree in Japan. As one Japanese scientist explained:

I worked at the Carnegie Institution in Washington, and I knew two eminent scientists who were good friends, but once it came to their work, they would have severe debates, even in the journals. That kind of thing happens in the United States, but in Japan, never.[72]

It turns out that too much harmony is not conducive to scientific breakthroughs: it discourages the pursuit of bold new approaches and ideas that go against the grain, and it limits the kind of sharp critical debate that roots out wrong ideas. As with other areas of Japanese education and society, harmony is a double-edged sword.

On a positive note, the number of Japanese Nobel Prize winners has picked up considerably in recent years. Though most of the prizes have been won by very senior scientists, some breakthroughs by younger researchers in emerging fields have captured the attention of both the scientific community and the nation. These include ground-breaking findings by Shinya Yamanaka, who won the Nobel Prize in 2012 for stem-cell research conducted when he was in his forties, and by Haruko Obokata, who shook up the scientific world with a new approach to stem cells, published in 2013 when she was only 30. Their accomplishments have sparked much discussion and debate in Japan on how to support other young scientific researchers, as well as on the role of women in science.[73]

Conclusion

In many senses, Japanese education is extraordinary. Student achievement rates in math, science, and literacy are among the best in the world, and the country also has one of the world's highest rates of tertiary education. Japan's exceptionally high level of human capital has undoubtedly helped make possible the country's economic success in the last half-century.

Yet just as educational success has contributed to the country's growth, so educational shortcomings have contributed to its stagnation. The Japanese are shockingly bad at English, which has become a vital tool for international communication in today's globalized society and economy. Perhaps more surprisingly, Japanese students are also falling behind in technology skills, as compared to students in other nations. And Japanese universities are far from being the required centers of innovation – either in undergraduate education or in scientific research.

The Abe government has the right instincts in education: it stresses English teaching, technology integration, and higher education reform. But at the same time, the strong nationalism of Abe and his cabinet works against the educational reforms they are promoting. For within the Ministry of Education, it is the forces of nationalism that have been most jealously protective of traditional values and most hesitant to emphasize foreign languages, new technologies, and new kinds of critical thinking. This captures the more general contradiction of Abe – between traditionalism and globalism. And it is a contradiction that has yet to be resolved.

Shaking Up Japan

Millions of words have been written about Japanese society and culture. Perhaps the most famous of all were published in a book by American anthropologist Ruth Benedict in 1946. Benedict had planned a trip to Japan to study the country's culture for the US State Department and Office of War Information. Because of the war, she was unable to travel to Japan, and instead completed her investigation with materials available in the United States. Furthermore, Benedict spoke no Japanese and relied on translators. To carry out her study, Benedict read translated novels, watched movies, examined propaganda, and spoke with Japanese Americans interned in relocation camps. A white paper by Benedict, entitled 'Japanese Behavior Patterns,' was expanded after the war into a book entitled *The Chrysanthemum and the Sword*.[1]

In spite of never having set foot in Japan and not speaking the language, Benedict's work won worldwide acclaim and greatly influenced scholarly and popular opinion of Japanese society. Millions of copies of her book were sold in the United States and around the world, including 2 million copies of a translated version in Japan.

As we do in this book, Benedict described the Japanese as highly paradoxical. Yet she describes their contradictions in ways that are very different from the way we see things today:

The Japanese are, to the highest degree, both aggressive and unag-
gressive, both militaristic and aesthetic, both insolent and polite,
rigid and adaptable, submissive and resentful of being pushed
around, loyal and treacherous, brave and timid, conservative
and hospitable to new ways. They are terribly concerned about
what other people will think of their behavior, and they are also
overcome by guilt when other people know nothing of their
misstep. Their soldiers are disciplined to the hilt but are also
insubordinate.[2]

If Benedict traveled to Japan today, she would not recognize the
nation she described in 1946. It is as paradoxical as ever, and still
values honor, hierarchy, and order; but 'aggressive,' 'militaristic,' and
'treacherous' are not words that would typically be used to describe
its people (at least outside Japan's immediate neighbors, with their
powerful wartime memories). Perhaps a title of 'The Chrysanthemum
and the Double-Edged Sword' would better describe the culture of
Japan today.

Cultures endure, but they are not etched in stone. They evolve as
people live out their lives in changing social and economic contexts.
A half-century after Benedict, the sociologist Manuel Castells
analyzed Japanese culture and society in the last volume of his widely
read trilogy on the information age.[3] He describes Japanese culture as
being entwined with the country's socioeconomic organization in
the postwar period. From this view, certain elements of Japanese
culture, such as militarism, faded away as they no longer served the
new economic order. Others, such as patriarchy, were strengthened
precisely because they matched with economic imperatives. And
Japan's orderly system of hierarchy has been vigorously reproduced
by the Education Ministry through its emphasis on rigid examina-
tions and moralistic training.

If Japan went through one major change after the Second World
War, another new era began in the 1990s. The postwar boom ended,

partly due to internal contradictions, but largely because of global economic trends. With the high cost of labor and real estate in Japan and increasing international competition, Japanese multinational corporations were increasingly forced to seek production, investments, and markets abroad. This in essence broke the postwar compact, in which corporations could promise stable lifelong employment in exchange for close labor–capital cooperation. Young people increasingly turned away from an inflexible system that could promise them neither stability nor happiness. Further political, economic, and cultural adjustments followed.

Harmony's paradox

Taking a long view of Japan's postwar development, how then might we characterize the country's 'paradox of harmony' today? Simply put, *whereas harmony helped make the country wealthy and prosperous, today that same harmony threatens the nation's future.*

The national compact of the postwar period – everyone working together to raise the nation – resulted in the most rapid economic ascent ever achieved until that time. Japan's GDP per capita rose from less than $1,500 in 1946 to more than $30,000 in 1991, an astounding twenty-fold. If the United States were to go through the same level of economic growth over the next 45 years, each man, woman, and child in the country would be producing a million dollars of wealth a year.

In Japan, this economic growth brought the population from impoverishment and malnutrition to join the ranks of the most prosperous people in the world. The Japanese live longer than people in any other country, and nearly five years longer than Americans.[4] This is, in part, thanks to Japan's excellent universal healthcare system, which reaches the entire population yet costs less than half what the US system does. The country has little poverty and low socioeconomic inequality: its ratio of the income of the wealthiest 10 percent to the poorest 10 percent is the lowest in the world, only 4.5, compared to 15.9 in the United States.[5] Its students consistently score among the best in the world in math, science, and reading – far above the levels found in the United States. Its high-school and college graduation rates are also among the world's highest – and again, well above those in the United States. The country has a world-class transportation system, with the world's fastest and most reliable intercity train service and highly efficient and well-organized subway systems in its major cities. Japan's crime rate is also among the lowest in the world: in 2011, the country experienced only 2.9 robberies per 100,000 population, compared to 113.2 per 100,000 in the United States.[6] Finally, Japan has become a world trendsetter in fashion, entertainment, and cuisine.

And make no mistake – Japan's culture of *wa* has contributed mightily to these gains. Its consensus-based system brought people together to fight for the survival of the nation after the terrible defeat of the Second World War. Labor joined with capital, women with men, and urban with rural. It was as if tens of millions of hearts beat as one, while the nation feverishly sought to rise from the ashes of war. None of this would have been possible without the nation's traditions of loyalty, service, honor, commitment, and hard work. These same traits held crime and other social ills at bay and supported Japan's strong family life and commitment to education.

How, then, can we say that harmony can destroy the nation? Because in Japan, harmony is the enemy of flexibility; harmony is the enemy of openness; and harmony is increasingly the enemy of innovation. Flexibility, openness, and innovation were not particularly necessary in the 1950s, 1960s, and 1970s; however, in today's era of globalization they are essential.

Japan's harmony and consensus in the postwar period demanded sacrifices – huge sacrifices, as salarymen worked 60–80 hour weeks, while women abandoned opportunities for a career and raised their children without help from their husbands. This harsh life contributed to one of the highest suicide rates in the world. It also eventually contributed to a decline in economic growth, as the productivity of Japan's overworked labor force lagged. People in Japan have to work nearly 12 hours to produce what Americans can in eight, and annual average pay for men in their thirties fell by nearly 50 percent from 1997 to 2007.[7] Japan's growing economy eventually required a larger workforce; but with women staying at home and with the country closed to immigrants (who might disrupt the harmonious nation), this workforce was not to be found. The heavy burden on families eventually took its toll on the birth rate, which reached a low of 1.26 children per family in 2005. Though by 2013 it had picked up to 1.41, it is still perilously low for a country that accepts almost no immigrants.[8] Given the late age of marriage in Japan, the birth rate is not likely to increase much any time soon.[9]

Combine a perilously low birth rate and a society closed to immigrants, and what do you get? An old and tired nation. By 2060, some 40 percent of the population is predicted to be aged 65 or older. Each senior citizen will be supported by only 1.25 working-age individuals – that's not *working* individuals, but merely individuals *of working age*. The country's population is expected to decline from 128 million in 2010 to 94.6 million in 2060. In other words, while Japan today is struggling with having 29.5 million people over 65 compared to 98.5 million people under 65, in 2060 it is expected to have 9 million *more* people over 65, and 42 million people *fewer* under that age. Barring some serious changes, that could be a crushing demographic burden.

The country experienced almost no economic growth for a decade and a half, with GDP per capita lower in 2009 than in 1995.[10] Recent reforms known as 'Abenomics' show some promise of shaking things up. However, broad structural problems persist. Abe has made no move yet to ease immigration restrictions; this potentially most important policy issue thus remains the 'missing arrow' of Japanese reform (see the 'three arrows' of chapter 1).[11] Japan remains isolated from the kind of global interaction needed for economic success and social reform.

The English language skills of Japan's population are far below those required for international communication; and in terms of the number of its students who study abroad, it has fallen behind its Asian competitors. The nation's youth are boxed in between the harsh lifestyle of the *freeter* and the exhausting career of the salaryman. Even if young people are lucky enough to secure a salaryman position, the inflexible seniority-based system means that they may have little voice or influence on the job during the very years that their ideas and energy are most needed.

Meanwhile, though Japan is in great need of improved international partnerships and collaboration, it pushes its neighbors away with needlessly provocative language and historic claims. And while there will be ongoing debate on this issue, many believe that the cozy relationship between a corporation and its supposed regulators led to the worst nuclear accident in history – one that has cost the country scores of billions of dollars in clean-up efforts, resulted in the shutdown of a large part of the country's energy capacity, and has contributed to global warming, due to a subsequent large-scale shift from nuclear to carbon-based energy production.

Japan's culture of *wa*, and particularly its insularity and inflexibility, contributes to all of this too. Harmony among insiders comes with fear of outsiders. Devotion to consensus comes with resistance to innovation. Loyalty to authority figures comes with unwillingness to challenge them when wrong. Without natural outlets for expression, conflicts go unresolved. Many of the problems that Japan faces – such as an aging society, economic stagnation, and an inability to incorporate immigrants – challenge other developed countries as well; but Japan's social norms amplify these problems and make them especially difficult to overcome.

Shaking up Japan

The last 20 years have seen Japan move gradually and fitfully toward reform. The Liberal Democratic Party, which had led the government without interruption since 1955, finally fell in 1993 (though it has been back in power for most of the time since). A number of recent prime ministers have pursued reformist agendas in various ways, none more so than Prime Minister Shinzo Abe, who returned for a second spell as prime minister in December 2012. Abe has pushed hard to stimulate the economy through the easing of monetary restrictions, massive fiscal stimulus, and sweeping structural reforms. 'Abenomics' has borne some early fruit, overcoming deflation, bringing down the overvalued yen, stimulating the stock market, and increasing the growth rate.

Abenomics may be helping Japan emerge from its prolonged deflation, but its effects have not yet been felt by most *freeters* or *haken* (temp workers). Some of these marginalized workers are hopeful that economic improvement may help them get full-time positions. Others fear that the liberalization of Japan's employment system could make them even more vulnerable to quick dismissals from jobs.

Abe has also sought to shake up education, by making Japanese universities more globally competitive, improving English teaching, sending more Japanese to study abroad, and recruiting more international students and faculty to Japan. At the same time, he has strongly supported 'patriotic education,' which appears to contradict these goals.

Abe has likewise spoken up on behalf of greater female participation in the workforce, with the government setting a 30 percent target for women in management.[12] However, little has been done to remove the structural impediments in the way of this.

In foreign policy, Abe has sought to 'normalize' Japan by revising Article 9 of the constitution, which severely limits the activities of the country's self-defense forces. This goal chimes with that of many other reformers, who hope that Japan might contribute more to international efforts led by the United Nations or Western alliances. However, in Abe's case, the motivation appears to be nationalism as much as internationalism. He has even flirted with historical revisionism on issues ranging from Japan's treatment of Second World War 'comfort women' to the controversial Yasukuni Shrine. These political stances also run counter to Abe's economic agenda, as they irritate some of Japan's principal trading partners.

Though neither Abe nor any other recent prime minister has had a consistent reform agenda, some of the steps he (and indeed his predecessors) has taken suggest that the country is at least gradually moving in the direction of economic and social liberalization. Whether changes occur fast enough to keep Japan from steadily becoming a grayer and less prosperous nation remains to be seen.

In considering Abe and his reforms, many hark back not to the postwar period, but to an earlier era of dramatic reform in Japan – the Meiji Restoration that began in the 1860s. The Meiji era was marked not just by a sudden openness to the West, but also by tremendous social and political upheaval inside Japan. The end of feudalism meant that millions of people were suddenly free to choose their occupation and move about without restriction. By providing an environment of political and financial security, the government made possible a sharp rise in investment in new technologies and industries: large amounts of infrastructure and dozens of new industries were created. Then, when government funds were exhausted, the industries were sold to private investors, decentralizing economic development and raising much needed capital. A national education system and a new constitution were introduced, creating an elected parliament and furthering the development of the nation. Unfortunately, by the turn of the new century, Japan had started to turn to militarism and colonialism, eventually with disastrous consequences. Some of Japan's neighbors likely fear that history could repeat itself.

Going for gold

In 2020, Japan will have a peaceful way to reassert itself in the global arena – through the Summer Olympiad. When the International Olympic Committee (IOC) voted for Tokyo to host the 2020 games, it was actually the third time the city had been awarded the honor, each occasion giving rise to expectations and conflict over what the games would mean for Japan.

Tokyo's first push to host the Olympics began in March 1930, when the city held a 'Reconstruction Festival' to celebrate its recovery after the Great Kanto Earthquake of 1923.[13] Tokyo's mayor at the time planned a massive national festival for ten years hence, in 1940, to commemorate the 2,600th anniversary of the establishment of the Japanese empire, and hoped to host the Olympic games that same summer in an extravaganza of celebration. Though the national government was lukewarm to the idea, preferring to concentrate on its military buildup, Tokyo did eventually win the right to host the 1940 games in an IOC vote taken at the 1936 Berlin Olympiad, following a backdoor agreement to secure Mussolini's support. Tokyo erupted with joy as the first non-Western city to host the games.

Yet it was not to be. Japan's war with China, which broke out in July 1937, placed great demands on the country for men and materiel. As the war intensified, funds for the Olympics dried up and other countries planned boycotts. In May 1938, the Japanese government cancelled the Tokyo Olympiad and instead, in a display of bravado, offered to host the games in 1944. The 1940 games were first rescheduled for Helsinki, Finland, but in the end both the 1940 and the 1944 games were cancelled.

When the Olympics resumed in London in 1948, Japan was an occupied country and excluded from participation. The Allied occupation officially ended in April 1952, and less than a month later Tokyo's new governor proposed a new application to host the Olympics.[14] The effort quickly won the support of Japanese officials, who were seeking ways to project a positive Japanese identity after the tragedy of the war and occupation. Though Tokyo failed in its bid for the 1960 games, in 1959 it won a first-ballot victory to host the 1964 Summer Olympiad. Once again, Tokyo was designated as the scene of the first Olympics to be held outside Europe and North America.

In contrast to 1936, however, the country's response was hesitant, due to the difficult economic times that Japan was emerging from. However, by the time 1964 came around, Japan was hitting its economic stride. The preparations for the Olympics themselves proved a stimulus, and the associated infrastructure greatly assisted Japan's continued boom over the next quarter of a century. Many train and subway lines were built, as was a highway system that criss-crossed the metropolitan area. Haneda International Airport in Tokyo was modernized so that it could handle the new jet airliners and welcome foreign visitors. Most importantly, Japan's first bullet train line was completed just nine days before the opening cere-mony.[15] This was the fastest train in the world and demonstrated Japan's re-emergence as a technological leader, both symbolizing and helping make possible Japan's ongoing economic growth. The Olympics were integrated into Prime Minister Hayato Ikeda's plan to double the national income in ten years – a goal that was reached in little more than five.[16]

The Olympics provided the perfect vehicle to promote patriotism in a non-militaristic fashion. Japanese spectators stepped up and cheered Japan in a way that had not been possible since the war. Artistic and cultural exhibits during the games emphasized themes of nature, harmony, and friendship, and excluded anything that conjured up images of the Japanese Empire.

The games themselves were a great success. Decolonization meant that a large number of new countries had emerged in Asia and Africa, and a record 94 nations ended up participating. They were the first Games broadcast live via global satellite, as well as the first to be broadcast in color. The whole world – or at least much of it – could watch the Olympics, as no international event had ever previously been watched.

The Games served as a critical transition from the militaristic and anachronistic Japan of mid-century to the successful Japan of the boom years.[17] They helped show that Japan had rebuilt itself from wartime destruction and, through such achievements as the bullet train, was now a global scientific and technological leader. They showcased Japan as a country with a mixture of Western modernity and Eastern tradition that made it 'uniquely suited to be an interlocutor between West and non-West.'[18] And they demonstrated that Japan was no longer the despised enemy from the Second World War, but a peaceful, internationalist country.

Now, more than a half-century later, Tokyo once again has the Summer Olympics. It is the first city ever to have been awarded the modern Games three times. And, once again, they come at an important time in Japan's history, as it tries to break free of its period of lengthy economic stagnation and to revitalize its society and economy.

One can imagine circumstances in which the 2020 Games could be a failure: there could be another major earthquake, unleashing massive radiation from Fukushima or otherwise wreaking havoc in Tokyo. Or Japan could spend itself into even more serious deficit problems without developing any important new infrastructure; could drive its workforce to exhaustion; or could engender opposition and boycotts through nationalist policies.

And yet the Japanese have a good track record of setting collective goals and working to achieve them. So let us imagine for a moment what a highly successful 2020 Olympics could look like. What if Tokyo took the opportunity to revamp its identity, as it did in 1964?

Imagine a country that set and achieved the goal of dramatically improving the teaching and learning of English and other foreign languages – not merely to welcome Olympic athletes and tourists, but also to participate more fully in world affairs. Imagine a country that used the occasion to radically revise its immigration policies, so that instead of shrinking and becoming grayer, it maintained its population and became younger. Imagine a country that, once and for all, turned its back on nationalistic rhetoric and behavior, so that its leaders could effectively reach out to Asian counterparts, rather than needlessly angering them. Imagine a country that curbed its protectionist agricultural policies, so that it could serve the interests of its tens of millions of consumers, rather than its half million or so full-time farmers. Imagine a country that rededicated itself to fulfilling the hopes of its young, rather than being paralyzed by the fears of its old.

To achieve these ends, Japan need not abandon such admirable cultural traits as honesty, hard work, service, self-sacrifice, respect, and commitment to education. Indeed, those are sources of the nation's strength. Rather, as in 1964, the country needs to become a better version of itself – a more confident, open, flexible, and outward-looking Japan. If that can be achieved, it will represent the true gold medal for Japan in 2020 and beyond.

Notes

Introduction

1. Martin Fackler, 'Severed from the world, villagers survive on tight bonds and to-do lists,' *New York Times*, 21 March 2011, http://www.nytimes.com/2011/03/24/world/asia/24isolated.html?pagewanted=all
2. 'Hinanjo de rida ni natta [We became leaders at an evacuation center],' *Asahi Shimbun Weekly AERA*, 2–9 May 2011, pp. 29–33.
3. Krista Mahr, 'Takeshi Kanno, Doctor,' *Time* magazine, 21 April 2011, at: http://content.time.com/time/specials/packages/article/0,28804,2066367_2066369_2066313,00.html
4. Translation courtesy of Wikipedia, http://en.wikipedia.org/wiki/Ame_ni_mo_Makezu
5. J. Bolt and J.L.van Zanden, 'The first update of the Maddison Project: Re-estimating growth before 1820,' Maddison Project Working Paper 4, 2013, at: www.ggdc.net/maddison/maddison-project/data.htm
6. Norimitsu Onishi, 'As Japan works to patch itself up, a rift between generations opens,' *New York Times*, 12 February 2012, at: www.nytimes.com/2012/02/13/world/asia/amid-japan-reconstruction-generational-rift-opens.html
7. World Earthquakes website, at: www.world-earthquakes.com/index.php?option=ethq_statistics
8. Bill Caraway, 'Journey to Asia: Japan,' at: www.koreanhistoryproject.org/Jta/Jp/JpGEO1.htm
9. 'List of earthquakes in Japan,' Wikipedia, at: http://en.wikipedia.org/wiki/List_of_earthquakes_in_Japan
10. 'Hiroo Onoda, Japan's last WWII soldier to surrender, dies,' CBC News website, 17 January 2014, at: http://www.cbc.ca/news/world/hiroo-onoda-japan-s-last-straggling-wwii-soldier-dies-1.2500510
11. For example, the Iwakura Mission sent a group of more than a hundred top governmental leaders and students to the United States and/or a dozen European countries in the early 1870s. The primary purposes of this mission were to acquire knowledge about Western society and pave the way for renegotiation of the unequal treaties Japan had been forced to make with the United States and other European countries following the arrival of Commodore Perry. Meiji leaders who traveled abroad were impressed with the modernity of Western society and were inspired to accelerate the process of *bunmei*

kaikoku (civilization and the opening of the country), all with the aim of making Japan strong.

12. Joshua Hammer, 'The great Japan earthquake of 1923,' *Smithsonian* magazine, May 2011, at: www.smithsonianmag.com/history-archaeology/The-Great-Japan-Earthquake-of-1923.html

13. Thomas P. Rohlen, *For Harmony and Strength: Japanese white-collar organization in anthropological perspective*, University of California Press, Berkeley and Los Angeles, 1974.

14. Robert Whiting, *You Gotta Have Wa*, Vintage, New York, 2009.

15. Nicholas Kristof, 'Your comments on my Japan column,' *New York Times* website, 19 March 2011, at: http://kristof.blogs.nytimes.com/2011/03/19/your-comments-on-my-japan-column/?_r=0

16. See humorous discussion of this in 'Japanese preschool, 12 things that stunned Chinese mom,' ChinaSmack website, 20 March 2010, at: www.chinasmack.com/2010/stories/chinese-mom-japanese-preschool.html

17. See humorous description and categorization in Eryk Salvaggio, *This Japanese Life*, CreateSpace Self-publishing, 2013.

18. United Nations Development Programme, *Human Development Report, 2009*, UNDP, New York, 2009.

19. Much of our own earlier academic research is marked by sociological and political analysis of the bitter conflicts in Japanese society over the country's national identity. See, for example, K. Hirata, 'Who shapes the national security debate? Divergent interpretations of Japan's security role,' *Asian Affairs: An American Review*, 35:3 (2008), pp. 123–51.

20. Ronald Dore, *Shinohata: Portrait of a Japanese village*, Allen Lane, London, 1978, p. 266. See also Ellis S. Krauss, Thomas P. Rohlen, and Patricia G. Steinhoff (eds.), *Conflict in Japan*, University of Hawaii Press, Honolulu, 1984.

21. V. Lee Hamilton, *Everyday Justice: Responsibility and the individual in Japan and the United States*, Yale University Press, New Haven, CT, 1992.

22. 'Tattoo ban at bathhouses raises concern in Japan over 2020 Tokyo Olympics,' ABC10 News website, 13 September 2013, at: www.10news.com/around-the-web/tattoo-ban-at-bathhouses-raises-concern-in-japan-over-2020-tokyo-olympics09132013

23. Jake Adelstein and Nathalie-Kyoko Stucky, 'I'll have the whale please: Japan's unsustainable whale hunts,' *Daily Beast*, 5 February 2013, at: www.thedailybeast.com/articles/2013/02/05/i-ll-have-the-whale-please-japan-s-unsustainable-whale-hunts.html

24. In Japan, whales are generally considered a type of fish rather than a mammal – a view that is reflected and reinforced in Japan's writing system, in which the symbol for whale includes within it a component that means fish. For background on Japanese whaling policy, see K. Hirata, 'Why Japan supports whaling,' *Journal of International Wildlife Law & Policy*, 8 (2005), pp. 1–21; and K. Hirata, 'Beached whales: Examining Japan's rejection of an international norm,' *Social Science Japan Journal*, 7:2 (2004), pp. 177–97.

25. Adelstein and Stucky, 'I'll have the whale please.'

26. Ansuya Harjani, 'Adult diapers will soon outsell baby nappies in Japan,' CNBC website, 3 September 2013, at: www.cnbc.com/id/101003141

Chapter 1 The Whistleblower

1. Masaharu Hamada, *Orinpasu no yami to tatakai tsuzukete* [*Fighting the Darkness of Olympus*], Kobunsha, Tokyo, 2012.

2. Yuri Kageyama, 'Whistleblower: Olympus ignores Japan court order,' Yahoo News! website, 29 July 2013, at: http://news.yahoo.com/whistleblower-olympus-ignores-japan-court-104355484.html

3. 'Whistle-blower defeats Japan Inc. for first time,' *Japan Times*, 1 July 2012, at: http://info.japantimes.co.jp/text/nn20120701a2.html

4. Including former Berkeley professor Chalmers Johnson.

5. Klaus Petersen, 'Japan – from greatness to decline?' *Valueinvest* 1 (2012), p. 16–22.

6. The US was first, with 132 companies on the list; China was second with 73, followed by Japan with 68. See 'China passes Japan for first time in Fortune 500 list of biggest companies,' *Japan Times*, 11 July 2012.

7. 'A game of leapfrog,' *The Economist*, 28 April 2012, at: www.economist.com/node/21553498

8. David H. Slater, 'The making of Japan's new working class: "Freeters" and the progression from middle school to the labor market,' *Asia-Pacific Journal*, 4 January 2010.

9. A growing number of women are entering the workforce, as discussed later in this chapter, and are referred to as *sogoshoku* (full-time management-track employees). Japanese men still constitute the vast majority of full-time employees and are called *sarariman* (salaryman). *Haken* include both men and women.

10. 'Taking a break: Employees in 24 countries tell us if they use up all of their holidays granted by their organization,' IPSOS/Reuters, August, 2010, at: www.ipsos-na.com/download/pr.aspx?id=9817

11. Catherine Rampell, 'Suicide rates, around the world,' *New York Times*, 3 December 2009, at: http://economix.blogs.nytimes.com/2009/12/09/suicide-rates-around-the-world/; Joe Chen, Yun Jeong Choi, Yasuyuki Sawada, 'How is suicide different in Japan?', *Japan and the World Economy*, 21:2 (2009), pp. 140–50.

12. 'McDonald's employee "died of overwork",' *Sydney Morning Herald*, 28 October 2009, at: http://news.smh.com.au/breaking-news-world/mcdonalds-employee-died-of-overwork-20091028-hkt0.html

13. 'Death by overwork in Japan: Jobs for life,' *The Economist*, 19 December 2007, at: www.economist.com/node/10329261

14. 'Nagoya court rules Toyota employee died from overwork,' *Japan Times*, 1 December 2007, at: www.japantimes.co.jp/text/nn20071201a9.html; also 'Overwork blamed in death of a top Toyota engineer,' *New York Times*, 10 July 2008, at: www.nytimes.com/2008/07/10/business/worldbusiness/10iht-overwork.1.14389149.html?_r=1

15. In 2006, Japan's labor productivity per hour was only 70 percent that of the United States and also far behind that of the UK and France. See Gilbert Cette, Yusuf Kocoglu, Jacques Mairesse, 'Productivity growth and levels in France, Japan, the United Kingdom and the United States in the twentieth century,' NBER Working Paper No. 15577, 2009, at: www.nber.org/papers/w15577. By 2011, its productivity had fallen to less than 66.8 percent of that of the United States: see '2011 international comparison of labor productivity,' Japan Productivity Center website, 2012, at: www.jpc-net.jp/eng/research/2012_02.html

16. Though OECD data suggest that US employees work on average longer than Japanese (see http://stats.oecd.org/Index.aspx?DataSetCode=ANHRS), the data are misleading because they include both full- and part-time workers, and also exclude unpaid overtime work. According to a study by a University of Tokyo researcher, Japanese *full-time* workers work about two hours more per day than their American counterparts. Shoko Kuroda, 'Nihonjin no rodo jikan: Jitan-seisaku donyu mae to sono 20-nengo no hikaku o chushin ni [Japanese working hours: Comparing the time before the introduction of a working hour reduction policy and 20 years after the policy introduction],' Research Institute of Economy, Trade, and Industry Policy Discussion Paper 10-P-002, 2010.

17. 'No overtime day,' Gaijin Days website (personal blog of unidentified American who used to live in Japan), 2 July 2009, at: http://gaijindays.blogspot.com/2009/07/no-overtime-day.html

18. Noel Williams, *The Right to Life in Japan*, Routledge, London, 1997.

19. 'Kareinaru kaishain no ichiniti [A day in the life of a glamorous salaryman],' Menet blog, 19 April 2010, reproduced at: http://detail.chiebukuro.yahoo.co.jp/qa/question_detail/q1132745756

20. Reiko Kosugi, *Frita to iu ikikata* [*The Freeter's Way of Life*], Keiso Shobo, Tokyo, 2003.
21. Mitsuko Uenishi, 'Freeter to iu hataraki kata [The *freeter's* way of working],' in Reiko Kosugi (ed.), *Jiyu no daisho – frita: Gendai wakamono no shushoku ishiki to kodo* [*The Price of Freedom – Freeter: Young people's attitudes towards employment and behavior*], Nihon rodo kenkyu kiko [Japan Labor Research Institute], Tokyo, 2002, pp. 55–74.
22. Stephanie Assmann and Sebastian Maslow, 'Dispatched and displaced: Rethinking employment and welfare protection in Japan,' *Asia-Pacific Journal*, 12 April 2010.
23. Emilie Guyonnet, 'Young Japanese temporary workers create their own unions,' *Asia-Pacific Journal*, 18 April 2011.
24. Japanese Ministry of Health, Labor, and Welfare, 'Heisei 24-nen chingin kozo kihon tokei chosa [Basic statistical survey on wage structure, 2012],' 2012, at: http://www.mhlw.go.jp/toukei/itiran/roudou/chingin/kouzou/z2012/index.html
25. Martin Fackler, 'In Japan, young face generational roadblocks,' *New York Times*, 27 January 2011, at: www.nytimes.com/2011/01/28/world/asia/28generation.html?pagewanted=all
26. ibid.
27. See http://himasoku123.blog61.fc2.com/blog-entry-691.html
28. Masahiro Abe, 'Hi-seiki koyo zoka no haikei [The background behind the increase of non-regular employment],' Economic and Social Research Institute website, at: http://www.esri.go.jp/jp/others/kanko_sbubble/analysis_06_13.pdf
29. 'Hi-seiki no yaku nana-wari wa josei ga shimeru [About 70 percent of non-regular workers are women],' Ministry of Internal Affairs and Communications Statistics Bureau, 19 February 2013, at: www.stat.go.jp/data/roudou/pdf/point16.pdf
30. Abe, 'Hi-seiki koyo zoka no haikei.'
31. Ames Gross and John Minot, 'The strengthening of the toothless lion: Japan's new gender equality law,' Asian HR Publications, November 2007, at: www.pacificbridge.com/publications/the-strengthening-of-the-toothless-lion-japans-new-gender-equality-law/
32. Tomoko A. Hosaka, 'Shiseido exec aims to elevate women,' *Seattle Times*, 21 November 2011, at: http://seattletimes.com/html/businesstechnology/2016821484_apasjapanworkingwomen.html
33. Megan Starich, 'The 2006 revisions to Japan's equal opportunity employment law: A narrow approach to a pervasive problem,' *Pacific Rim Law & Policy Journal*, 16:2 (2007), pp. 551–78.
34. Hiroko Tabuchi, 'In a culture clash, Olympus ousts its British chief,' *New York Times*, 15 October 2011, at: www.nytimes.com/2011/10/15/business/global/in-rare-move-olympus-fires-its-chief.html?scp=4&sq=Japan&st=cse
35. Yoshimasa Yamaguchi, *Samurai to orokamono: Anto, Orinpasu jiken* [*Samurai and Fools: Secret strife, the Olympus incident*], Kodansha, Tokyo, 2012; Hugh Cortazzi, 'Olympus case a black mark for Japan,' *Japan Times*, 24 October 2011, at: www.japantimes.co.jp/opinion/2011/10/24/commentary/olympus-case-a-black-mark-for-japan/#.UkcaKbzgLoB
36. Michael Woodford, *Kainin* [*Dismissal*], Hayakawa Shobo, Tokyo, 2012.
37. Yamaguchi, *Samurai to orokamono.*
38. Karl Taro Greenfeld, 'The story behind the Olympus scandal,' *Bloomberg Businessweek*, 16 February 2012, at: www.businessweek.com/articles/2012-02-16/the-story-behind-the-olympus-scandal
39. Hiroko Tabuchi, 'Corporate Japan rocked by scandal at Olympus,' *New York Times*, 9 November 2011, at: www.nytimes.com/2011/11/10/business/global/corporate-japan-rocked-by-scandal-at-olympus.html?pagewanted=all
40. 'Cosmetic firm in accounts scandal,' BBC News, 13 April 2005, at: http://news.bbc.co.uk/2/hi/business/4439615.stm

41. Gus Lubin, 'Here's why corporate fraud is easier in Japan,' *Business Insider*, 15 March 2012, at: http://articles.businessinsider.com/2012-03-15/strategy/31195434_1_japanese-stocks-japanese-media-tsuyoshi-kikukawa

42. Nathaniel Parish Flannery, 'Problems at Olympus a sign of investor risk at major Japanese companies,' *Forbes*, 25 October 2011, at: www.forbes.com/sites/nathanielparishflannery/2011/10/25/a-setting-sun-recent-scandal-at-olympus-a-sign-of-deeper-governance-issues-at-japanese-companies/

43. Michiyo Nakamoto, 'Japan tries to limit Olympus fallout,' *Financial Times*, 11 November 2011, at: www.ft.com/intl/cms/s/2/027066f4-0c20-11e1-9310-00144feabdc0.html#axzz1dufeKiPR

44. 'Arrested development,' *The Economist*, 16 February 2012, at: www.economist.com/blogs/banyan/2012/02/olympus-scandal

45. Allison Jackson, 'Japan: Olympus whistleblower Michael Woodford wins millions in settlement as company announces job cuts,' Global Post website, 8 June 2012, at: www.globalpost.com/dispatch/news/regions/asia-pacific/japan/120608/japan-olympus-whistleblower-michael-woodford-wins-mi

46. 'Michael Woodford gives up Olympus leadership bid,' video of Woodford's press conference statement at the Japan National Press Club, Shingetsu News Agency, 6 January 2012, available at: www.youtube.com/watch?v–NXZA08x4HZA

47. 'Hello world: Japanese firms are waking up to the merits of hiring globe-trotting recruits,' *The Economist*, 25 August 2011, at: www.economist.com/node/21526941

48. Miki Tanikawa, 'More young Japanese heading abroad to study,' *New York Times*, 24 May 2013, at: www.nytimes.com/2013/03/25/world/asia/25iht-educside25.html. During this same five-year period, the youth population fell (http://www8.cao.go.jp/youth/whitepaper/h23honpenhtml/index.html), but not by nearly as much as did the number of overseas students. In addition to the general fall in overseas studies, the proportion of overseas students choosing the United States has decreased, in part due to the rising costs of tuition in the United States and in part due to an increased interest in studying in China; see Peter Ford, 'For study abroad, more Japanese prefer Chinese university over US one,' *Christian Science Monitor*, 19 May 2010, at: www.csmonitor.com/World/Asia-Pacific/2010/0519/For-study-abroad-more-Japanese-prefer-Chinese-university-over-US-one

49. Ronald Yates, 'Japan's returnees face rejection,' *Chicago Tribune*, 23 September 1990.

50. The three arrows and their expected overlapping effects are explained in a very clear chart at the Quartz website: http://qz.com/70866/its-hard-to-explain-what-abenomics-is-so-we-drew-you-a-picture/

51. Paul Krugman, 'Japan the model,' *New York Times*, 23 May 2013, at: www.nytimes.com/2013/05/24/opinion/krugman-japan-the-model.html

52. Kenji Nishizaki, Toshitaka Sekine, Yuichi Ueno, and Yuko Kawai, 'Chronic deflation in Japan,' Bank for International Settlements (BIS) Papers No. 70, 2013, at: https://www.bis.org/publ/bppdf/bispap70c.pdf

53. Gwynn Guilford, 'Japan is finally escaping its deflation vortex. But it's not in the clear just yet,' Quartz website, 30 August 2013, at: http://qz.com/120039/japan-is-finally-escaping-its-deflation-vortex-but-its-not-in-the-clear-just-yet/

54. 'Japan approves $117 billion stimulus as PM Abe aims to boost economy,' CNBC website, 10 January 2013, at: www.cnbc.com/id/100371478

55. Aya Takada and Yuriy Humber, 'Japan's free-trade nemesis built on part-time farmers empire,' Bloomberg News website, 2 August 2012, at: www.bloomberg.com/news/2012-08-02/japan-s-free-trade-nemesis-built-on-part-time-farmers-empire.html

56. Hiroko Tabuchi, 'Japan's farmers oppose Pacific free-trade talks,' *New York Times*, 11 November 2010, at: www.nytimes.com/2010/11/12/business/global/12yen.html

57. In spring 2012, Japan's powerful National Central Union of Agriculture Co-operatives took its campaign against the agreement to the US, running a full-page advertisement in the *Washington Post* with the title 'Don't let the TPP rob your future.' With the Japanese farm lobby so passionate about defeating the TPP, they failed to realize that most Americans have no idea what the TPP is.

58. 'Sacred cows, rice and the rest of them,' *The Economist*, 9 October 2013, at: www.economist.com/blogs/banyan/2013/10/japan-and-trans-pacific-partnership

59. Mohammed Aly Sergie, 'Japan boosts the Trans-Pacific Partnership,' Council on Foreign Relations website, 9 August 2013, at: www.cfr.org/japan/japan-boosts-trans-pacific-partnership/p31206

60. 'Japan and Abenomics: Once more with feeling,' *The Economist*, 16 May 2013, at: www.economist.com/news/briefing/21578052-shinzo-abe-shaking-up-japans-economy-seems-different-man-one-whose-previous

61. 'The world's 20 hottest startup scenes,' *Entrepreneur*, 14 August 2013, at: www.entrepreneur.com/article/227832

Chapter 2 Grass-eating Girly Men

1. Maki Fukasawa, 'U35 danshi maketingu zukan, dai 5-kai: soshokukei danshi [An illustrated guide for marketing for men under 35, the fifth essay: herbivore men],' Nikkei Business Online website, 13 October 2006, at: http://business.nikkeibp.co.jp/article/skillup/20061005/111136/?rt=nocnt

2. Richard Lloyd Perry, *The Times*, quoted in 'Soshokukei Danshi,' *New York Times*, 10 November 2009, at: http://schott.blogs.nytimes.com/2009/11/10/soshokukei-danshi/

3. Chris Deacon, 'All the world's a stage: Herbivore boys and the performance of masculinity in contemporary Japan' in Brigitte Steger and Angelika Koch (eds), *Manga Girl Seeks Herbivore Boy: Studying Japanese gender*, Lit Verlag, Zurich, 2013, pp. 129–76.

4. Masahiro Morioka, 'A phenomenological study of "herbivore men",' *Review of Life Studies*, 4 (2013), pp. 1–20, at: http://www.lifestudies.org/press/rls0401.pdf

5. T. Otake, 'Blurring the boundaries,' *Japan Times*, 10 May 2009, at: http://www.japantimes.co.jp/life/2009/05/10/life/blurring-the-boundaries/#.UtEz1PRdU8o

6. Deacon, 'All the world's a stage.'

7. Alexander Harney, 'The herbivore's dilemma,' Slate website, 15 June 2009, at: www.slate.com/articles/news_and_politics/foreigners/2009/06/the_herbivores_dilemma.html

8. Masahiro Morioka, *Soshoku-kei danshi no renai-gaku* [*Love Science on Herbivore-Type Men*], Media Factory, Tokyo, 2008.

9. Morioka, 'A phenomenological study of "herbivore men."'

10. 'Soshoku-kei danshi no konkatsu [Marriage-hunting activities by herbivore-type men],' Soshoku-kei danshi no jittai [The reality of herbivore-type men] blog, at: http://www.so-shoku.net/36.html

11. Mark Hanrahan, 'Japan population decline: Third of nation's youth have "no interest" in sex,' *Huffington Post* website, 30 January 2012, at: http://www.huffingtonpost.com/2012/01/30/japan-population-decline-youth-no-sex_n_1242014.html; data taken from Kunio Kitamura, 'Dai 5-kai danjo no seikatsu to ishiki ni kansuru chosa no kekka hokoku [Report on the fifth survey on men and women's lives and views],' *Gendai seikyoiku kenkyu janaru* [*Journal on Modern Sex Education*], July 2011, at: http://www.jase.faje.or.jp/jigyo/journal/seikyoiku_journal_201110.pdf; see also Kunio Kitamura, *Sekkusu–girai na wakamono tachi* [*The Youth Who Don't Like Sex*], Media Factory, Tokyo, 2011.

12. National Institute of Population and Social Security Research, 'The fourteenth Japanese national fertility survey in 2010: Attitudes toward marriage and family among Japanese singles,' 2011, at: http://www.ipss.go.jp/site-ad/index_english/nfs14/Nfs14_Singles_Eng.

pdf; another survey, this time conducted by the Meiji Yasuda Life Welfare Research Institute in 2013, found that more than 30 percent of single men in their twenties and thirties have no dating experience, and that 27.9 percent of single women in their twenties, and 14.8 percent of single women in their thirties, have had no boyfriend. Meiji Yasuda Seikatsu Fukushi Kenkyujo [Meiji Yasuda Life Welfare Research Institute], 'Dai-nana-kai "Kekkon Shussan ni kansuru chosa" kekka gaiyo [Summary report on the seventh survey on marriage and birth]', 18 March 2013, at: www.myilw.co.jp/life/enquete/pdf/22_01.pdf

13. William Pesek, 'The lust beneath Japan's sex drought', Bloomberg Opinion, 25 October 2013, at: www.bloomberg.com/news/2013-10-25/the-lust-beneath-japan-s-sex-drought-.html

14. For an excellent overview of the work of Johnny and Associates and its relationship to gender issues in Japan, see Lucy Glasspool, 'From boys next door to boy's love: Gender performance in Japanese male idol media', in Patrick Galbraith and Jason Karlin (eds), *Idols and Celebrity in Japanese Media Culture*, Palgrave MacMillan, London, 2012, pp. 113–30.

15. Declan Hayes, *The Japanese Disease: Sex and sleaze in modern Japan*, iUniverse, Lincoln, NE, 2005.

16. Karl Taro Greenfeld, 'The incredibly strange mutant creatures who rule the universe of alienated Japanese zombie computer nerds', *Wired*, March/April 1993, at: www.wired.com/wired/archive/1.01/otaku.html

17. Robert Michael Poole, 'Why it's better to date an otaku guy: Eight reasons Japanese nerds are the best boyfriends around', CNN website, 25 January 2011, at: www.cnngo.com/tokyo/life/why-its-better-date-otaku-guy-591862#ixzz1CVTUbage

18. Goo Ranking, 'Joshi ga "tsukiaitai!" to omou otaku danshi no miryoku ranking [Top reasons that women want to date otaku men]', 5 March 2013, at: http://ranking.goo.ne.jp/column/article/goorank/32355/ For an English translation, see www.jefusion.com/2013/03/top-20-reasons-why-women-would-date-an-otaku-guy.html

19. Toko Shirakawa, 'Figyua to tabisuru otoko to ayumu ni wa? [How to move forward with a man who travels with a figurine?]', Spice Komachi, *Yomiuri Shimbun*, 25 June 2012.

20. ibid.

21. 'AKB48', The Top Tens website, undated, at: www.the-top-tens.com/items/akb48-381555.asp

22. Megumi Ushikubo, *Yuruota-kun to kekkon shiyo!* [*Let's Marry Light* Otaku], Kodansha, Tokyo, 2012.

23. Mizuho Aoki, 'Poverty a growing problem for women', *Japan Times*, 19 April 2012, at: www.japantimes.co.jp/text/nn20120419f1.html

24. 'Yamaguchi Yoshie no Nazo no Shi ni Miru Josei Kodoku-shi [Women's solitude deaths as exemplified in the death of Yoshie Yamaguchi]', Infoseek Woman website, 10 March 2012, at: http://woman.infoseek.co.jp/news/entertainment/menscyzo_10Mar2012_9536; see also the blog posting by a conservative commentator, translated as 'Learn from Yoshie Yamaguchi: A solitary death awaits happy-go-lucky women', 21 March 2012, at: http://blog.goo.ne.jp/grk39587/e/361e0378b3f05dd83b7142c0b095ac13

25. Takuro Morinaga, *Hikon no susume* [*Bachelorhood Recommended*], Kodansha, Tokyo, 1997.

26. Junko Sakai, *Makeinu no toboe* [*Distant Howling of the Loser Dogs*], Kodansha, Tokyo, 2003.

27. Taro Fujimoto, 'Helping women get back into the workplace', *Japan Today*, 16 July 2008, at: www.japantoday.com/category/lifestyle/view/helping-women-get-back-into-the-workplace

28. Japan Ministry of Internal Affairs and Communications, *Heisei 22-nen kokusei chosa* [*2010 Census*], 2011, at: www.stat.go.jp/data/kokusei/2010/users-g/qa-1.htm

29. Wendy Nelson Tokunaga, *Marriage in Translation: Foreign wife, Japanese husband interviews on cross-cultural relationships*, CultureWave Press, Half Moon Bay, CA, 2011.

30. Anne Allison, 'Japanese mothers and obentos: The lunch-box as ideological state apparatus,' *Anthropological Quarterly*, 64:4 (1991), pp. 195–208.

31. Risa Ishihara, *Kutabare! Sengyo-shufu [Give Me A Break, Full-Time Housewife]*, Kobunsha, Tokyo, 2003.

32. Fumiko Hayashi, *Ishhokenmei tte suteki na koto [Doing One's Best is a Wonderful Thing]*, Soshisha, Tokyo, 2006.

33. Myra H. Strober and Agnes Miling Kaneko Chan, *The Road Winds Uphill All the Way: Gender, work and family in the United States and Japan*, MIT Press, Cambridge, MA, 1999, p. xi.

34. Fukuko Yoshimori, '80-nendai no kozure shukkin ronso ni manabu [Learning from the 1980s' controversy over bringing a child to the workplace],' All About website, 25 November 2005, at: http://allabout.co.jp/gm/gc/224965

35. Sylvia Ann Hewlett, 'Japan's working-woman problem,' *Time*, 11 December 2011, at: http://ideas.time.com/2011/12/11/japans-working-woman-problem/

36. Yoshie Komuro, *Naze ano bumon wa 'zangyo nashi' de 'ko seiseki' nanoka. 6-ji ni kaeru chimu-jutu [Why that division can perform well without working overtime: Technique to go home at 6 p.m.]*, JMA Management Center, Tokyo, 2008.

37. Japan Ministry of Health, Labor, and Welfare, 'Jinko dotai tokei [Demographic statistics],' 2012, at: www.mhlw.go.jp/toukei/saikin/hw/jinkou/geppo/nengai12/dl/gaikyou24.pdf

38. Japan Cabinet Office, *Heisei 24-nendo-ban kodomo kosodate hakusho [White Paper on Children and Childrearing]*, Tokyo, 2012, chapter 2, at: www8.cao.go.jp/shoushi/whitepaper/w-2012/24pdfhonpen/pdf/1-2-1-2.pdf

39. National Institute of Population and Social Security Research, 'Dai-14-kai shussei doko kihon chosa: Kekkon to shussan ni kansuru zenkoku chosa dokushinsha chosa no kekka gaiyo [The 14th basic survey on birth trends: National survey on marriage and birth – summary of survey results on single people],' 2011, at: www.ipss.go.jp/ps-doukou/j/doukou14_s/doukou14_s.pdf

40. Technically referring back to the era of Emperor Showa, who died in 1989.

41. Some single women request partners who have older siblings, since marrying the first son brings the risk of caring for in-laws, the traditional responsibility of the first son's wife.

42. Carmen Solomon-Fears, 'Teenage pregnancy prevention: Statistics and programs,' Congressional Research Service, 19 June 2013, at: www.fas.org/sgp/crs/misc/RS20301.pdf

43. US Census Bureau, 'Marriage and divorce rates by country,' Table, 2012, at: www.census.gov/compendia/statab/2012/tables/12s1336.pdf

44. ibid.

45. United Nations Office on Drugs and Crimes, 'Crime and criminal justice statistics: sexual violence,' Table, 2013, at: www.unodc.org/documents/data-and-analysis/statistics/crime/CTS_Sexual_violence.xls

46. In spite of tolerant attitudes, same-sex marriage is not legal in Japan. To make it legal would require revision of the Japanese constitution, which is very difficult to amend and has not been revised since it took effect in 1947. See Miho Inada and Phred Dvorak, 'Same-sex marriage in Japan: A long way away?', *Wall Street Journal*, 20 September 2013, at: http://blogs.wsj.com/japanrealtime/2013/09/20/same-sex-marriage-in-japan-a-long-way-away/

Chapter 3 Graying and shrinking

1. 'The alarm bells of Nagasaki,' *The Economist*, 13 January 2011, at: www.economist.com/node/17909982

2. 'Nagasaki-ken, Kyushu ichi no koreika-ken [Nagasaki to be the most aged prefecture in the Kyushu region],' *Asahi Shimbun*, 3 April 2013, at: http://digital.asahi.com/

area/nagasaki/articles/SEB201304020030.html?ref=comkiji_txt_end_s_kjid_
SEB201304020030

3. National Institute of Population and Social Security Research, *Nihon no shorai suikei jinko hokoku-sho* [*Report on Japan's Estimated Future Population*], 2012, at: www.ipss.go.jp/syoushika/tohkei/newest04/hh2401.asp

4. Floria Coulmas, *Population Decline and Ageing in Japan: The social consequences*, Routledge, London, 2007.

5. Monaco, however, is a statistical anomaly; its tiny population (just over 30,000) consists mostly of wealthy European seniors attracted by its tax-haven status.

6. Rajeshni Naidu-Ghelani, 'Countries with aging populations,' CNBC website, 2012, at: www.cnbc.com/id/46010334/Countries_With_Aging_Populations?slide=

7. Chico Harlan, 'Japan's rural voters cling to the principle of power to the countryside,' *Guardian*, 9 July 2013, at: www.theguardian.com/world/2013/jul/09/japan-rural-voters-tokyo-abe

8. Fumio Ohtake, 'On increasing political power of senior voters in Japan,' Global Communications Platform website, 24 October 2008, at: www.glocom.org/opinions/essays/20081024_ohtake_on/

9. 'More Chinese, Japanese CEOs have science backgrounds,' *Chosunilbo*, 1 December 2009, at: http://english.chosun.com/site/data/html_dir/2009/12/01/2009120100386.html

10. Statistics and quotation (by Manabu Shimasaw, a professor of social policy at Akita University) in Fackler, 'In Japan, young face generational roadblocks.'

11. Report on *Good Morning, Japan*, NHK TV, 13 September 2012.

12. Sanya covers an area in the Taito and Arakawa districts of Tokyo. It is traditionally known as home to Japan's poor day laborers, tanners, and leather makers. Sanya was split into smaller neighborhoods in the mid-1960s, so the name does not officially exist any more; but it is still used informally.

13. Report on *Good Morning, Japan*, NHK TV, 13 September 2012.

14. 'Crimes by elderly on the rise,' *Japan Times*, 3 December 2012, at: www.japantimes.co.jp/text/ed20121203a2.html

15. Minako Tamaki, 'Yonin ni hitori wa saihan 10-kai ijo [A quarter (of the seniors imprisoned) has committed a crime more than 10 times],' *Business Journal*, 7 May 2012, at: http://biz-journal.jp/2012/05/post_98.html

16. Rie Horita and Etsuko Yuhara, 'Korei ni natte hajimete hanzai nit e o someta josei hanzaisha ni kansuru kenkyu [Research on female offenders who commit a crime for the first time at a senior age],' Japan Welfare University Ronshu Collection No. 123, September 2010, pp. 69–83.

17. Midori Kotani, 'Hitori de kurasu koreisha no mondai [The problem of elderly people living alone],' Life Design Report 1 (2012), pp. 16–23.

18. National Institute of Population and Social Security Research, 'Nihon no setai-su no shorai suikei [Estimate of numbers of households in Japan in the future],' 2008, at: www.ipss.go.jp/pp-ajsetai/j/HPRJ2008/t-page.asp

19. Non-interest spending is all expenditure except that which is used to pay interest on the national debt.

20. Kenichiro Kashiwase, Masahiro Nozaki, and Kiichi Tokuoka, 'Pension reforms in Japan,' IMF Working Paper 12/285, 2012, at: www.imf.org/external/pubs/ft/wp/2012/wp12285.pdf

21. Robert D. Retherford and Naohiro Ogawa, 'Japan's baby bust: Causes, implications, and policy responses,' East-West Center Population and Health Series No. 118, April 2005, at: http://scholarspace.manoa.hawaii.edu/bitstream/handle/10125/3757/POPwp118.pdf?sequence=1

22. 'Fertility rate expected to remain flat,' *Japan Times*, 6 June 2012, at: www.japantimes.co.jp/news/2012/06/06/national/fertility-rate-expected-to-remain-flat/#.UkfFoKBgMlI

23. Ryusaburo Sato, 'Nihon no "cho-shoshika": Sono genin to taisaku o megutte [Japan's "ultra-low birth rates": Concerning the reasons and appropriate policy measures],' *Jinko Mondai Kenkyu* [*Journal of Population Problems*], 62:2 (2008), pp. 10–24; see also Ryota Isobe, Masahiro Kaneko, Daisuke Sawa, and Takuro Sugimoto, 'Nihon o mushibamu teikonka gensho: Rodo-shijo no kaikau o tsuji teinenka no kaisho o [Taikonka – the phenomenon of giving up marriage – undermines Japan: The elimination of taikonka through reform of the labor market],' Japan Center for Economic Research, 2011, at: http://www.jcer.or.jp/report/econ100/pdf/econ100bangai20110714data.pdf

24. Japan Ministry of Internal Affairs and Communications, *Heisei 22-nendo kokusei chosa.*

25. Japan Ministry of Health, Labor, and Welfare, 'Jinko dotai tokei.'

26. Japan Prime Minister's Office, *Heisei 23-nendo-ban kodomo kosodate hakusho* [*White Paper on Children and Childrearing*], 2011, at: www8.cao.go.jp/shoushi/whitepaper/w-2011/23webhonpen/index.html

27. Kitamura, 'Dai 5-kai danjo no seikatsu to ishiki ni kansuru chosa no kekka hokoku'; see also Miho Iwasawa, 'Kinnen no TFR hendo ni okeru kekkon kodo oyobi fufu no shussei kodo no henka no kiyo nit tsuite [About the impact of the change in nuptiality patterns and married couples' reproduction behavior on the recent change in TFR (total fertility rate)],' *Jinko Mondai Kenkyu* [*Journal of Population Problems*], 58:3 (2002), pp. 15–44.

28. Japan Ministry of Health, Labor, and Welfare, *Kosei rodo hakusho* [*White Paper on Health, Labor, and Welfare*], 2013, at: www.mhlw.go.jp/wp/hakusyo/kousei/13/; see also Toru Suzuki, 'Lowest-low fertility in Korea and Japan,' *Jinko Mondai Kenkyu* [*Journal of Population Problems*], 59:3 (2003), pp. 1–16, at: www.ipss.go.jp/syoushika/bunken/data/pdf/17268901.pdf

29. AIU Insurance Co., *Gendai kosodate keizai-ko* [*Thoughts on Modern Child-Raising Economics*], AIU, Tokyo, 2005.

30. National Institute of Population and Social Security Research, 'Dai-14-kai shussei doko kihon chosa: Kekkon to shussan ni kansuru zenkoku chosa, fufu chosa no kekka gaiyo [The 14th basic survey on birth trends: National survey on marriage and birth – summary of survey results on married couples],' 2010, at: www.ipss.go.jp/ps-doukou/j/doukou14/doukou14.pdf

31. 'Densha-nai no bebi-ka riyo ni sanpi ryoron: Keihatsu posta hikigane [Approvals and disapprovals of stroller use in railways],' *Asahi Shimbun*, 25 August 2012, at: www.asahi.com/edu/kosodate/news/TKY201208250290.html; 'Densha-nai de no bebi-ka riyo o megutte no ronso ... Anata no kangae wa? [Controversy over the use of strollers on trains. What is your view?],' BLOGOS website, at: http://blogos.com/discussion/2012-09-01/baby_car/

32. Kevin O'Neil, 'Stroller wars continue on CTA,' CTA Tattler website, 23 April 2012, at: www.chicagonow.com/cta-tattler/2012/04/stroller-wars-continue-on-cta/

33. Japan Ministry of Health, Labor, and Welfare, 'Heisei 23-nen Jinko Dotai Tokei Geppo Nenkei no Gaikyo [2011 population statistics monthly report – summary],' 2012, at: www.mhlw.go.jp/toukei/saikin/hw/jinkou/geppo/nengai11/index.html

34. Masami Ito, 'Late pregnancies, little financial aid for fertility treatments conspire against rise: Revival eludes nation's birthrate,' *Japan Times*, April 28, 2012, at: www.japantimes.co.jp/text/nn20120828i1.html

35. 'Top court upholds surrogate ruling,' *Japan Times*, 25 November 2005, at: www.japantimes.co.jp/news/2005/11/25/national/top-court-upholds-surrogate-ruling/

36. Melissa Ahlefeldt, 'Less than family: Surrogate birth and legal parent–child relationships in Japan,' *Journal of Japanese Law*, 16:32 (2011), pp. 65–96, at: sydney.edu.au/law/anjel/documents/2012/ZJapanR32_12_Ahlefeldt_Endf3.pdf

37. One institution in Japan, the Suwa Maternity Clinic in Nagano Prefecture, defies the JSOG guidelines and offers fertility treatment using donated eggs and surrogate mothers. The clinic is led by maverick Dr Yahiro Netsu, an ardent advocate of surrogacy

and the use of egg donation for infertile women – especially those who do not have a uterus. Netsu gained notoriety in 1998 when he announced that he had performed IVF with donated eggs for infertile couples. He was expelled from JSOG after the announcement. Operating outside of JSOG guidelines can cause doctors to lose their license, so this was a great risk. However, he was reinstated by JSOG, and he oversaw the country's first successful surrogate birth in 2001. Since then, he has delivered babies using surrogate mothers, many of whom carry babies for their own biological daughters. But his clinic is rather small and operates in a limited capacity, and simply cannot handle the many Japanese women suffering from infertility. Mizuho Aoki, 'When a baby can't come naturally. Quest by Noda, other women to get pregnant yields success stories, failures, risks, controversy,' *Japan Times*, 8 September 2010, at: www.japantimes.co.jp/text/nn20100908f1.html

38. Japan Government Gender Equality Bureau, 'National machinery for the promotion of the formation of a gender-equal society,' 2011 at: http://www.gender.go.jp/english_contents/about_danjo/prom/national_machinery.html
39. Michael Hoffman, 'Only immigrants can save Japan,' *Japan Times*, 21 October 2012.
40. Kenji Toda, 'Jiminto "imin 1000-man-nin ukeire" no jitsugen-sei [The feasibility of the LDP's proposal to welcome 10 million immigrants],'*Nikkei Business*, 19 June 2008, at: http://business.nikkeibp.co.jp/article/topics/20080617/162440/?rt=nocnt
41. Minoru Matsutani, 'Keidanren: Immigrant worker influx vital to halt labor shortage,' *Japan Times*, 15 October 2008, at: www.japantimes.co.jp/text/nn20081015a1.html
42. 'Trouble haunts foreign trainee program,' *Japan Times*, 23 September 2007, at: www.japantimes.co.jp/text/nn20070913f2.html
43. Koichi Yasuda, *Gaikokujin kenshusei satsujin-jiken* [*A Murder Case Involving a Foreign Trainee*], Nanatumori Shokan, Tokyo, 2007.
44. Satoshi Kamata, 'Japan's internship training program for foreign workers: Education or exploitation?' *Shukan Kinyobi*, 25 April 2008, trans. Nobuko Adachi, *Asia-Pacific Journal*, 15 July 2008, at: www.japanfocus.org/-Kamata-Satoshi/2820#
45. Japan Ministry of Health, Labor, and Welfare, 'Gaikokujin koyo jokyo no todokede jokyo [The status of reported employment of foreign workers],' 2011, at: www.mhlw.go.jp/stf/houdou/2r98520000020ns6.html
46. Japan International Training Cooperation Organization (JITCO), 'Kenshusei ginou-jishusei no koshu-teate, kenshu-teate, chingin joho ni tsuite [Information about trainees' class-attendance rewards, in-service trainee rewards, and wages],' 2011, at: www.jitco.or.jp/stop/teate-chingin.html
47. Koichi Yasuda, *Sabetsu to hinkon no gaikokujin rodosha* [*Discriminations and Poverty That Foreign Workers Face*], Kobunsha, Tokyo, 2010.
48. ibid.
49. Hiroshi Matsubara, 'Training scheme exploits foreigners,' *Japan Times*, 7 April 2000, at: www.japantimes.co.jp/text/nn20000407b1.html
50. Hiroko Tabuchi, 'Japan training program is said to exploit workers,' *New York Times*, 20 July 2010, at: http://www.nytimes.com/2010/07/21/business/global/21apprentice.html?pagewanted=all&_r=0
51. '"Karoshi" claims first foreign trainee,' *Japan Times*, 3 July 2010, at: www.japantimes.co.jp/text/nn20100703a4.html
52. 'Trouble haunts foreign trainee program,' *Japan Times*, 23 September 2007.
53. Philip Brasor, 'Foreign trainees easily exploited as bosses take advantage of system,' *Japan Times*, 14 February 2010, at: www.japantimes.co.jp/text/fd20100214pb.html
54. 'UN rights rapporteur says end foreign trainee program "slavery",' *Japan Times*, 1 April 2010, at: www.japantimes.co.jp/text/nn20100401a6.html
55. US Department of State, *Trafficking in Persons Report 2011*, 2011, at: www.state.gov/j/tip/rls/tiprpt/2011/

56. Yasuda, *Gaikokujin kenshusei satsujin-jiken.*
57. Kamata, 'Japan's internship training program for foreign workers: Education or exploitation?'
58. Yasuo Kuwahara, 'Migrant workers in the post-war history of Japan,' *Japan Labor Review*, 2:4 (2005), pp. 25–47.
59. Yasushi Inoguchi, *Gaikokujin rodosha shinjidai* [*The New Age of Foreign Workers*], Chikuma Shobo, Tokyo, 2001.
60. Matsubara, 'Training scheme exploits foreigners.'
61. Coco Masters, 'Japan to immigrants: Thanks, but you can go home now,' *Time*, 20 April 2009, at: www.time.com/time/world/article/0,8599,1892469,00.html#ixzz292DoPS3a
62. Hiroko Tabuchi, 'Japan pays foreign workers to go home,' *New York Times*, 22 April 2009, at: www.nytimes.com/2009/04/23/business/global/23immigrant.html?pagewanted=all
63. Yasuda, *Sabetsu to hinkon no gaikokujin rodosha.*
64. Minority Rights Group International, 'State of the world's minorities and indigenous peoples 2011 – Japan,' 2011, at: www.unhcr.org/refworld/docid/4e16d36dc.html
65. Kazuo Watanabe, 'Brazil-hatsu. Dekasegi gensho no kaiko to tenbo. Kodomo no kyoiku sekinin wa dare ni [From Brazil. Reflections of the migrant phenomena and the future prospects. Who is responsible for migrant children's education?],' *Nikkei Shimbun*, 13 June 2009, at: www.nikkeyshimbun.com.br/090613rensai-rondan.html
66. Toshi Maeda, 'Japanese-Brazilians go "home" to tap economic boom,' AFP, 12 April 2012, at: www.google.com/hostednews/afp/article/ALeqM5gh9Mm9IIozBRMrk7k_ ePxZuVreyw?docId=CNG.ef219419e3c05e20659f6300c1e4136d.6c1
67. Japan Institute for Labor Policy and Training, 'Dai-9 koyo sokushin kihon keikaku [The ninth basic plan of employment measures],' 1999, at: www.jil.go.jp/jil/kisya/ syokuan/990813_01_sy/990813_01_sy_bessi.html
68. Japan Student Services Organization, 'Part-time work,' 2009, at: www.g-studyinjapan. jasso.go.jp/en/modules/pico/index.php?content_id=30
69. Ministry of Health, Labor, and Welfare, 'Gaikokujin koyo jokyo hokoku (Heisei 24-nen 10-gatsu-matsu genzai) no kekka ni suite [About the report on the situation of the employment of foreigners as of the end of October 2012],' 2012, at: www.mhlw.go.jp/stf/ houdou/2r9852000002ttea-att/2r9852000002tthv.pdf
70. Ministry of Education, Culture, Sports, Science, and Technology, 'Kongo no ryugakusei seisaku ni suite [About the future policy on foreign students],' 2013, at: www.mext.go. jp/a_menu/koutou/ryugaku/1338568.htm
71. Hitomi Hirose, 'Gaikokujin no kangofu-san, kaigo-fukushi-san [Foreign nurses, foreign caregivers],' NHK News Commentators Bureau website, 29 November 2012, at: www. nhk.or.jp/kaisetsu-blog/700/139513.html
72. Rumiko Inoue and Kumiko Miyashita, 'Kaigo gyokai no kyuyo soba [Average wage in the senior care sector],' All About website, 1 October 2009, at: http://allabout.co.jp/gm/ gc/298164/
73. Ho Al Li, 'Barriers deter Asian nurses from Japan,' *Straits Times*, 15 October 2012, at: www.asianewsnet.net/news-37635.html
74. Linda H. Aiken, James Buchan, Julie Sochalski, Barbara Nichols, and Mary Powell, 'Trends in international nurse migration,' *Health Affairs*, 23:3 (2004), pp. 69–77.
75. 'Indonesia no kangoshi koho gokaku Devi-san [Indonesian nurse candidate Dewi passes examination],' *Kango kaigo zenkoku nyusu* [*National News on Nursing and Senior Care*], 124 (2011), at: www.bimaconc.jp/beritaperawatan1104.html#news04
76. 'Futan omoku ukeire keien: Gaikokujin kaigosi gokakuritu 37.9%, hitode busoku shinkoku [Avoiding foreign caregivers due to the burden of hosting them: the success rate of foreign caregivers (in passing the national exam) at 37.9%],' Sankei News, 29 March 2012, at: http://sankei.jp.msn.com/life/news/120329/bdy12032914250003-n1. htm

77. Hitomi Hirose, 'Kaigo fukushi-shi: Gaikokujin ukeire no kadai [Caregivers: the challenges of hosting foreigners],' NHK News Commentators Bureau website, 29 March 2012, at: www.nhk.or.jp/kaisetsu-blog/100/115321.html

78. 'Futan omoku ukeire keien,' Sankei News.

79. Japanese Nursing Association, 'Indoneshia-jin kango kohosha ukeire ni atatte Nihon Kango Kyokai no kenkai [The view of the Japanese Nursing Association on hosting Indonesian nursing candidates],' Press release, 17 June 2008, at: www.nurse.or.jp/home/opinion/press/2008pdf/0617-4.pdf; 'EPA-waku no gaikokujin kangoshi: Shikaku shutoku no shien susumu [Foreign nurses in the EPA program: Extending support for their acquisition of qualification certificate],' Yomiuri Shimbun, 16 April 2012, at: www.yomidr.yomiuri.co.jp/page.jsp?id=57457

80. Takashi Yamasaki, 'Kango kaigo bunya ni okeru gaikokujin rodosha no ukeire mondai [The problem of allowing foreign workers in the fields of nursing and senior care],' Refarensu [Reference], February 2006, pp. 5–24, at: www.ndl.go.jp/jp/data/publication/refer/200602_661/066101.pdf

81. Hitomi Hirose, 'Gaikokujin kaigo fukushi-shi: Ukeire no kadai wa [Foreign caregivers: the challenges of hosting them],' NHK News Commentators Bureau, 3 April 2012, at: www.nhk.or.jp/kaisetsu-blog/450/116067.html

82. Japan Ministry of Health, Labor, and Welfare, 'Gaikokujin koyo taisaku no kihonteki na kangae-kata [The basic stance on policy on the employment of foreigners],' 2010, at: www.mhlw.go.jp/bunya/koyou/gaikokujin17

83. Hirose, 'Gaikokujin kaigo fukushi-shi.'

84. ibid.

85. Hirose, 'Gaikokujin no kangofu-san, kaigo-fukushi-san.'

86. 'Foreign caregiver exits put program in doubt,' Japan Times, 20 June 2012, at: www.japantimes.co.jp/text/nn20120620f1.html

87. 'Betonamu-jin kangoshi, kaigoshi kouhosha no hounichi-mae Nihongo kenshu kaimakushiki o kaisai [Holding a ceremony for the start of a Japanese language training program for Vietnamese nursing and caregiving candidates prior to their visit to Japan],' Viet Jo website, 28 November 2012, at: www.viet-jo.com/news/nikkei/121127024652.html; Noriyuki Wakisaka, 'Foreign nurses and care workers in Japan: Reform needed,' Nippon.com website, 13 June 2012, at: www.nippon.com/en/currents/d00034/

88. Nobue Suzuki, 'Outlawed children: Japanese Filipino children, legal defiance and ambivalent citizenships,' Pacific Affairs, 83:1 (2010), pp. 31–50.

89. 'Aratana kaigo no ninaite,' NHK.

90. Gaikokujin kangoshi kaigo fukushi shien kyogikai [Cooperation for Overseas Nurses and Care Workers], 'Nichi-Hi EPA: Wakugumi ni genkai [Japan–Philippine EPA: Limits to the framework],' Kango kaigo zenkoku nyusu [National News on Nursing and Senior Care], 123 (2011), at: www.bimaconc.jp/beritaperawatan1103.html#news06

91. Hirose, 'Gaikokujin kaigo fukushi-shi.'

92. Ministry of Justice, Immigration Bureau, 'Points-based preferential immigration treatment for highly skilled professionals,' April 2012, at: www.immi-moj.go.jp/english/topics/120502_en.html; for the points calculation table, see: www.immi-moj.go.jp/english/topics/pdf/120502/02_e.pdf

93. Norifumi Mizoue, 'Roson-ryu "daibashiti saiyo" [Lawson-style "diversity hiring"],' President, 11–14 (2011), at: www.president.co.jp/pre/backnumber/2011/20111114/21082/21087/

94. 'Shukatsu isso kibishiku,' Sankei News, 24 March 2012, at: http://sankei.jp.msn.com/economy/news/120324/biz12032420200020-n1.htm

95. Kenji Nanbu, 'Ryugakusei saiyou ga moogataru kigyo no uchimuki-do [Hiring of foreign students tell the degree of introvertedness among Japanese companies],' Yomiuri Online, 22 March 2012, at: http://www.yomiuri.co.jp/net/global/20120322p02.htm

96. Paul. J. Scalise, 'Japan's phony solution,' *Newsweek*, 9 May 2010, at: http://www.news-week.com/scalise-economics-japanese-immigration-70193

97. Japan Student Services Organization, 'Heisei 23-nen gaikokujin zaiseki jokyo chosa kekka [The 2011 survey results on enrollment of foreign students (at Japanese universities and professional schools),' 2 May 2012, at: www.jasso.go.jp/statistics/intl_student/data11.html

98. Japan Economic Research Institute, 'Gaikokujin rodosha ukeireno seisaku no kadai to houkou [The challenges and direction of policy on admitting foreign workers],' 2008, at: www.nikkeicho.or.jp/report/kono080916_all.pdf

99. Robert Lenzner, '40% of the largest US companies founded by immigrants or their children,' *Forbes*, 25 April 2013, at: www.forbes.com/sites/robertlenzner/2013/04/25/40-largest-u-s-companies-founded-by-immigrants-or-their-children/. The five firms listed were all founded or co-founded by first-generation immigrants.

100. Yasuda, *Sabetsu to hinkon no gaikokujin rodosha*.

101. Ministry of Health, Labor, and Welfare, 'Shikyu kaishi nenrei nit suite [About pension eligibility age],' 2011, at: www.mhlw.go.jp/stf/shingi/2r9852000001r5uy-att/2r9852000001r5zf.pdf

102. OECD, *OECD Skills Outlook 2013: First results from the survey of adult skills*, 2013, at: http://skills.oecd.org/OECD_Skills_Outlook_2013.pdf; American Chamber of Commerce in Japan, *Charting a New Course for Growth: Recommendations for Japanese leaders*, American Chamber of Commerce in Japan, Tokyo, 2010, at: iis-db.stanford.edu/res/2323/ACCJ_CHARTING_A_NEW_COURSE_FOR_GROWTH.pdf

Chapter 4 Getting Along with the Neighbors

1. Hirata, 'Who shapes the national security debate?'

2. Ministry of Foreign Affairs of Japan (MOFA), 'Statement by Prime Minister Tomiichi Murayama "On the occasion of the 50th anniversary of the war's end", 15 August 1995, at: www.mofa.go.jp/announce/press/pm/murayama/9508.html

3. Kobayashi Yoshinori, *Sensoron [On War]*, Gentosha, Tokyo, 1998.

4. The exact number of victims is unclear. Western media typically report about 200,000 comfort women in total, but some Japanese scholars claim there were only about 20,000. For diverse claims, see 'Sex slaves put Japan on trial,' BBC News, 8 December 2000, at: http://news.bbc.co.uk/2/hi/asia-pacific/1061599.stm; 'Japan's NHK boss apologises for "comfort women" comments,' BBC News, 27 January 2014, at: http://www.bbc.co.uk/news/world-asia-25880481; and Ikuhiko Hata, *Ianfu to senjo no sei [Comfort Women and Sex in the Battlefield]*, Shincho sensho, Tokyo, 1999.

5. 'Exchanges between Mr. Hashimoto and reporters,' *Asahi Shimbun*, 14 May 2013, at: http://digital.asahi.com/articles/TKY201305140366.html

6. Toko Sekiguchi, 'Japanese prime minister stokes wartime passions,' *Wall Street Journal*, 25 April 2013, at: http://online.wsj.com/news/articles/SB10001424127887324743704578444273613265696?mg=reno64-wsj&url=http%3A%2F%2Fonline.wsj.com%2Farticle%2FSB10001424127887324743704578444273613265696.html%2GTH%2F

7. Justin McCurry, 'Is Japan's Shinzo Abe finally acting on his true nationalist colors?,' *Christian Science Monitor*, 25 April 2013, at: http://www.csmonitor.com/World/Asia-Pacific/2013/0425/Is-Japan-s-Shinzo-Abe-finally-acting-on-his-true-nationalist-colors

8. 'We challenge Takaichi to raise "aggression" argument in Japan's neighbors, US,' *Asahi Shimbun*, 15 May 2013, at: http://ajw.asahi.com/article/views/editorial/AJ201305150047

9. David Pilling, 'How will Abe spend his political capital?' *Financial Times*, 21 July 2013, at: www.ft.com/intl/cms/s/0/d062f318-f1ef-11e2-8e04-00144feabdc0.html

10. ibid.

11. Linda Sieg, 'Japan PM Abe seeks personal redemption in upper house election,' Reuters, 7 July 2013, at: www.reuters.com/article/2013/07/07/us-japan-election-abe-idUSBRE9660I720130707. Keiko Hirata, in 'Who shapes the national security debate?', divides the normalists in Japan into three categories: US-leaning normalists, global-leaning normalists, and nationalist-leaning normalists. According to her definitions, Abe would fall into the third camp, rather than into a separate ultra-nationalist group.

12. Jong's case became well known through a 2011 documentary called *Tese*, directed by Nariaki Kang and distributed on CD by Kadokawa Shoten, Tokyo.

13. Rennie Moon, 'Koreans in Japan,' *Spice Digest*, Freeman Spogli Institute for International Studies, Stanford University, 2010, at: http://iis-db.stanford.edu/docs/507/Koreans_inJapan.pdf

14. Sonia Ryang, 'The North Korean homeland of Koreans in Japan' in Ryang (ed.), *Koreans in Japan: Critical voices from the margin*, Routledge, London, 2000.

15. 'Kokuseki wa Kankoku, shozoku wa Kitachosen no Jong Tese, soshite haha, Li Jongumu-san [Jong Te-se with South Korean nationality, but belonging to North Korea. And his mother, Mrs. Li Jongumu],' *Korea Joongang Daily*, 14 July 2010, at: http://japanese.joins.com/article/191/131191.html?sectcode=&servcode=600

16. Du-jin Park, *Chosen Soren: Sono kyozo to jittai* [*Chongryon: Its false image and reality*], Chuko Shinsho, Tokyo, 2008.

17. Sonia Ryang, 'Indoctrination or rationalization? The anthropology of "North Koreans" in Japan,' *Critique of Anthropology*, 12:2 (1992), pp. 101–32.

18. Gwang Hee Han, *Waga Chosen-soren no tsumi to batsu* [*The Crimes and Punishments of Our Chongryon*], Bungei Shunju, Tokyo, 2005.

19. ibid.

20. Yong Hun Kim, 'Debts, mergers, collapses and foreclosures,' Daily NK website, 23 November 2009, at: www.dailynk.com/english/read.php?cataId=nk00400&num=5681

21. Gwang Hee Han, *Waga Chosen-soren no tsumi to batsu*.

22. Blair McBride, 'Young "Zainichi" Koreans look beyond Chongryon ideology,' *Japan Times*, 16 December 2008, at: www.japantimes.co.jp/community/2008/12/16/issues/young-zainichi-koreans-look-beyond-chongryon-ideology/#.UQwCJqBgNSU

23. 'Pro-North schools to lose tuition waiver: Lack of progress on abductions to hit Chongryon,' *Japan Times*, 29 December 2012, at: www.japantimes.co.jp/text/nn20121229a3.html

24. Susan Menadue-Chun, 'Chongryon students as scapegoats,' *Japan Times*, 3 January 2013, at: www.japantimes.co.jp/text/rc20130103a6.html

25. Kirk Spitzer, 'N. Korea crisis: A view from Tokyo,' *The Diplomat*, 12 April 2013, at: http://thediplomat.com/2013/04/12/north-korea-crisis-a-view-from-tokyo

26. Eiko Osaka, 'Kanryu to Kankoku, Kankoku-jin imeji [The Korean Wave and images of South Korea and Korean people],' *Suruga Daigaku Ronso*, 36 (2008), pp. 24–47.

27. Norimitsu Onishi, 'What's Korean for "real man?" Ask a Japanese woman,' *New York Times*, 23 December 2004, at: www.nytimes.com/2004/12/23/international/asia/23JAPAN.html?_r=2&

28. Osaka, 'Kanryu to Kankoku, Kankoku-jin imeji.'

29. Onishi, 'What's Korean for "real man?" Ask a Japanese woman.'

30. Nabeela On, 'Exploring the "Japan Brand": K-Pop won't live up to the hype forever,' Seoulbeats website, 4 April 2012, at: http://seoulbeats.com/2012/04/exploring-the-japan-brand-kpop-wont-live-up-to-the-hype-forever/

31. Onishi, 'What's Korean for "real man?" Ask a Japanese woman.'

32. 'Japan's first lady takes flak for attending South Korean musical,' *Asahi Shimbun*, 11 May 2013, at: http://ajw.asahi.com/article/behind_news/social_affairs/AJ201305110051

33. 'Korean singers dropped from yearend NHK music show,' *Japan Times*, 28 November 2012, at: www.japantimes.co.jp/text/nn20121128a4.html

34. 'Shin-Okubo aikawarazu oonigiwai: Kanryu fan wa Takeshima-mondai dokofuku kaze [Shin-Okubo is bustling as usual: The Takeshima problem falls on deaf ears of K-Wave fans],' JCAST News website, 29 August 2012, at: www.j-cast.com/2012/08/29144457. html?p=all

35. Tetsushi Kajimoto and Izumi Nakagawa, 'Japan firms say China protests affect business plans: Reuters poll,' Reuters, 20 September 2012, at: www.reuters.com/article/2012/09/20/ us-japan-china-poll-idUSBRE88J1CH20120920

36. 'Tettai ga dekinai. Chugoku shinshutsu Nikkei kigyo no kuno [Cannot withdraw. The plight of Japanese firms that made inroads in China],' Close-up Gendai, NHK TV, 2 October 2012.

37. 'Teaching manuals modified to describe Senkakus, Takeshima as Japan's territory,' Asahi Shimbun, 28 January 2014, at: http://ajw.asahi.com/article/behind_news/politics/ AJ201401280051

38. Linus Hagström and Jon Williamsson, ' "Remilitarization," really? Assessing change in Japanese foreign security policy,' Asian Security, 5:3 (2009), pp. 242–72.

39. Moriteru Arasaki, 'The struggle against military bases in Okinawa: Its history and current situation,' Inter-Asia Cultural Studies, 2 (2001), pp. 102–08.

40. Steve Rabson, 'Okinawa's Henoko was a "storage location" for nuclear weapons: Published accounts,' Asia-Pacific Journal, 14 January 2013, at: www.japanfocus.org/-Steve-Rabson/3884

41. Nakaima won a financial package from the Abe government, worth about 300 billion yen each year until 2021, and a promise that the Futenma base would be closed within five years. See 'Nakaima OKs offshore work at Nago base site,' Japan Times, 27 December 2013, at: http://www.japantimes.co.jp/news/2013/12/27/national/nakaima-oks-offshore-work-at-nago-base-site/#.UtCVRqBgMlI

42. Yoshio Shimoji, 'Futenma: Tip of the iceberg in Okinawa's agony,' Asia-Pacific Journal, 24 October 2011, at: www.japanfocus.org/-Yoshio-SHIMOJI/3622

43. 'Armitage says Japan's ban on collective self-defense "impediment",' Global Post website, 24 June 2013, at: www.globalpost.com/dispatch/news/kyodo-news-international/ 130624/armitage-says-japans-ban-collective-self-defense-imped

44. Richard L. Armitage and Joseph S. Nye, The US–Japan Alliance: Anchoring stability in Asia, Center for Strategic and International Studies, Washington, DC, 2012.

45. Advisory Panel on Reconstruction of the Legal Basis for Security, 'Report of the Advisory Panel on Reconstruction of the Legal Basis for Security,' 24 June 2008, at: www.kantei.go.jp/jp/singi/anzenhosyou/report.pdf

46. Yuki Tatsumi and Andrew Oros (eds.), Japan's New Defense Establishment: Institutions, capabilities, and implications, Stimson Center, Washington, DC, 2007.

47. Yutaka Oishi, 'Seron chosa to shimin ishiki [Public opinion polls and citizens' level of awareness],' Keio Gijuku Daigaku Media Komyunikeshon Kenkyujo Kiko [Keiko University Media Communication Research Institute Journal], 55 (2005), pp. 49–62, at: http://www.mediacom.keio.ac.jp/publication/pdf2005/kiyou55/ooishi.pdf

48. Tatsumi and Oros (eds.), Japan's New Defense Establishment.

49. G. John Ikenbery, 'Japan's history problem,' Washington Post, 17 August 2006, at: www. washingtonpost.com/wp-dyn/content/article/2006/08/16/AR2006081601427.html

Chapter 5 Meltdown

1. Kiyoshi Kurokawa, 'Message from the Chairman' in Kurokawa et al., The Official Report of the Fukushima Nuclear Accident Independent Investigation Commission, Executive Summary, National Diet of Japan, Tokyo, 2012, at: warp.da.ndl.go.jp/info:ndljp/ pid/3856371/naiic.go.jp/wp-content/uploads/2012/09/NAIIC_report_hi_res10.pdf

2. Richard J. Samuels, 3.11: Disaster and change in Japan, Cornell University Press, Ithaca, New York, 2013.

3. Gerald Curtis, 'Stop blaming Fukushima on Japan's culture,' *Financial Times*, 10 July 2012, at: www.ft.com/intl/cms/s/0/6cecbfb2-c9b4-11e1-a5e2-00144feabdc0. html#axzz2rpTxvhAP

4. Wayne Drash, 'Why Japan relies on nuclear power,' CNN website, 15 March 2011, at: http://edition.cnn.com/2011/WORLD/asiapcf/03/14/japan.nuclear.history.qa/

5. Toru Takeda, *Watashitachi wa koshite 'genpatsu taikoku' wo eranda* [*This is How We Chose to Become a Nuclear Powerhouse*], Chuo Koron Shinsha, Tokyo, 2011.

6. *OECD Environmental Performance Reviews: Japan 1994*, reported in Mick Corliss, 'OECD asks how green is Japan,' *Japan Times*, 2 June 2001, at: www.japantimes.co.jp/ news/2001/06/02/news/oecd-asks-how-green-is-japan/

7. 'The OECD environment programme: Environmental performance review of Japan – Executive Summary,' 2002, at: www.oecd.org/environment/country-reviews/2110905. pdf

8. Mariko Shinju, *Mottainai Basan* [*Mottainai Grandma*], Kodansha, Tokyo, 2004; also David Kestenbaum, 'Mottainai Grandma reminds Japan, "Don't waste"', NPR website, 8 October 2007, at: http://www.npr.org/templates/story/story.php?storyId=14054262

9. 'Mottainai! "Reduce, reuse, recycle" gets ethical in Japan and beyond,' Treehugger website, 26 September 2008, at: www.treehugger.com/culture/mottainai-reduce-reuse-recycle-gets-ethical-in-japan-and-beyond.html

10. See: www.city.shinjuku.lg.jp/foreign/english/pdf/other/gomi2013_e.pdf

11. John Olmsted, 'Japan's recycling: More efficient than USA,' *University of Wisconsin-Stout Journal of Undergraduate Research*, 2007, at: minds.wisconsin.edu/handle/ 1793/52921

12. UN Statistics Division, 'Greenhouse gas emissions per capita,' July 2010, at: http:// unstats.un.org/unsd/environment/air_greenhouse_emissions.htm

13. Yoichi Funabashi, *Kaunto daun: Meruto daun jo* [*Countdown: Meltdown*, Vol. 1], Bungei Shunju, Tokyo, 2012.

14. NHK Supesharu Merutodaun Shuzai-han [NHK Special TV Crew on the Meltdowns], *Merutodaun rensa no shinso* [*The Truth Behind the Chain of Meltdowns*], Kodansha, Tokyo, 2013.

15. In Units 1 and 3, hydrogen released as a result of the damage to the core of these reactors filled the buildings and exploded. Unit 4, which had no fuel in its reactor and thus no source of hydrogen, also suffered a similar explosion – either because hydrogen from the Unit 3 building entered Unit 4 through connected pipes, or because the spent-fuel pool in Unit 4 got overheated and generated hydrogen. These explosions exacerbated the crisis, but were not as catastrophic as the worst-case scenario that TEPCO and Japanese government officials feared: explosions in the nuclear containment vessels. Such explosions would have released an enormous amount of radioactive materials into the environment, making at least one-third of Japan uninhabitable. See Funabashi, *Kaunto daun: Meruto daun jo*; also 'Causes of Unit 4 explosion revisited,' SimplyInfo: The Fukushima project website, 21 January 2013, at: www.simplyinfo.org/?page_ id=9326

16. NHK Supesharu Merutodaun Shuzai-han, *Merutodaun rensa no shinso*.

17. Yasuaki Oshika, *Merutodaun: Dokyument Fukushima Daiichi genpatsu jiko* [*Meltdowns: Documentary on the Fukushima Daiichi nuclear accident*], Kodansha, Tokyo, 2013.

18. Oshika, *Merutodaun*. Some media reported that about 50 remained. ' "Eiyu Fukushima 50" Obei media genpatsu no sagyoinra shosan ["Heroic Fukushima 50": Western press praise workers at nuclear plant],' *Asahi Shimbun*, 18 March 2011. While hundreds of workers evacuated from Fukushima Daiichi, many of them soon returned to the plant and the number of workers at the plant fluctuated.

19. Ryusho Kadota, *Shi no fuchi o mita otoko* [*The Man Who Stared Down Death*], PHP Institute, Tokyo, 2012.

20. Oshika, *Merutodaun*.
21. The hydrogen explosion at the Unit 1 building removed the blowout panel in the walls of the Unit 2 building, allowing the escape of hydrogen vented from Unit 2 and preventing a hydrogen explosion at the reactor. Funabashi, *Kaunto daun: Meruto daun jo*.
22. The Unit 3 explosion also caused the water injection pumps that had been got ready to cool the Unit 2 reactor to be buried in the resultant debris, delaying the process of water injection. See 'Fukushima genpatsu no 101-jikan (3) [The first 101 hours of the Fukushima nuclear accident, (3)]', *Kahoku Shimbun*, 9 August 2012, at: www.kahoku. co.jp/spe/spe_sys1106/20120809_01.htm
23. When the safety relief valve is opened, high-pressure steam is injected from the pressure vessel into the water in the suppression chamber of the containment vessel. This process provides depressurization.
24. *NHK supesharu genpatsu jiko 1*.
25. Oshika, *Merutodaun*.
26. 'NRC chair: "No water in the spent fuel pool" at Unit 4,' ABC News, 16 March 2011, at: http://abcnews.go.com/blogs/politics/2011/03/nrc-chair-no-water-in-the-spent-fuel-pool-at-unit-4/
27. Matthew L. Wald, 'Report gives new details of chaos at stricken plant,' *New York Times*, 11 November 2011, at: http://www.nytimes.com/2011/11/12/world/asia/report-details-initial-chaos-at-fukushima-daiichi-nuclear-plant-in-japan.html?_r=0
28. *NHK supesharu genpatsu jiko 1*.
29. Yuji Okada, 'Fukushima dismantling to start as cold shutdown announced,' *Bloomberg Businessweek*, 19 December 2011, at: http://www.businessweek.com/news/2011-12-19/fukushima-dismantling-to-start-as-cold-shutdown-announced.html
30. TEPCO says Yoshida's death a couple of years after the Fukushima Daiichi nuclear accident had nothing to do with the nuclear radiation he was exposed to during the crisis, as he received a total of 70mSv of radiation, well below the 100mSv threshold for heightened cancer risk. His cancer was esophageal cancer, which requires several years to develop. But his friends and some medical experts say the excessive level of stress he endured during the crisis may have shortened his life. Kenichi Omae, 'Yoshida shocho no si, genpatujiko no eikyo wa [The death of plant manager Yoshida: Any impact of the nuclear accident?],' *ZakZak*, 21 July 2013, at: www.zakzak.co.jp/economy/ecn-news/news/20130721/ecn1307210735000-n1.htm
31. Yoichi Funabashi, *Kaunto daun: Meruto daun ge* [*Countdown: Meltdown*, Vol. 2], Bungei Shunju, Tokyo, 2013.
32. Fukushima Daiichi is often contrasted with its sister plant, Fukushima Daini, which is only 12km to the south of Daiichi. Daini was also struck by the tsunami, but it sustained less damage thanks to the improved plant design, which strengthened its resistance to flooding. Generators and other electrical distribution equipment were stored in the watertight reactor building. Fukushima Daini stayed on the grid and avoided station blackout. Three of the four reactors at Daini failed in the tsunami, but they were soon restored to operation. See Junichi Taki, 'Jonetsu kino o soshitsu, girigiri no fukkyuu sagyo: Fukushima Daini de nani ga okita ka, jo [Losing the function of heat removal, repair work reaching the limit: What happened at Fukushima Daini, first series],' *Nihon Keizai Shimbun*, 3 May 2013, at: www.nikkei.com/article/DGXNASFK3002L_R00C13A5000000/
33. 'Toden, Fukushima Daiichi de takasa 15m no tsunami yosoku shiteita [TEPCO had predicted 15-meter tsunami at Fukushima Daiichi],' *Yomiuri Shimbun*, 24 August 2011, at: www.yomiuri.co.jp/science/news/20110824-OYT1T00991.htm?from—ain1
34. Funabashi, *Kaunto daun: Meruto daun jo*.

35. Investigation Committee on the Accident at the Fukushima Nuclear Power Stations of Tokyo Electric Power Company, 'Executive summary of the final report,' 23 July 2012, via: www.cas.go.jp/jp/seisaku/icanps/post-3.html
36. Section 3.1 of the Japanese Act on Compensation for Nuclear Damage 1961.
37. Oshika, *Merutodaun.*
38. At Reactor Unit 3, an emergency coolant system (the High-Pressure Coolant Injection or HPCI system) was working, but the operators stopped it for fear that it might break down. They tried to restart it, but it never worked again. They did not have the necessary knowledge to operate it in an emergency. Fukushima Daiichi Plant Manager Yoshida did not know for more than an hour that Unit 3's HPCI had stopped working, because of the lack of communication by the operators. Also, the operators erroneously assumed that the emergency cooling system of the isolation condenser (IC) at Unit 1 was working. The IC was designed to cool Unit 1 for at least eight hours. This wrong assumption delayed the water injection for core cooling and venting of the primary containment vessel (to depressurize the reactor vessel to allow water injection). 'As a result, an earlier opportunity for core cooling was missed' (Investigation Committee on the Accident at Fukushima Nuclear Power Stations of Tokyo Electric Power Company, 'Executive summary,' p. 7). Unit 1 had a meltdown within half a day of the tsunami. See Funabashi, *Kaunto daun: Meruto daun jo.*
39. Tokyo Electric Power Company (TEPCO), 'Fukushima nuclear accident analysis report,' 20 June 2012, at: www.tepco.co.jp/en/press/corp-com/release/betu12_e/images/120620e0104.pdf
40. TEPCO is not the only Japanese firm that has had serious nuclear accidents. In 1999, for example, fuel-reprocessing workers at Tokaimura plant used buckets to hand-mix uranium, in violation of safety standards. Later, two of the workers died from exposure to radioactive materials. These workers lacked basic technical background and understanding of nuclear safety. In 2004, there were five casualties at Kansai Electricity Mihama Nuclear Plant Unit 3 due to a non-radioactive steam leak from a broken pipe. Whenever a problem occurred, NISA dealt with the crises and focused its energy on how to restart the nuclear power plant. See James Brooke, '4 die in accident at Japan nuclear power plant,' *New York Times* Learning Network website, 10 August 2004, at: www.nytimes.com/learning/teachers/featured_articles/20040810tuesday.html
41. Ikuko Kao, 'Japan's TEPCO admits 1978 nuclear criticality,' Reuters, 22 March 2007, at: http://uk.reuters.com/article/2007/03/22/japan-tepco-nuclear-idUKT16854920070322
42. Office of Nuclear Data and Information [Genshiryoku Shiryo Joho-shitsu], *Kensho: Toden genpatsu toraburu kakushi* [*Examination: TEPCO's cover-ups of nuclear power plant troubles*], Iwanami Shoten, Tokyo, 2002; Norimitsu Onishi and Ken Belson, 'Culture of complicity tied to stricken nuclear plant,' *New York Times*, 27 April 2011, at: www.nytimes.com/2011/04/27/world/asia/27collusion.html?pagewanted=2&_r=4&src—e
43. Funabashi, *Kaunto daun: Meruto daun jo.*
44. Because Yoshida ignored TEPCO/Takekuro's order and did not immediately report to TEPCO headquarters the continual seawater injection into the reactor, the then vice-president of the company, Sakae Muto, did consider reprimanding Yoshida, even though Moto himself thought Yoshida's decision the correct one at the time. Prime Minister Kan defended Yoshida a couple of months after the disaster, saying that the onsite manager was authorized to take independent decisions and that Yoshida's decision to continue with seawater injection had not been mistaken. Kan argued that Yoshida should not be reprimanded and TEPCO went along with the prime minister's argument. 'Fukushima Daiichi no kaisui chuyu chudan sezu, Toden shocho, honsha ni mudan [Seawater injection never halted, TEPCO's director made the decision without

headquarter's approval],' *Asahi Shimbun*, 27 May 2011, at: http://www.asahi.com/special/10005/TKY201105260339.html; 'Fukushima Daiichi Genpatsu shocho no shobun fuyo shusho ga ninshiki [The prime minister recognizes there is no need to reprimand the manager at Fukushima Daiichi Nuclear Plant],' *Nihon Keizai Shimbun*, 28 May 2011, at: http://www.nikkei.com/article/DGXNASFS2801C_Y1A520C1000000/

45. Oshika, *Merutodaun*.
46. National Diet of Japan, *The Official Report of the Fukushima Nuclear Accident Independent Investigation Commission*, 2012, chapter 3, at: http://warp.da.ndl.go.jp/info:ndljp/pid/3856371/naiic.go.jp/en/report/
47. Funabashi, *Kaunto daun: Meruto daun jo*.
48. NHK Supesharu Merutodaun Shuzai-han, *Merutodaun rensa no shinso*.
49. According to TEPCO's report, these batteries could not be delivered on the freeway due to a lack of administrative permission, and so had to be delivered via land freight to the Onahama Coal Center, TEPCO's emergency storage place for Fukushima Daiichi, before being sent on to Daiichi.
50. NHK Supesharu Merutodaun Shuzai-han, *Merutodaun rensa no shinso*.
51. *NHK supesharu genpatsu jiko 1: Genpatsujiko 100 jikan no kiroku*.
52. National Diet of Japan, *The Official Report of the Fukushima Nuclear Accident Independent Investigation Commission*, chapter 3.
53. Tomohiko Shinoda, 'DPJ's political leadership in response to the Fukushima nuclear accident,' *Japanese Journal of Political Science*, 14:2 (2013), pp. 243–59.
54. Oshika, *Merutodaun*; Keiji Takeuchi, '"Tettai suru ka, nokoru ka," Toden to shusho ga chokumenshita kyukyoku no sentaku ["Withdrawal or remaining," the ultimate choice faced by TEPCO and the prime minister],' Web Ronza website, 21 March 2012, at: http://astand.asahi.com/magazine/wrscience/2012032000009.html
55. Mari Yamaguchi, 'Ex-PM slams utility over Japan nuke crisis video,' AP News website, 8 August 2012, at: http://bigstory.ap.org/article/ex-pm-slams-utility-over-japan-nuke-crisis-video
56. Oshika, *Merutodaun*.
57. Boric acid was used at the plant in an attempt to stop nuclear fission reactions.
58. Funabashi, *Kaunto daun: Meruto daun jo*.
59. Oshika, *Merutodaun*.
60. Kan's visit to TEPCO led to the creation of a joint command center in TEPCO head-quarters, which significantly improved communication. A private-sector panel investigating the nuclear crisis praised both Kan's call for TEPCO not to withdraw from the plant and the establishment of the joint command center that followed his visit, saying those actions helped contain the crisis. Kan later claimed that the visit was useful in getting a grip on the crisis.
61. Oshika, *Merutodaun*.
62. Onishi and Belson, 'Culture of complicity tied to stricken nuclear plant.'
63. Funabashi, *Kaunto daun: Meruto daun jo*.
64. James M. Acton and Mark Hibbs, 'Opinion: Preventing another Fukushima,' Kyodo News English webiste, 13 March 2012, at: http://english.kyodonews.jp/news/2012/03/146800.html
65. Funabashi, *Kaunto daun: Meruto daun ge*.
66. 'Hoan iincho, "naze netako o okosu" [Director of the Nuclear and Industry Safety Agency, "Why wake a sleeping child?"],' NHK Kabun [NHK Science and Culture] website, 2012, at: http://www9.nhk.or.jp/kabun-blog/200/113325.html
67. Yuri Oiwa and Jin Nishikawa, 'NISA obstructed adoption of IAEA guidelines for nuclear accidents,' *Asahi Shimbun*, 15 March 2012, at: http://ajw.asahi.com/article/behind_news/politics/AJ201203150089
68. 'Hoan iincho, "naze netako o okosu?"'

69. Suzanne Goldenberg, 'Japan's nuclear crisis: Regulators warned of reactor risks,' *Guardian*, 14 March 2011, at: www.theguardian.com/environment/2011/mar/14/nuclearpower-energy

70. Haruki Madarame and Koji Okamoto, *Shogen Madarame Haruki: Genshiryoku Anzen Iinkai wa nani o machigaeta no ka [What Mistake Did the Nuclear Safety Committee Make?]*, Shinchosha, Tokyo, 2012.

71. Oshika, *Merutodaun*.

72. This information was handled by MEXT because of its role in science and technology affairs.

73. Asahi Shimbun Tokubetsu Hodobu [Asahi Shimbun Special Report Unit], *Purometeusu no wana [Prometheus's Trap] 1*, Gakken, Tokyo, 2012.

74. Katsuhiko Ishibashi, 'Why worry? Japan's nuclear plants at grave risk from damage,' *Asia-Pacific Journal*, 11 August 2007, at: www.japanfocus.org/-Ishibashi-Katsuhiko/2495

75. Madarame and Okamoto, *Shogen Madarame Haruki*.

76. During the crisis, the NSC stopped functioning, as Prime Minister Kan lost faith in the committee's chairman, Haruki Madarame. Madarame accompanied Kan to Fukushima Daiichi on 12 March. During the flight, Kan asked him if there could be an explosion of any sort at the plant. Madarame said 'no,' and explained that there was no oxygen to cause any explosion. Just hours later, a hydrogen explosion destroyed the building of Unit 1. Watching the explosion on TV, Kan fumed: 'Isn't that an explosion? You said there would be no explosion.' At that point, the prime minister's trust in Madarame evaporated and he started looking around for other nuclear experts to advise him. The problem with Madarame was that he lacked appropriate communication skills to clearly and succinctly explain technical matters to highly stressed politicians who had no nuclear expertise. See Funabashi, *Kaunto daun: Meruto daun jo*; Oshika, *Merutodaun*.

77. Funabashi, *Kaunto daun: Meruto daun jo*.

78. *NHK supesharu Iitate-mura ichinen: Ningen to hoshano no kiroku [NHK Special: Iitate Village, One Year Since the Disaster: The record of humans and radiation]*, NHK TV, 23 July 2012.

79. 'Hoan iincho, "naze netako o okosu?"'

80. Joshua Norman, 'Report: Japanese mafia providing quake relief,' CBS News website, 19 March 2011, at: www.cbsnews.com/8301-503543_162-20045060-503543/report-japanese-mafia-providing-quake-relief/

81. 'Hoan iincho, "naze netako o okosu?"'

82. Ryujiro Komatsu, 'TEPCO rejects compensation settlement for radiation anxiety,' *Asahi Shimbun*, 27 June 2013, at: http://ajw.asahi.com/article/0311disaster/fukushima/AJ201306270078

83. Kyung Lah, 'Husband of Fukushima suicide victim demands justice,' CNN website, 20 June 2012, at: www.cnn.com/2012/06/20/world/asia/japan-fukushima-suicides

84. *News Watch* report, NHK TV, 6 September 2013.

85. The data were collected on 31 March 2013. Reconstruction Agency of Japan, 'Higashi Nihon Daishinsai ni okeru shinsai kanren shi no shisha-su [The number of deaths related to the Great East Japan Earthquake],' 10 May 2013, at: www.reconstruction.go.jp/topics/20130510_kanrenshi.pdf

86. 'Shinsai kanren-shi 2,688-nin ni, fukko-cho matome [The deaths related to the disaster total 2,688, the Reconstruction Agency summarizes],' *Asahi Shimbun*, 11 May 2013, at: www.asahi.com/national/update/0511/TKY201305100536.html

87. Reconstruction Agency of Japan, 'Zenkoku no hinansha-to no kazu [The number of evacuees, etc., throughout the nation],' 2013, at: www.reconstruction.go.jp/topics/main-cat2/sub-cat2-1/20130822_hinansha.pdf

88. Asahi Shimbun Tokubetsu Hodobu, *Purometeusu no wana 2*.

89. Takemichi Nishihori, 'Fukushima no yasai noka ga jisatsu [Suicide by a vegetable farmer in Fukushima],' *Asahi Shimbun*, 29 March 2011, at: www.asahi.com/special/10005/TKY201103280468.html

90. A video of the meeting is available on a personal blog site at: http://saigaijyouhou.com/blog-entry-838.html

91. Minoru Matsutani, 'Seniors urged to eat Fukushima rice to help farmers, protect young people,' *Japan Times*, 20 March 2012, at: www.japantimes.co.jp/news/2012/03/20/national/seniors-urged-to-eat-fukushima-rice-to-help-farmers-protect-young-people/#.Uiprw6BgNFI

92. Fukushima Prefecture Government, 'Shohisha no minasama e [To consumers],' 4 September 2013, at: wwwcms.pref.fukushima.jp/download/1/130904pamph-marinfish_and_shellfish.pdf

93. Chico Harlen, 'S. Korea expands ban on fish from northeastern Japan, citing radiation concerns,' *Washington Post*, 6 September 2013, at: www.washingtonpost.com/world/s--korea-expands-ban-on-fish-from-northeastern-japan-citing-radiation-concerns/2013/09/06/d19c5650-16d6-11e3-a2ec-b47e45e6f8ef_story.html

94. Oshika, *Merutodaun*.

95. 'Toden, 30-nendai zenhan ni datsu kokuyuka: Shin-saiken keikaku no zenyo hanmei [TEPCO, post-nationalization in the early 2030s: The whole picture of the new reconstruction plan became known],' *Tokyo Shimbun*, 27 December 2013, at: http://www.tokyo-np.co.jp/s/article/2013122701001813.html

96. 'Higashi Nihon Daishinsai kara ni-nen han [Two and a half years since the Great East Japan Earthquake],' NHK TV *News Watch*, 11 September 2013.

97. Linda Sieg, 'Insight: Japan ponders Fukushima options, but Tepco too big to fail,' Reuters, 10 September 2013, at: www.reuters.com/article/2013/09/10/us-japan-fukushima-tepco-insight-idUSBRE9891C520130910

98. ibid.

99. Ida Torres, 'NRA chief says situation at Fukushima "exaggerated",' *Japan Daily Press* website, 5 September 2013, at: http://japandailypress.com/nra-chief-says-situation-at-fukushima-exaggerated-0535399/

100. Toru Takeda, *Watashitachi wa koshite 'genpatsu taikoku' to eranda [This is How We Chose the Path Towards 'a Large Nuclear Energy State]'*, Choshinsho, Tokyo, 2011.

101. Chisaki Watanabe, 'Japan's greenhouse gas emissions rose 3.9% on nuclear shutdowns,' Bloomberg News website, 5 December 2012, at: www.bloomberg.com/news/2012-12-05/japan-s-greenhouse-gas-emissions-rose-3-9-on-nuclear-shutdowns.html

102. Hiroko Tabuchi and David Jolly, 'Japan backs off from emissions targets, citing Fukushima disaster,' *New York Times*, 15 November 2013, at: www.nytimes.com/2013/11/16/world/asia/japan-shelves-plan-to-slash-emissions-citing-fukushima.html?smid=tw-share&_r=0

103. Samuels, *3.11: Disaster and change in Japan*.

104. Brett Wilkins, 'Tens of thousands protest against nuclear power in Tokyo,' Digital Journal website, 3 June 2013, at: http://digitaljournal.com/article/351473

105. Martin Fackler, '2 former premiers try to use Tokyo election to rally public against nuclear power,' *New York Times*, 7 February 2014, at: www.nytimes.com/2014/02/08/world/asia/2-former-premiers-try-to-use-tokyo-election-to-rally-public-against-nuclear-power.html?hpw&rref=science

106. The election took place in the midst of Tokyo's worst snowstorm in decades. Turnout was unusually low, which probably favored Masuzoe, the more conservative candidate. Hosokawa may also have been hurt by his late entry into the campaign, his age (76 at the time of the election), his lack of support for Tokyo's successful Olympic bid, and his damaged reputation from a prior corruption scandal that had forced him to resign as prime minister after only eight months in office in 1994. The winner of the election,

Masuzoe, was a flawed candidate as well. In 1989, he had argued that women should be kept out of top government posts because their menstrual cycle makes them irrational. He told a men's magazine at the time: 'Women are not normal when they are having a period . . . You can't possibly let them make critical decisions about the country [during their period] such as whether or not to go to war.' After the statement resurfaced during the gubernatorial campaign, a group of Japanese women threatened a 'sex boycott' against any man who voted for Masuzoe. See 'Tokyo women call for "sex strike" over sexist gubernatorial candidate,' *Guardian*, 7 February 2014, at: http://www.theguardian.com/world/2014/feb/07/tokyo-women-sex-strike-yoichi-masuzoe
107. James M. Acton and Mark Hibbs, *Why Fukushima was Preventable*, Carnegie Endowment for International Peace, Washington, DC, 2012.

Chapter 6 What We Learned at Lunch

1. Randall S. Jones, 'Education reform in Japan,' Economics Department Working Paper No. 888, Organisation for Economic Co-operation and Development, 2011, at: http://www.oecd-ilibrary.org/docserver/download/5kg58z7g95np.pdf?expires=1390234527&id=id&accname=guest&checksum=C232843579C81A65669A38ADCE1CA76D
2. Monbu Kagaku-sho (Ministry of Education, Culture, Sports, Science, and Technology (MEXT)), 'Koto gakko kyoiku no genjo [The present state of high-school education],' 2011, at: www.mext.go.jp/component/a_menu/education/detail/__icsFiles/afieldfile/2011/09/27/1299178_01.pdf
3. OECD, *Education at a Glance 2013: OECD indicators*, 2013, at: http://www.oecd.org/edu/eag2013%20(eng)—FINAL%2020%20June%202013.pdf Note that while there are 34 countries in the OECD, for statistics on teaching hours England and Scotland are reported separately, as are French Belgium and Flemish Belgium.
4. See, for example, Eisuke Saito and Masaaki Sato, 'Lesson study as an instrument for school reform: A case of Japanese practices,' *Management in Education*, 26:4 (2012), pp. 181–6.
5. Makoto Yoshida, 'Overview of lesson study in Japan,' 2013, at: www.rbs.org/SiteData/docs/yoshidaoverview/aeafddf638d3bd67526570d5b4889ae0/yoshidaoverview.pdf
6. ibid.
7. James W. Stigler and James Heibert, *The Teaching Gap*, Simon & Schuster, New York, 1999.
8. Kathleen Roth and Helen Garnier, 'What science teaching looks like. An international perspective,' *Educational Leadership*, 64:4 (2006/07), pp. 16–23.
9. OECD, *Reviews of National Policies for Education: Japan*, OECD, Paris, 1971.
10. MEXT, 'Seito shido teiyo ni tuite [About the Student Guidance Outline],' 2010, at: www.mext.go.jp/b_menu/houdou/22/04/1294538.htm. For the section on developing healthy attitudes, see chapter 8: www.mext.go.jp/b_menu/houdou/22/04/__icsFiles/afieldfile/2011/07/08/1294538_03.pdf
11. Alexis Agliano Sanborn, 'Flavoring the nation: School lunch in Japan,' MA thesis, Harvard University, March 2013, at: http://www.academia.edu/3129340/Flavoring_the_Nation_School_Lunch_in_Japan
12. Quotations are from 'Heisei nijuichi nendo gakko kyushoku shido nen keikaku, Higashi Hiroshima Shiritsu Kurosekiri Shogakko [2009 school lunch guidance yearly plan, East Hiroshima City Elementary School],' reproduced in ibid.
13. For a fascinating discussion of *shokuiku* and its relationship to social interaction and national cohesiveness, see Catherine L. Mah, 'Shokuiku: Governing food and public health in contemporary Japan,' *Journal of Sociology*, 46:4 (2010), pp. 393–412.

14. 'Kyushoku shokku-shi, nido to: Arerugi-ji taio isogu [Death from a shock, never again: Urgent need for measures to address children with allergies],' *Asahi Shimbun*, 4 February 2013, at: http://digital.asahi.com/articles/OSK201302030160.html?ref= comkiji_redirect

15. See discussion of cleaning time in Gail R. Benjamin, *Japanese Lessons: A year in a Japanese school through the eyes of an American anthropologist and her children*, New York University Press, 1997.

16. Justin McCurry, 'Fukushima 50: "We felt like kamikaze pilots ready to sacrifice everything," ' *Guardian*, 11 January 2013, at: www.theguardian.com/environment/2013/jan/11/fukushima-50-kamikaze-pilots-sacrifice

17. 'TEPCO begins power blackouts,' *Japan Today*, 14 March 2011, at: http://www.japantoday.com/category/national/view/tokyo-power-outages-to-start-later-than-planned-trains-reduce-services

18. National Police Agency, Juvenile Division, 'Situation of juvenile delinquency in Japan in 2006,' March 2007, at: www.npa.go.jp/english/syonen1/20070312.pdf

19. 'On being bullied in Japan,' This Japanese Life website, 12 June 2013, at: http://thisjapaneselife.org/2013/06/12/japan-ijime-bullies/

20. Jeanne M. Hilton, Linda Anngela-Cole, and Juri Wakita, 'A cross-cultural comparison of factors associated with school bullying in Japan and the United States,' *Family Journal*, 18:4 (2010), pp. 413–22.

21. 'On being bullied in Japan.'

22. Akiko Fujita, 'Kids and laughing teachers bullied suicide teen,' ABC News, 6 July 2012, at: abcnews.go.com/blogs/headlines/2012/07/kids-and-laughing-teachers-bullied-suicide-teen/ For a book on the case, see Kyodo Tsushin Osaka Shakaibu (Kyodo Osaka Social Division), *Otsu chu-2 ijime jisatsu [Suicide by an Otsu Second-Year Junior High Student, Due to Bullying]*, PHP Kenkyu-jo, Tokyo, 2013.

23. Ken Schoolland, 'Ijime: The bullying of Japanese youth,' *Japanese Education*, 15:2 (1986), pp. 5–28. For a book documenting the end of the student's life, see Mitsuru Toyota, *Soshiki gokko: Hachinen me no shogen [Pretend Funeral: Testimony eight years after]*, Fuga Shobo, Tokyo, 1994.

24. Britney Donald, '70% of teachers say they are unavailable to deal with bullying in classrooms,' *Japan Daily Press* website, 22 November 2012, at: http://japandailypress.com/70-of-teachers-say-they-are-unavailable-to-deal-with-bullying-in-classrooms-2218783/

25. Shoko Yoneyama, 'The era of bullying: Japan under neoliberalism,' *Asia-Pacific Journal*, 31 December 2008, at: http://www.japanfocus.org/-Shoko-YONEYAMA/3001

26. Takashi Naito and Uwe P. Gielen, 'Bullying and ijime in Japanese schools' in F.L. Denmark, H.H. Krauss, R.W. Wesner, E. Midlarsky, and U.P. Gielen, *Violence in Schools: Cross-national and cross-cultural perspectives*, Springer, New York, 2005; see also Yoneyama, 'The era of bullying.'

27. Joy Hendry, *Becoming Japanese: The world of the pre-school child*, University of Hawaii Press, Honolulu, 1986; Tamaki Mino, 'Ijime (bullying) in Japanese schools: A product of Japanese education based on group conformity' in Kate Bennett, Maryam Jamarani, and Laura Tolton, *Rhizomes: Re-visioning boundaries*, School of Languages and Comparative Cultural Studies, University of Queensland, 2006, at: http://espace.library.uq.edu.au/view/UQ:7721

28. ibid.

29. John Hofilena, 'Japan's anti-bullying law goes into effect, guidelines to follow,' *Japan Daily Press* website, 30 September 2013, at: http://japandailypress.com/japans-anti-bullying-law-goes-into-effect-guidelines-to-follow-3036793/; Justin McCurry, 'Long troubled by school bullying, Japan now eyes zero tolerance,' *Christian Science Monitor*, 9 May 2013, at: www.csmonitor.com/World/Asia-Pacific/2013/0509/Long-troubled-by-school-bullying-Japan-now-eyes-zero-tolerance

30. Ida Torres, 'Education taskforce suggests including moral education in Japan's official curriculum,' Japan Daily Press website, 12 November 2013, at: http://japandailypress.com/education-taskforce-suggests-including-moral-education-in-japans-official-curriculum-1239354/

31. 'Folk artist Peter Yarrow to release anti-bullying song in Japan next week,' Japan Times, 23 October 2013, at: www.japantimes.co.jp/news/2013/10/23/national/folk-artist-peter-yarrow-to-release-anti-bullying-song-in-japan-next-week/

32. Setsuko Kamiya, ' "Exam hell" now not so hot,' Japan Times, 20 January 2009, at: www.japantimes.co.jp/news/2009/01/20/reference/exam-hell-now-not-so-hot/#.UXtoTR38KSo

33. Minoru Matsutani, 'Student count, knowledge sliding,' Japan Times, 10 January 2012, at: www.japantimes.co.jp/news/2012/01/10/reference/student-count-knowledge-sliding/#.Uj6KpWQ4VAc

34. Carolyn Dweck, Mindset: The new psychology of success, Ballantine Books, New York, 2007.

35. Minako Sato, 'Cram schools cash in on failures of public schools,' Japan Times, 28 July 2005, at: http://www.japantimes.co.jp/life/2005/07/28/language/cram-schools-cash-in-on-failure-of-public-schools/#.Ut43YBDFLcs

36. MEXT, 'Report on children's out-of-school learning activities,' 2008, as cited in OECD, OECD Economic Surveys: Japan 2011, OECD Publishing, Paris, 2011, chapter 4.

37. ibid.

38. Sato, 'Cram schools cash in on failures of public schools.'

39. ibid.

40. For an in-depth look at class and inequality among Japanese youth, see Robert S. Yoder, Youth Deviance in Japan, Trans Pacific Press, Melbourne, 2004; Robert S. Yoder, Deviance and Inequality in Japan: Japanese youth and foreign migrants, Policy Press, Bristol, 2011. For an earlier work, see Thomas P. Rohlen, 'Is Japanese education becoming less egalitarian? Notes on high school stratification and reform,' Journal of Japanese Studies, 3:1 (1977), pp. 37–70.

41. OECD, OECD Economic Surveys: Japan 2011.

42. Private school subsidies are made directly to the schools, which use them to reduce the tuition for particular families. See MEXT, 'Making public high schools tuition-free and high school enrollment subsidies,' 2010, www.mext.go.jp/b_menu/hakusho/html/hpab200901/detail/1305888.htm

43. Keita Takeyama, 'The politics of international league tables: PISA in Japan's achievement crisis debate,' Comparative Education, 44:4 (2008), pp. 387–407.

44. National Center for Education Statistics, 'Program for International Student Assessment (PISA),' 2013, at: http://nces.ed.gov/surveys/pisa/pisa2012/

45. OECD, OECD Skills Outlook 2013: First results from the survey of adult skills.

46. Educational Testing Service, 'Test and score data summary for TOEFL iBT® tests and TOEFL® PBT tests,' 2013, at: www.ets.org/s/toefl/pdf/94227_unlweb.pdf

47. John Dougill, 'Japan and English as an alien language,' English Today, 24:1 (2008), pp. 18–22.

48. Salvaggio, This Japanese Life.

49. Tim Murphey, The Tale That Wags, Perception Press, Nagoya, 2011.

50. Reiji Yoshida, 'To communicate in English, TOEFL is vital: LDP panel,' Japan Times, 5 April 2013, at: www.japantimes.co.jp/news/2013/04/05/national/to-communicate-in-english-toefl-is-vital-ldp-panel

51. Minoru Matsutani, 'Plan to introduce TOEFL to universities has its merits,' Japan Times, 6 May 2013, at: http://www.japantimes.co.jp/life/2013/05/06/language/plan-to-introduce-toefl-to-universities-has-its-merits/

52. Daisuke Igarashi, 'Rakuten to make English official language,' Asahi Shimbun, 2 July 2010.

53. OECD, *OECD Skills Outlook 2013: First results from the survey of adult skills.*

54. ibid., Figure 4.10, p. 155.

55. '2011 international comparison of labor productivity,' Japan Productivity Center website, 2012, at: www.jpc-net.jp/eng/research/2012_02.html

56. Brian McVeigh, *Japanese Higher Education as a Myth*, M.E. Sharpe, Armonk, New York, 2002.

57. Kariya Takehiko, 'Higher education and the Japanese disease,' Nippon.com website, 16 April 2012, at: www.nippon.com/en/in-depth/a00602/

58. Nicolas Gattig, 'Failing students: Japanese universities facing reckoning or reform,' *Japan Times*, 13 November 2012, at: www.japantimes.co.jp/community/2012/11/13/issues/failing-students-japanese-universities-facing-reckoning-or-reform

59. Takehiko, 'Higher education and the Japanese disease.'

60. Type and number of educational institutions in 2009 from MEXT, Statistical Abstract, 2010 edition, as cited in Yasuo Saito, 'Higher education in Japan,' National Institute for Educational Policy Research, undated, at: www.nier.go.jp/English/EducationInJapan/Education_in_Japan/Education_in_Japan_files/201109HE.pdf

61. Takehiko, 'Higher education and the Japanese disease.' The percentage that are private ranges by type of institution, from about 77 percent of universities to 93–94 percent of junior colleges and vocational schools.

62. Waseda University Circle Database, at: http://e-mile.com/cdb/

63. Maho Yoshida, 'Recruit Rhapsody,' on YouTube, at: www.youtube.com/watch?feature=player_embedded&v—6rb6kknj3A

64. J.S. Eades, Roger Goodman, and Yumiko Hada (eds.), *The 'Big Bang' in Japanese Higher Education: The 2004 reforms and the dynamics of change*, Trans Pacific Press, Melbourne, 2005.

65. Miki Tanikawa, 'More young Japanese heading abroad to study,' *New York Times*, 24 May 2013, at: www.nytimes.com/2013/03/25/world/asia/25iht-educside25.html

66. Suvendrini Kakuchi, 'Call for world's top researchers to collaborate,' *University World News*, 31 January 2014, at: http://www.universityworldnews.com/article.php?story=20140129112214210

67. Suvendrini Kakuchi, 'Boosting foreign student numbers to 300,000,' *University World News*, 31 January 2014, at: http://www.universityworldnews.com/article.php?story=20140129160918747

68. Information on the Global 30 Project, and a list of the 13 universities, is available on the MEXT website at: www.uni.international.mext.go.jp/

69. Norifumi Mizoue, 'Beyond the University of Tokyo? Universities evaluated highly by corporate personnel divisions,' President Online website, 15 October 2013, at: http://president.jp/articles/-/10892

70. Beckie Smith, 'Internationalisation key to Japan's Abeducation,' PIE News, 16 August 2013, at: http://thepienews.com/news/internationalisation-key-to-japans-abeducation/

71. Richard E. Nisbett, *Intelligence and How to Get It: Why schools and cultures count*, W.W. Norton, New York, 2009.

72. ibid., p. 169.

73. After Obokata's publication, the education minister issued a statement saying that the government would further contribute to the creation of a positive environment where young and/or female researchers could actively conduct research: 'Monkasho: Wakate, josei kenkyu-sha ga Katsuyaku shiyasui kankyo o [Ministry of Education, Culture, Sports, Science, and Technology: Creating an environment where young and/or female researchers can play an active part],' Livedoor news website, 31 January 2014, at: http://news.livedoor.com/article/detail/8489570/ See also 'Editorial: Young researcher challenges conventional science with STAP cell study,' *Asahi Shimbun*, 31 January 2004, at: ajw.asahi.com/article/views/editorial/AJ201401310182

Conclusion

1. Ruth Benedict, *The Chrysanthemum and the Sword: Patterns of Japanese culture*, Houghton-Mifflin, Boston, 1946.
2. ibid., pp. 2–3.
3. Manuel Castells, *End of Millennium: The information age*, Blackwell, Malden, MA, 1998.
4. United Nations Department of Economic and Social Affairs, 'World population prospects: The 2012 revision,' 2013, at: http://esa.un.org/wpp/Documentation/pdf/WPP2012_%20KEY%20FINDINGS.pdf
5. United Nations Development Programme, *Human Development Report, 2009.*
6. United Nations Office on Drugs and Crime, 'Robbery at the national level, number of police-recorded offences,' 2012, at: www.unodc.org/documents/data-and-analysis/statistics/crime/CTS_Robbery.xls
7. '2011 comparison of labor productivity.'
8. Faith Aquino, 'Japan's birthrate drops to 1.03 million, number of deaths keep increasing,' *Japan Daily Press* website, 7 June 2013, at: http://japandailypress.com/japans-birthrate-drops-to-1-03-million-number-of-deaths-keep-increasing-0730181/
9. Buerk, 'Japan singletons hit record high.'
10. 'GDP per capita (current US$),' World Bank website, at: http://data.worldbank.org/indicator/NY.GDP.PCAP.CD
11. Joseph Sternberg, 'Mr. Abe's Missing Arrow,' *Wall Street Journal*, 26 June 2013, at: http://online.wsj.com/article/SB10001424127887324637504578568613127577972.html
12. Lillian Cunningham, 'Will the bedroom or boardroom save Japan,' *Washington Post*, 13 September 2013, at: www.washingtonpost.com/blogs/on-leadership/wp/2013/09/13/will-the-bedroom-or-boardroom-save-japan/
13. Sandra Collins, *The 1940 Tokyo Games: The missing Olympics – Japan, the Asian Olympics and the Olympic movement*, Routledge, London, 2007.
14. Paul Droubie, 'Playing the nation: 1964 Tokyo Summer Olympics and Japanese identity,' unpublished dissertation, University of Illinois at Urbana-Champaign, 2009.
15. Paul Droubie, 'Japan's rebirth at the 1964 Summer Olympics,' Japan Society website, 31 July 2008, at: http://aboutjapan.japansociety.org/content.cfm/japans_rebirth_at_the_1964_tokyo_summer
16. Richard Halloran, 'The rising east: 2020 in Tokyo cheers up a despondent Japan,' Honolulu Civil Beat website, 16 September 2013, at: www.civilbeat.com/posts/2013/09/16/19900-the-rising-east-2020-olympics-in-tokyo-cheers-up-a-despondent-japan/
17. Droubie, 'Playing the nation.'
18. ibid., p. ii.

Select Bibliography

The following are some recommended books on contemporary Japan.

Birmingham, Lucy and David McNeill. *Strong in the Rain: Surviving Japan's earthquake, tsunami, and Fukushima nuclear disaster*, Palgrave Macmillan, New York, 2012.

Brinton, Mary C. *Lost in Transition: Youth, work, and instability in postindustrial Japan*, Cambridge University Press, Cambridge, 2010.

Decoker, Gary and Christopher Bjork (eds.). *Japanese Education in an Era of Globalization: Culture, politics, and equity*, Teachers College Press, New York, 2013.

Dower, John W. *Ways of Forgetting, Ways of Remembering: Japan in the modern world*, The New Press, New York, 2012.

Goodman, Roger, Yuki Imoto, and Tuukka Toivonen (eds.). *A Sociology of Japanese Youth: From returnees to NEETs*, Routledge, London, 2012.

Hasegawa, Harukiyo and Glenn D. Hook (eds.). *Political Economy of Japanese Globalization*, Routledge, London, 2012.

Hendry, Joy. *Understanding Japanese Society*, Routledge, London, 2012.

Hook, Glenn D., Julie Gilson, Christopher W. Hughes, and Hugo Dobson. *Japan's International Relations: Politics, economics and security*, 3rd edn, Routledge, London, 2011.

Kingston, Jeff (ed.). *Natural Disaster and Nuclear Crisis in Japan: Response and recovery after Japan's 3/11*, Routledge, London, 2012.

Krauss, Ellis S. and Robert J. Pekkanen. *The Rise and Fall of Japan's LDP: Political party organizations as historical institutions*, Cornell University Press, Ithaca, NY, 2011.

Midford, Paul. *Rethinking Japanese Public Opinion and Security: From pacifism to realism?* Stanford University Press, Palo Alto, CA, 2011.

Pyle, Kenneth. *Japan Rising: The resurgence of Japanese power and purpose*, Public Affairs, New York, 2009.

Rosenbluth, Frances McCall and Michael F. Thies. *Japan Transformed: Political change and economic restructuring*, Princeton University Press, NJ, 2010.

Ryang, Sonia. *Koreans in Japan: Critical voices from the margin*, Routledge, London, 2013.

Samuels, Richard. *3.11: Disaster and change in Japan*, Cornell University Press, Ithaca, NY, 2013.

Soeya, Yoshihide. *Japan as a 'Normal Country'?: A nation in search of its place in the world*, University of Toronto Press, 2011.

Acknowledgements

We are grateful to the many people in Japan who have shared their lives and stories with us during our visits to Japan, and especially during and after the March 2011 earthquake, tsunami, and nuclear disaster. We spent the 2010–11 academic year in Japan as visiting scholars, Keiko at Waseda University and the University of Tokyo, and Mark at Waseda University. We are grateful to Chikako Ueki of the Waseda University Institute of Asia-Pacific Studies and Akira Suehiro of the University of Tokyo Institute of Social Science for hosting Keiko as a visiting scholar, and to Michiko Nakano, professor at Waseda University's School of Education and Director of its Distance Learning Center, for hosting Mark.

We also wish to thank Dean Stella Theodoulou and the California State University of Northridge College of Social and Behavioral Sciences, which provided funding to Keiko for this study through its summer research program, and to Dean Deborah Vandell and the School of Education at the University of California, Irvine, which provided sabbatical funding to Mark.

We are grateful to Tetsu Iwaya, a former employee of the Tokyo Electric Power Company (TEPCO), who provided invaluable background information for the chapter on the Fukushima nuclear crisis.

Yochiro Sato of Ritsumeikan Asia Pacific University provided much valuable information, and also commented in detail on a previous version of this manuscript. We greatly appreciate his help.

Parts of the education chapter draw on some prior work on educational and social inequality by Rachel Dunn. We thank her for her assistance.

Aileen Kawagoe runs the Education in Japan website, blog, and discussion forum. She and the many people who contribute to the discussion forum have been an enormous source of information, not only on education, but on a wide range of other topics, including gender, language, technology, immigration, and the Fukushima crisis. We appreciate the information she and all the members of her discussion forum have provided, and are also grateful for her comments on parts of the manuscript.

Other people who have given us suggestions and information include Jason Karlin of the University of Tokyo and Glenn Stockwell of Waseda University.

Of all the people who assisted in this effort, three stand out the most. Our editor at Yale University Press, Phoebe Clapham, provided amazing support throughout the process of our proposing, writing, and revising this book. The only thing that matched the speed of Phoebe's feedback to us was its degree of thoughtfulness. We are extremely appreciative of her superb advice and support. We are also greatly appreciative of our copy editor at the press, Clive Liddiard, whose very careful line-by-line editing of the completed manuscript resulted in improvements to virtually every paragraph. Finally, our deepest gratitude goes to Eryk Salvaggio, currently a graduate student at the London School of Economics and formerly a teacher and journalist who lived and worked in Japan for several years. Early on we hired Eryk as an editorial assistant, on account of his writing skills, editing, research ability, and keen insights into Japanese culture and society, as reflected in his blog postings and book, *This Japanese Life*. Eryk gathered background information for our book, shared some of his own stories and anecdotes with us, consulted closely on the education chapter, provided detailed feedback and suggestions on the book's contents, and carefully edited the entire manuscript. This book would not have come to fruition without his expert and tireless assistance, and we can't thank him enough.

Index

Abe, Akie 148
Abe, Shinzo, Prime Minister
    character 133–4
    and collective self-defense 159–60, 161
    economic reforms 55–8, 246
    and educational reforms 229, 239, 246
    nationalism of 132, 133, 134, 148, 246–7,
        329
    and relocation of US air base from
        Futenma to Henoko 157–8
    and Second World War 132–3
    and use of technology 232, 239
Abenomics 55–8, 246
age, deference within companies 39, 40
aging population 89–90, 244
    social welfare cost of 95–6
agriculture
    effect of Fukushima accident on farmers
        192–3
    limited arable land 6–7
    resistance to reform 56–7, 92
AIJ Investment Advisors 51
AKB48 girl group 71–2
Akihabara district, Tokyo 68–9, 71
Akita International University 236
American Chamber of Commerce in Japan
    125
anime culture, young men's fascination
    with 40, 61, 68–71
anti-nuclear energy protest movement
    165–6, 198–9

Anti-Terrorism Special Measures Law
    (2001) 160–1
Armitage, Richard, US Deputy Secretary of
    State 159, 161

Bae Yong-joon (Yon-sama), South Korean
    actor 146–7, 148–9
Bank of Japan 55
Bank of Tokyo-Mitsubishi UFJ, recruitment
    54
baseball 11
Basic Act for a Gender-Equal Society
    (1999) 47, 104
Basic Plan of New Economic Strategies
    118
Basic Space Law (2008) 145
Benedict, Ruth, *The Chrysanthemum and
    the Sword* 240–1
benefits
    cuts in 93
    for housewives 78
    lack of in part-time and temporary jobs
        36, 38
birth rate 244, 257–8n12
    declining 90
    low 64, 96–8
    measures to increase 104–5
    see also fertility treatment
Bloomberg Businessweek 50
bowing, ritualized 16
boy bands 66–7

Brazilians (of Japanese descent)
  menial labor 112
  repatriation program 111–12, 114
  social problems and discrimination
    113–14
  work visas for 111–14
Buddhism 7
bullying in schools
  as collective 213–15
  national task force on 215
burakumin (outcast group) 134–5
bureaucracy
  and failure of response to Fukushima
    accident 200
  and opposition to immigration 123
  permanent 8, 14–15
  power of 18–19
  and rigid orderliness 14–15
Bushido ('The Way of the Warrior') 8

career-track women 43–8
  and childcare 43–4
  long working hours 43–4
  transfers 44
Castells, Manuel 241
centenarians 88–9
Chan, Agnes, singer 79
child allowance program 105
childcare 43, 80
Childcare and Family Care Leave Laws
  (1991) 104
  (1999) 47
children
  cost of raising 98
  declining numbers 91, 217
  disincentives to having 98
  and pushchair controversies 99–100
China 27
  anti-Japanese protests 129, 130, 151–2
  and 'comfort women' 131
  declaration of 'maritime air defense zone'
    152
  and disputed Senkaku/Diaoyu islands
    151–3
  economic development 128
  foreign trainees from 107
  and Japanese history textbooks
    129–30
  and Japan's militarization 160
  Second World War 126–7, 151
Chizuko, Ueno, *A Guide for Singles* 76
Chongryon organization 138, 139–45

financial activities 141–2
  'repatriation' program 140–1
Chongryon (pro-North Korean) schools
  137–9, 140
  lack of public funding 142–3
Christian missionaries, suspicion of 8–9
citizenship 106
class system 7–8
Clinton, Bill, US President 160
Close-up Gendai TV program 108
collective resolve 4
collective self-defense 159–61
'comfort women' 130, 131–2, 265n4
companies
  age of CEOs 92
  corruption 48–53
  foreign workers 122–3, 236
  hierarchies 39–42
  insularity 53–5
  lifetime employment 19, 25, 30
  management style 26
  recruitment rules 35, 38, 39, 233–4
  right to impose overtime work 33
  and seniority 92–3
  staff transfers 44
  treatment of whistle-blowers 22–4
  and *wa* 11
  and workplace loyalty 15–16, 39–40
  see also Olympus
companies, foreign
  acquisitions by Japan (1990s) 42
  corporate culture 45, 58
  productivity and job-creation rates 125
computers, in schools 230–1
Confucianism 7
Constitution, Article 9 127, 159,
    161, 246
consumer expenditure 26
corporate culture 53–5, 62–3
  foreign companies foreign 45, 58
  TEPCO 196
  see also companies; salarymen
corporate governance 52
corruption 48–53
cosmetic companies 46, 51, 80
  and herbivore men 62
creativity, stifled within companies
    32, 41
crime
  against women 86
  low rates 212, 243
  by seniors 94–5

The Croissant Syndrome 75
cross-dressing 66
culture, national
    paradoxes of 241
    see also wa
currency exchange rate 57–8
Curtis, Gerald 165

Daio Paper company 51
Dalai Lama 215
DBSK (South Korean pop group) 146, 147–8
deference
    and scientific research 237
    to elderly 5
demography 88–125
depression, from overwork 31
Diaoyu/Senkaku islands *see* Senkaku/
    Diaoyu islands
Distant Howling of the Loser Dogs 75–6
divorce rate 86, 97
Dokdo/Takeshima islands 148–50

earthquake and tsunami (March 2011) 167–8
    economic recovery from 56
    scale of 175, 199–200
    social solidarity 1–3, 188–9
    and workplace loyalty 15
    see also Fukushima nuclear accident
earthquakes
    frequency of 6, 173
    Great Kanto (1923) 10, 248
East Asian Community, proposed 153
economic development zones 56
economic equality 16, 242–3
Economic Partnership Agreements
    with Philippines and Indonesia 116
    with Vietnam 119
The Economist 52, 53
economy
    1990–91 collapse 27–8, 241–2
    and education system 223
    and English language 229, 230
    fiscal debt 95
    improvements 57–8
    'lost decade' (stagnation) 27, 55, 244
    new stimulus (Abenomics) 55–8, 244
    post-war development 24–6, 242–3
    social welfare cost of aging population
        95–6
    and structural reform 56
education system 21, 202–39
    academic year 236–7

attempts at reform 223, 229, 235
    collectivism 204–8
    competition within 216–17, 219
    and egalitarianism 208, 221–2
    exam culture 215–19
    and focus on hard work and
        perseverance 218
    international comparisons 204, 223–32,
        238, 243
    juku cramming schools 219–23
    and learning in precise order 227
    mathematics 206–7, 238
    organization 204–5
    power of tradition in 237
    rote learning 206
    science teaching 207, 238
    see also schools; universities
elderly
    caregivers for 116
    centenarians 88–9
    deference to 5, 92
    health and welfare needs 93
    homeless 93–4
    numbers of 20
    political power of 91–2
    poverty 94
    proportion of 89–90
    serial petty crimes by 94–5
electoral system
    influence of seniors in 91–2
    and policy choices 92
    rural bias 56, 91–2
    voter turnout 91
employment
    lifetime 19, 25, 30
    menial labor 112
    part-time or temporary 27–8, 34–9
energy sector 197
    natural gas 197
    proportion of nuclear electricity
        generation 197
    renewables 197
    see also nuclear energy
English language
    and exam system 225–6, 228
    failures in teaching and learning 224–30,
        239, 245
    as mandatory in private companies
        229–30
    as means of communication 227–8
entrepreneurs 93
environmentalism 166–7

Equal Employment Opportunity Law
    (1986) 43, 47
equality
    economic 16, 242–3
    education system and 208, 221–2
    enforced 15
ethics, and corporate loyalty 51
ethnicity, homogeneity of 8, 228
exhaustion
    of salarymen 30–1
    of schoolchildren 203–4, 219
expansionismm 10

Fackler, Martin 38–9
FACTA magazine 49
families
    extended 98
    single-parent 86
    see also households
Family Planning Association 65
Family Registration Law 102, 103
fashion
    men's 60
    men's interest in 61
fatalism 7
fax machines, in schools 231
fertility treatment
    egg donation 102
    IVF 102, 103
    for older women 101–3
    surrogate motherhood 102–3,
        261–2n37
feudal social system 7–8
fishing, effect of Fukushima accident on
    193–4
food education, at school lunch 209
Food Education Act (2005) 209
foreign policy 20, 126–63, 245
    and nationalism 246–7
foreign students, employment of 115–16, 236
foreign trainee programs 107–11
    court cases against employers 110
    as illegal workers 111
foreigners, suspicion of 8–9
Four Leaves boy band 66–7
fraud, accounting, penalties 52
free trade 56–7
freeters (part-time or temporary workers)
    34–6, 245, 246
Freitas, Francisco 111–12
Fukasawa, Maki 61
Fukuda, Yasuo, Prime Minister 106

Fukushima Daiichi nuclear power plant,
    accident (March 2011) 164–201,
    268n18, 269n30
    attempts to cool reactors 169–70
    blamed on culture 164–5
    boiling water reactors 168–9, 185
    causes of 199–200
    decommissioning 195–6
    decontamination 95, 191, 193
    effect on farmers 192–3
    effect on fishermen 193–4
    evacuation 185–6, 268n18
    and evacuation zone 187–9, 191
    first week 168–72
    groundwater contamination 194,
        195–6
    heroism 172–3
    leaks of contaminated water 194, 195
    legacy of 197–9
    poor contingency planning 173, 174–8
    Reconstruction Agency 190–1
    regulatory failures 183–7, 200
    scale of 168
    suicides and indirect deaths 190–1
    Unit 1 268n15, 269n21, 270n38
    Unit 2 171
    Unit 3 268n15, 269n22, 270nn38, 40
    Unit 4 172, 268n15
Fukushima Daini nuclear power plant 170,
    173, 269n32
Fukuyama, Tetsuro, Deputy Chief Cabinet
    Secretary 181–2

geeks see otaku
Gender Equality Bureau, and work-life
    balance 47
gender inequality 105
    measures to combat 47, 104
gender relations 20
gender roles
    rejection of 59–87
    rigidity of 5, 86–7
    women and 5, 243
Germany, birth rate 90
girl bands 71–3, 150
globalization 243
    and education 229–30, 231–2, 239
    loss of competitive edge 55
GMI research group, on corporate
    governance 52
Good Morning, Japan news show 120
Google 58

Government Investigation Committee (on accident at Fukushima) 175–6
Great Kanto Earthquake (1923) 10, 248
greenhouse gas emissions 167, 198
grooming, herbivores 61–2
Guam, US base 157

Hadenya 5
    March 2011 earthquake 1–2
haken (dispatch workers) 36–9, 246
    women as 42
Hamada, Masaharu, and Olympus 22–4
Haneda International Airport 249
harmony
    crisis of 5–6, 19
    as enemy of flexibility, openness and innovation 243
    and scientific research 238
Hashimoto, Toru 131
Hatoyama, Yukio, Prime Minister 153, 157
Hayashi, Fumiko 81
headhunting, illegal from client firms 22–3
healthcare 242
    for seniors 93
Henoko, Okinawa 156–7
herbivore men 61–5
    as androgynous 62
    and male celebrities 66–7
    passivity 65, 87
    rejection of corporate norms 62–3
    relations with women 63–5, 257–8n12
hierarchies 11, 16–17, 241
    within companies 39–42, 92
    within schools 211
Hiraoka, Eiji, vice-director of NISA 185
Hirohito, Emperor 130
Hirose, Kenkichi, NISA director 184
Hirose, Naomi, new president of TEPCO 195
historical revisionism 129–30, 237
homeless, elderly as 93–4
homosexuality, tolerance of 86, 259n46
Hong Kong 27
honor 11–12
Hosokawa, Morihoro 199, 273n106
household budgets 29
households
    single-parent 86
    two-generation nuclear 95, 98
    two-income 47–8, 78–9

housewives 76–9
    image of 77–8
    part-time workers 42, 77, 78
    traditional role of 29, 76–7
    as working mothers 79–81
housing, renting 37

IAEA (International Atomic Energy Agency) 184
Ienaga, Saburo 129
Iijima, Ai, actress 75
Iitate (village), and Fukushima accident 187–9
Ikenberry, John 161
immigrants 105–25, 244
    Brazilian *Nikkeijin* 111–15
    and cultural friction 124
    foreign students 115–16
    Korean 17, 105–6, 124
    need for 106
    nurses and caregivers 116–21
    points-based system 121–2
    policy on 114–15
    popular opposition to 123–5
    professionals 121–3
Immigration Control Law (2005) 119
    amendment (1989) 121
    amendment (2008) 120
Immigration Control and Refugee Recognition Law (1990) 112
income, per capita 27
independence, Japanese concept of 13
India, gestational surrogacy 103
Indonesians, as nurses and caregivers 116–18
Industrial Training Program (ITP) 107–8, 110–11
industrialization 10
infertility, and pregancy 101–3
inflation, new target 55
information technology 125
innovation
    lack of 27, 58, 123, 243
    tax breaks to encourage 124–5
Inoguchi, Kuniko 81
Inoguchi, Yasushi 111
insider/outsider distinctions 5–6, 163, 245
    sharp boundaries 17–18, 126
institutional shareholders, and corruption 53
insularity 6, 18
    of corporations 53–5

International Military Tribunal for the Far East (1946–48) 130
internet
English language and 229–30, 231–2
websites for career women 44
internet cafes, overnight accommodation in 37–8
interns, foreign 108
ippanshoku (non-career) jobs, women in 42–3
Iraq Special Measures Law (2003) 161
Ishihara, Shintaro, governor of Tokyo 131, 151
Italy, birth rate 90

Jaczko, Gregory, US Nuclear Regulatory Commission 172
Japan, geographical hostility of land 6–7
Japan Atomic Industrial Forum 198
Japan International Training Cooperation Organization 108
Japan Restoration Party 131–2
Japan Society of Obstetrics and Gynecology (JSOG) 102
Japanese Exchange and Teaching (JET) Programme 229
Japanese language
requirements for immigrant workers 113, 117, 121–2
teaching of 206
Japanese Nursing Association 118
Johnny & Associates, talent agency 66–7
The Johnny's, pretty and androgynous men 67
Jong Te-se, football player 135–6, 138, 139, 144
juku cramming schools 219–23
costs 220

K-Pop 146, 148, 149
K-Wave (South Korean culture) 146–8, 150
Second Wave 147–8
Kadota, Ryusho, on Masao Yoshida 173
Kan, Naoto, Prime Minister
and Fukushima nuclear accident 170, 176, 179
and head of NSC 272*n*76
and NISA 185
and TEPCO 180–2, 270*n*40
visit to Fukushima 181–2, 271*n*60
Kanebo cosmetics group 51, 52
Kanno, Takeshi 3

Kansai Electricity Mihama Nuclear Plant 270*n*40
KARA (South Korean girl band) 150
karo-jisatsu (suicide from overwork) 31
karoshi (death from overwork) 31–2
foreign trainees 109
Kashiwazaki Kariwa nuclear power plant 196
Kato, Sogen, oldest man 88
Kato, Toru 28–9
Katsumata, Tsunehisa, chairman of TEPCO 176, 178, 182, 195
Kawasaki, Jiro 112
Keidanren (Federation of Business Organizations) 57, 106
Keynes, John Maynard 55
Kikukawa, Tsuyoshi, president of Olympus 23, 48–9, 50, 51
Kim Il-sung, and Chongryon organization 141
Kim Jang-hoon, South Korean singer 149
Kishi, Nobusuke 134
Kitagawa, Johnny 67
Koizumi, Junichiro, Prime Minister 116, 130, 199
Komori, Akio, Managing Executive Officer of TEPCO 178
Komuro, Yoshie, CEO Work Life Balance Co. Ltd. 80–1
Kondo, Shunsuke, chair of Japan Atomic Energy Commission 171
kone (connections) 35
konkatsu (marriage hunting) 81–6
net (online) 84–5
Kono, Yohei, apology for 'comfort women' 131, 132
Korea
and 'comfort women' 131
Japanese annexation (1910) 137
Second World War 126–7
see also North Korea; South Korea
Korean residents 17, 105–6
assimilation 144, 162
and Chongryon schools 138–9
and Japanese citizenship 137
and Japanese relations with Korea 135–7
Korean War 155
Kristof, Nicholas 12
Krugman, Paul 55
Kurokawa, Kiyoshi, chairman of Nuclear Accident Independent Investigation Commission 164–5
Kushioka, Hiroaki, whistle-blower 23–4

labor exploitation, of foreign trainees 107–11
labor market 27
  rigidity of 40–2
labor productivity 32, 124–5, 231–2, 244, 254n15
labor shortage 20
  managerial posts 46
  need for immigrant workers 106–7, 118–19
  see also immigrants
labor unions 23, 38
land reforms, postwar 56–7
land values 26
  collapse 27
languages see English language; Japanese language
Lawson convenience stores 115, 122
Lee Myung-bak, South Korean President 149
Lee, Tadanari, football player 144
Liberal Democratic Party 128, 245–6
life expectancy 242
lifetime employment 19, 25, 30
literacy 4, 223, 238
loneliness
  of single elderly 95
  of single women 74–6
loyalty
  extreme 8, 15–16, 245
  to employer 15–16
lunch boxes (bento) 29, 77, 147

McDonalds, overwork 31–2
McVeigh, Brian, Japanese Higher Education as a Myth 232–3
Madarame, Haruki, chairman of NSC 272n76
Mainichi Shimbun newspaper 120
Manchuria, Japanese invasion 152
marriage, age at 81–2, 97, 244
marriage brokers, professional 83
marriage hunting (konkatsu) 81–6
  omiai (matchmaking) 83–4
  online matchmaking sites 84–5
  speed-dating parties 83–4
masuku (surgical masks) 11–12
Masuzoe, Yoichi 199, 273–4n106
mathematics, teaching of 206–7
Meiji Restoration 9, 133, 247, 252–3n11
men
  fall in salaries 82
  herbivores 61–5

new voluntary and involuntary roles 87
  and otaku (homebound lifestyle) 61, 67–71
  part-time or temporary employment 27–8, 34–6
  single 85
  see also salarymen
Michishita, Hiroshi 35
middle class 16
militarism 241
militarization, pressure for 20–1, 159–60, 161, 163
military
  changes to security policy 160–1
  and collective self-defense 159–61
  missile defense program with USA 145
  security alliance with USA 153–61
  self-defense forces 127
Mindan, pro-South Korean organization 142
Ministry of Economy, Trade and Industry (METI) 183
Ministry of Education (MEXT)
  and economic inequalities 222–3
  and goals for school lunch 208–9, 210
  and national cultural standards 207–8, 209–10
Ministry of the Environment, and Nuclear Regulation Authority (NRA) 187
Miyazaki, Tsutomu, serial killer 68
Miyazawa, Kenji, 'Not Losing to the Rain' (poem) 3–4
mortality rate, foreign trainees 109
mottainai (disapproval of waste) 166
Mukden Incident (1931) 152
Murayama Statement (1995), apology for Second World War 128
Murayama, Tomiichi, Prime Minister 128
Muto, Sakae, vice-president of TEPCO 270n44

Nabokov, Vladimir, Lolita 68
Nagadoro, and Fukushima accident 186, 189–90
Nagasaki
  aging population 89
  Christian rebellion (17th century) 9
Nakaima, Hirokazu, governor of Okinawa 157
Nakasone, Yasuhiro, Prime Minister 130
Nakayama, Tatsumi 119
Nanjing Massacre (1937) 130
Narisawa, Hironobu 105

National Defense Program Outline (1976) 160

National Institute of Population and Social Security Research 65
  on aging demographic 89–90
  on birth rate 96–7, 101

National Pension Law, 1986 amendment 42

nationalism 9–10
  and education 239
  and 'normalism' 132, 162, 266n11
  and prospects for 2020 Olympic Games 250–1
  and warrior wa 127

natural gas, imported 197

NEETs (not in education, employment or training) 40

Nikkeijin, Latin Americans of Japanese descent 111–15

Nikkeijin, New (Filipino-Japanese children) 119–21

Ninth Basic Plan of Employment Measures (1999) 114–15

NISA (Nuclear and Industrial Safety Agency) 174
  conflicts of interest in 184
  failures of 184–7
  and jurisdiction of METI 183
  lack of expertise 183–4
  lack of neutrality 183
  revelations of cover-up 178
  and TEPCO 180

Nisbett, Richard 237

Nixon, Richard, US President 155

'No Overtime Days' 30, 32–4
  failure of 33

Nobel Prizes for science 237, 238

Noda, Seiko 102

Noda, Yoshihiko, Prime Minister 53

normalism 132, 162, 266n11

North Korea 135
  abduction of Japanese citizens 142, 143–4
  military threat to Japan 144–5
  Workers' Party control of Chongryon 137
  zainichi affinity with 135–9

Nuclear Accident Independent Investigation Commission (NAIIC) 164–5, 174
  and responsibility of TEPCO 175

nuclear accidents, small 167–8

Nuclear Damage Liability Facilitation Corporation 195

Nuclear Emergency Response Headquarters 181

nuclear energy 165–6, 167
  debate on future of 198–9
  lax regulatory system 174, 183–7
  suspension after Fukushima 197–9
  see also Fukushima nuclear accident

Nuclear Regulation Authority (NRA)
  creation of 187
  and TEPCO 196–7

Nuclear Safety Commission (NSC) 184, 187
  failings of 186, 272n76

nuclear weapons, held by USA on Okinawa 155–6

nurses and caregivers
  immigrants as 116–19
  and New Nikkei Filipinos 120
  resistance of Japanese to employment as 118

nursing, national certification exams 116–17

obedience
  reflexive 164
  at work 34

Obokata, Haruko, scientist 238, 277n73

Ohara, Reiko, actress 74–5

Ohitorisama, TV drama 76

Okinawa 154–9
  Futenma Base 156–7
  Kadena US Air Base 154
  relations with Japanese government 158
  reversion to Japan (1972) 156
  US Camp Schwab at Henoko 156–7

Okinawa, Battle of (1945) 154–5

Olympic Games
  1940 (cancelled) 248
  1964 249–50
  2020 17, 248, 250–1

Olympus
  corruption scandal 48–53
  and whistleblowing 22–4

omiai (matchmaking) 83–4

orderliness, rigid 13–15

organized crime syndicates, yakuza (mafia) groups 51

Osaka 89

otaku (homebound lifestyle) 40
  advice for women dating otaku men 69–70

idol 71–3
  men and 61, 67–71
overtime 28–9, 33
  unpaid 46
overwork 29, 30–2, 243–4
  and blind obedience 34
  and lack of ideas 32

Pacific Ring of Fire 6
pacifism 127
part-time or temporary employment 27–8,
    34–6
  haken 36–9
  income gap 37
  lack of benefits 36, 38
paternity leave 105
pato (housewife part-time workers) 42
patriarchy 241
  see also gender roles
pension fraud, claims for dead relatives 88
pensions 42, 93
  raising age of eligibility 124
Perry, Commodore Matthew, US Navy 9
perseverance 7, 8, 30, 210, 218
Philippines
  New Nikkei children from 119–21
  nurses and caregivers from 116–18
PISA (Program for International Student
    Assessment) 223
Plaza Accord (1985) 26
pop music, South Korean 146, 147–8
population
  aging 89–90, 244
  shrinking 90, 217, 244
poverty 16, 242
  single women and 74–5
prices
  and deflation 55
  increasing 57
PriceWaterhouseCoopers 49
private schools 217, 222
private sector
  Nikkeijin broker companies 120–1
  use of English language 229–30
private universities 233
productivity rates 32, 124–5, 244, 254n15
  and low technology skills 231–2
professionals, as immigrants 121–3
prohibitions 14
Public Investigation Committee (on
    Fukushima accident) 176
public opinion

anti-Korean sentiment 149–50
  and nuclear power after Fukushima 198–9
  opposition to immigration 123–5
public sector employment 42, 45
pushchairs, controversies over 99–100

railways
  bullet train line 249
  pushchairs on 99–100
Rakuten online retailer 229–30
Reconstruction Agency, Fukushima 190–1
recycling 166–7
rice, price of 57
Ritsumeikan Asia Pacific University 236
Ryang, Sonia 138
Ryukyu Kingdom (Okinawa) 154
Ryutaro, Hashimoto, Prime Minister 160

Saito, Hidekazu 101
Sakanaka, Hidenori 106
sakoku, policy of isolation 9
salarymen 19, 243
  as absentee fathers 60
  characteristics of 41, 60
  extreme exhaustion 30–1
  life of 28–32
  obligatory games of golf 29
  overtime work 28–9
Samuels, Richard 198–9
samurai warrior class 8
San Francisco Peace Treaty (1951) 155
Sanya, elderly housing 94
Sato, Eisaku, Prime Minister 155–6
Sato, Mitsuru 110
Sato, Yuhei, governor of Fukushima 194
schools
  and bullying 17, 213–15
  children's cleaning tasks 12–13, 203, 210,
    211
  effect of falling population on 217
  entrance tests 215–17
  extracurricular classes 202
  group unity 211–12, 214–15
  high schools 204–5, 222
  homeroom system 202–3, 207–8
  lack of computers in 230–1
  lunchtimes 208–11
  and moral education 210–11, 212
  private 217, 222
  requirements for pre-school 13–14
  role of teachers 205–6, 210–11
  school day 202–4

schools (*cont.*)
  uniforms 212
  and *wa* 11
science
  research 237–8, 277*n*73
  teaching of 207
Second World War 126–7, 128–30
  government apologies 128, 131
  Japanese revisionism 129–30, 237
  rebuilding after 4, 24–5, 162
  and view of Japan as aggressor 133–4,
    162
self-defense forces 127
self-reliance 12–13
Senkaku/Diaoyu islands 151–3
  Japanese government purchase of 151
September 11, 2001 attacks on USA, and
  'War on Terror' 160
service, concept of 12–13
sex
  indifference to 65
  infrequency of 97–8
  premarital and extramarital 86
Shimizu, Masataka, President of TEPCO
  178, 181
Shimokobe, Kazuhiko, new chairman of
  TEPCO 195
Shirakawa, Toko, journalist 71, 101
Shiseido cosmetics company 46
  provision of childcare 80
shoes, rules about 14
Shotoku, Prince, first constitution 7
Shukan Shincho newspaper 150
Singapore 27
single women 74–6
  advice against careers 75–6
  and independence 85
  stigmatized 81
small businesses 41–2
social norms, *wa* and 10
social solidarity 1–3
Song Il-gook, South Korean actor 149
Sony, market value decline 230
South Korea
  ban on fish from northeastern coasts of
    Japan 194
  and disputed Dokdo/Takeshima islands
    148–50
  economic growth 127–8
  and Japanese history textbooks 129
  and Japan's militarization 160
  K-Wave 146–8

  origin of most *zainichi* 135
  relations with Japan 136
Soviet Union, fall of 128
speech, indirect manner of 8
SPEEDI (System for Prediction of
    Environmental Emergency Dose
    Information) 185–6
  models 189
sports
  at universities 234
  and *wa* 11
students
  foreign 115–16, 236
  job hunting 234, 235
  recruitment by companies 35, 38, 39, 234
  studying abroad 53–5, 228, 236, 256*n*48
Suga, Yoshihide 57
Sugaoka, Kei, GEC inspector 177–8
suicides
  after bullying in schools 213
  after Fukushima 190–1
  from overwork 31
  rates 243
supermoms 81
Support Plan for Children and Parenting
    104–5
Supreme Court, and Olympus whistle-
    blowing case 23

Taiwan 27
Takahashi, Kotoro, MEXT official 218
Takaichi, Sanae 133
Takehiko, Kariya, on higher education
    233–4
Takekuro, Ichiro, TEPCO expert 179, 180
Takeshima/Dokdo islands *see* Dokdo/
    Takeshima islands
Tanaka, Hideyuki 33
Tanaka, Hiroshi 111
Tanaka, Shunichi, head of NRA 196–7
Tanimura, Shiho, *The 'I May Not Marry'
    Syndrome* 75
tattoos, negative view of 17–18
teachers
  cooperation between 205–6
  role of 205–6
  rotation between high schools 222–3
  and teaching of English 225
  working hours 205
teaching, career for women 45
Technical Internship Program (TIP) 107–8,
    110–11

technology, weaknesses in teaching and use of 230–2, 239
tenkin (geographical transfers) 44, 46–7
TEPCO (Tokyo Electric Power Company) 169, 170, 270*nn*40, 44, 271*n*60
  compensation 176, 189, 192, 195
  corporate culture 196
  corporate failure at time of accident 178–82
  cover-up of previous accidents 177–8
  and deference to prime minister's office 178–9, 180–2, 200
  future of 194–7
  government bailout 182, 194–5
  links with METI 183
  nationalization 195
  poor contingency planning 174–8
  reluctance to share information 180–2
  responsibility for decontamination and decommissioning 195–6
  and safety myth 177
Terasaka, Nobuaki, director of NISA 185, 186
Test of English as a Foreign Language (TOEFL) 224–5, 229
textbooks
  and disputed islands 152
  limited range 208
  on Second World War 129–30
Tohoku region 3
  earthquake and tsunami (March 2011) 2, 168
Tokaimura nuclear plant, 1999 accident 184–5, 270*n*40
Tokugawa Shogunate 9
Tokyo 4, 89
  2014 gubernatorial election 199, 273–4*n*106
tourism, foreign shopping 26
Toyota
  overwork 32
  treatment of foreign trainees 108–9
trade
  protectionism 56
  surpluses (1980s) 25
Train Man, TV drama 69
trainees, exploitation of foreign 107–11
Trans-Pacific Partnership (TPP) 57
transgender people 86
  role models 66
transport 243
  and Olympic Games 249
tsunamis 6
March 2011 1–3
  provision against at Fukushima 174–5
typhoons 6

UN Charter, and right of defence 159
Unit 731, chemical and biological warfare experiments 130
United Nations
  Committee on the Elimination of Discrimination against Women 105
  report by migrant rights rapporteur (2010) 110
United States
  Armitage Report on collective self-defense 159–60
  bases on Okinawa 154–9
  education system compared with Japan 206–7, 324
  fertility treatment in 103
  and Fukushima accident 180
  Japanese acquisitions in 26
  and joint missile defense program 145
  and nuclear weapons on Okinawa 155–6
  and post-war reconstruction 25
  and pressure for remilitarization 21
  proportion of elderly 91
  reaction to economic boom 25–6
  security alliance with Japan 153–61
  Trafficking in Persons Report 110
universities 232–7
  choice of 234–5
  courses taught in English 236
  deregulation 235
  effect of falling population on 217–18
  enrolment rates 217–18
  entrance exams 216, 217–19
  lack of quality 233
  private 233
  scientific research 237–8
  sports and clubs 234
  see also students
US Atomic Energy Commission (AEC) 185
US Nuclear Regulatory Commission, and Fukushima nuclear accident 172
US-Japan Joint Declaration on Security (1996) 160
Ushikubo, Megumi 61, 63, 73
Ustonomiya, Kenji 199

Vietnam, Economic Partnership Agreement with 119

Vietnam War 155
volcanoes 6

wa (social harmony)
  components of 10–19
  and gender and family 86–7
  history of 7–10, 243
  and inside/outside distinctions 5–6,
    17–18, 126, 163
  see also harmony
wages
  fall of 82, 97, 244
  skilled workers 123
  trainees and interns 108–9
war criminals 134
  at Yasukuni Shrine 130
Waseda University 234, 236
waste, disapproval of 166
welfare
  effect of low birth rate on 104
  for seniors 93, 95–6
whaling policy 18–19, 253*n*24
whistle-blowing 22–4
  and workplace loyalty 15–16
Whiting, Robert 11
Wired magazine 68
women
  age of childbearing 97, 101–2
  in careers 43
  fertility treatment for older women
    101–3
  and gender roles 5, 243
  ideal number of children 98
  'office ladies' 26, 27
  and pushchair controversies
    99–100
  supermoms 81
  unrealistic expectations of marriage 82
  and work-life balance 47–8
  in workforce 42–8, 246, 254*n*9
  working mothers 79–81
  see also housewives; young women
Woodford, Michael C., and Olympus
    scandal 48–50, 52–3
work-life balance 47, 80–1, 98
workaholics, Japan as nation of 30
Worker Dispatching Act (1985) 37
workforce participation, measures to
    increase 124
workforce population, declining 89–90
working hours 28–9, 30, 254*n*16
  extreme exhaustion 30–1

five-day working week 33
  'No Overtime Days' 30, 32–4
  overwork 29, 30–2, 34
  and peer pressure to work late 33
  'service overtime' 28–9
  teachers 204
working mothers 79–81
  and childcare 80
  taking babies to work 79
workplace loyalty 15–16, 39–40
World Economic Forum 105

yakuza (mafia) groups 51
Yamada, Kosaku 215
Yamada, Masahiro 74
Yamaguchi Gumi, *yakuza* (mafia)
    group 51
Yamaguchi, Yoshie, newscaster 75
Yamaichi Securities 50
Yamamoto, Kenta 34–5
Yamanaka, Shinya, scientist 238
Yarrow, Peter 215
Yasuda, Koichi 110
Yasukuni Shrine, controversy over
    130, 132
Yoshida Doctrine 25
Yoshida, Masao, manager of Fukushima
    Daiichi 169, 181, 182, 269*n*30
  attempts to cool reactors 170,
    173, 270*n*44
  heroism 173
  request for emergency generators
    179–80, 271*n*49
Yoshida, Shigeru, Prime Minister 25
Yoshizawa, Atsufumi, TEPCO 180
young men
  idol *otaku* 72–3
  otaku men 67–71
  see also herbivore men
young people
  employment opportunities 92–3,
    245
  irregular work 36–9
  less competitive 64
  and male celebrities 66–7
  NEETs 40
  overnight accommodation in internet
    cafes 37–8
  proportion of 90, 244
  rejection of gender roles 59–87
  see also herbivore men; young men;
    young women

young women
    choice of men 64
    and dating *otaku* men 69–70, 72–3
    diversification 73–81
    single 74–6, 257–8n12
Yukan Fuji newspaper 149–50

zainichi (Korean residents)
    affinity with North Korea 135–9
    assimilation 144, 162
    and Chongryon schools 137–9, 140
    membership of Chongryon 139–40, 144
    and South Korea 142